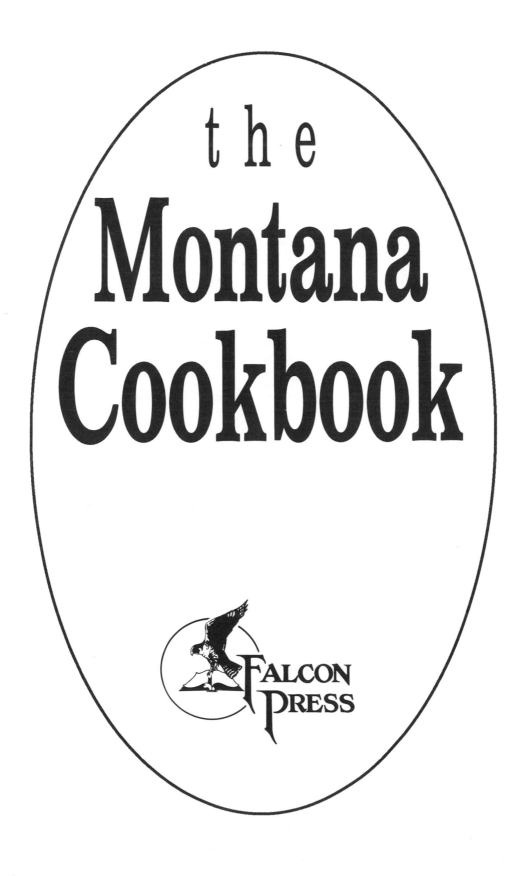

the
Montana
Cookbook

FALCON PRESS

Published in cooperation with the Helena *Independent Record*, *The Billings Gazette*, the Butte *Montana Standard*, the *Bozeman Daily Chronicle*, *The Missoulian*, the *Great Falls Tribune*, and Kalispell's *The Daily Inter Lake*.

Design, typesetting, and other prepress work by Falcon Press, Helena, Montana

Editor: Gayle C. Shirley
Consulting editor: Mary Ellen Holverson
Cover and inside artwork: DD Dowden

Printed in the United States of America

Library of Congress Number: 90-83661
ISBN 1-56044-037-6

For extra copies of this book, please check with your local bookstore or write to Falcon Press, P.O. Box 1718, Helena, MT 59624. You also may call toll-free 1-800-582-BOOK, and please ask for a free Falcon Press catalog.

Contents

The Flavor of Montana

In 1813, in a crude fort at the base of the Bitterroot Mountains, a hardy band of mountain men celebrated one of the first Christmases in what is today Montana. The wintering trappers brought in a number of mountain sheep for their Yuletide feast, and they washed down the meat with fifteen gallons of prime rum—a libation guaranteed to produce the jocularity fitting to the season. A party of Flathead Indians joined the celebration unexpectedly, and so they enjoyed a respite from the buffalo meat that was the mainstay of their diet.

Montana has changed dramatically since those days when wild game was the chief foodstuff and one's skill with a rifle meant the difference between eating and starving. Hard on the heels of the trappers came miners and settlers, packing their food preferences and their old family recipes with them. Cowboys began trailing cattle into the state, pausing to wolf down steak, beans, and coffee around the ever-popular chuckwagon. A century after the trappers' Christmas, homesteaders were pouring onto Montana's prairies by the thousands, planting crops and hoping to tame the land.

With this influx of people came an influx of ideas about how and what to eat. Many of the new Montanans came from foreign lands—farmers from Scandinavia and Germany; miners and smelter workers from Ireland, England, and central Europe; railroad workers from China. Sauerbraten, sarma, pasties, and chow mein joined the Montana menu.

Despite drought and pests, wheat flourished on the eastern plains, and so did the aromatic art of bread-making. Foods that could not be grown or raised here were available via the Sears Roebuck catalog and the newly laid rails.

Today, Montana Indians still treasure their ancestors' recipes for pemmican, even though buffalo no longer blacken the plains. Wild game is still popular among those lucky enough to bag their quarry, although the hunt lasts only a few weeks of the year. Ranch cooks still produce the hearty kind of fare that can fuel a full day's work, but technology has reduced the work force sitting around the kitchen table.

5

But, today too, as the recipes in this cookbook prove, the flavor of Montana remains as varied as its population. Montanans have eagerly expanded their culinary horizons. And, through this book, they and Falcon Press—with the help of the Helena *Independent Record*, the *Great Falls Tribune*, *The Missoulian*, the *Billings Gazette*, the *Montana Standard*, the *Bozeman Daily Chronicle,* and Kalispell's *The Daily Inter Lake*—have happily shared the resulting taste treasures with you.

When Falcon Press and Montana's major newspapers asked people to submit recipes for this cookbook, we were overwhelmed by the response. More than 1,200 recipes poured in from all parts of the state. Most were from individuals, but some represent specialities of popular Montana restaurants. We had to select from among them only enough to fit in these 352 pages—an awesome task.

Even more overwhelming was the job of choosing one recipe in each category to win a promised prize. How does one pick the best from among so many gems? Still, we cooked and we considered, and finally we selected thirteen winners. You will find the winning recipes specially marked where they appear in the cookbook.

You will also find sprinkled throughout the cookbook some fascinating historical tidbits related to food and cooking. The historical recipes are included for their entertainment value only; if you choose to try them, Falcon Press does not guarantee the results.

Falcon Press would like to thank consulting editor Mary Ellen Holverson for her help in selecting and testing the recipes to be included in *The Montana Cookbook*. A registered dietitian with a master's degree in food and nutrition, Mary Ellen owned and operated the Stovetop Restaurant in Helena for several years. She has created and developed recipes for her restaurant, taught cooking courses, operated a catering service, and worked as a public health nutritionist at the state and county level.

Falcon Press also extends its thanks to the many other people who helped make *The Montana Cookbook* possible—especially those of you who submitted recipes. We think the cookbook pleasantly reflects Montana's heritage, its cultural diversity, and its wholesome way of life. As you try the recipes we have included, savor the flavor of Montana. Or as an old cowboy cook would have put it, "Come an' git it or I'll spit in the skillet!"

6

Beverages

Switchel

8 cups water
1 cup sugar
1 cup apple cider
1/2 cup cider vinegar
1/2 cup molasses
1/4 tsp. ginger
1/4 tsp. cinnamon

Heat all ingredients together until sugar is dissolved. Chill before serving. Makes 9-10 cups.

Chef's note: "In earlier days, this beverage was kept in stoneware jugs in the root cellar and served to workers in the field with the noonday meal. It was a substitute for water, which the pioneers believed could cause sunstroke if consumed in great quantities. Switchel also was a popular drink to serve to guests, usually after adding hard cider or brandy."

Elaine Kyriss
Billings

Tart and Tangy Citrus Punch

1 (6-oz.) can frozen
  lemonade concentrate,
  thawed
1 (6-oz.) can frozen grapefruit
  juice concentrate, thawed
1 (6-oz.) can frozen
  pineapple juice
  concentrate, thawed
2 cups water
1 (28-oz.) bottle club soda,
  chilled
1 (28 oz.) bottle ginger ale,
  chilled

In a large punch bowl, combine lemonade, grapefruit juice, and pineapple juice concentrates. Add water and mix well. Refrigerate. Just before serving, add club soda and ginger ale; stir to blend. Garnish punch bowl with ice rings and fresh fruit slices if desired. Makes 25 (4-oz.) servings.

Julie Nielsen
Billings

Diet Cherry Punch

1 package cherry Kool-Aid
1 (12-oz.) can frozen
  pineapple juice concentrate
1 (12-oz.) can frozen orange
  juice concentrate
1 liter Diet Cherry 7-Up
1/2 cup lemon juice
1 gallon water

Mix all ingredients except 7-Up in large bowl. Add 7-Up right before serving. Makes about 24 cups.

Carol Hansen
Roundup

Banana Pineapple Punch

1 (12-oz.) can frozen orange
  juice concentrate,
  reconstituted
1 (12-oz.) can frozen
  lemonade concentrate,
  reconstituted
1 (48-oz.) can pineapple
  juice
3 ripe bananas, crushed
1 1/2 cups sugar
1 1/2 cups water
32 oz. 7-Up (more or less
  to taste)

Mix all ingredients together in large punch bowl. Makes about 1 1/2 gallons.

Barbara Wolfe
Lewistown

Almost Orange Julius

1 (6-oz.) can frozen orange
   juice concentrate
1 cup milk
1/4 cup sugar (optional)
1/2 tsp. vanilla
1 cup water
10 ice cubes

Mix all ingredients in blender until ice cubes are thoroughly crushed. Serve immediately. Makes 4-6 servings.

Diane Browder
Great Falls

Strawberry Watermelon Slush

2 cups cubed watermelon
1 pint fresh strawberries,
   cleaned
1/3 cup sugar
1/3 cup lemon juice
2 cups ice cubes

In blender, combine all ingredients except ice. Blend well. Gradually add ice, blending until smooth. Serve immediately. Makes 5 cups.

Patty Howse
Great Falls

Summer Slush

9 cups water
2 cups sugar
4 tea bags
1 (12-oz.) can frozen orange
    juice concentrate
1 (12-oz.) can frozen
    lemonade concentrate
2 cups gin or vodka
    (optional)
Club soda or 7-Up

Boil sugar in 7 cups of water for 5 minutes after sugar is dissolved. Cool. Pour 2 cups of boiling water over tea bags. Let steep until cool. Mix orange juice and lemonade together and then add other ingredients. Freeze. Put 1/4 to 1/2 cup of frozen slush into 8-oz. glass and fill with club soda or 7-Up. Makes 30-60 servings.

Rita Casagranda
Butte

Banana Strawberry Yogurt Shake

1 cup frozen whole
    strawberries, partially
    thawed
8 oz. plain yogurt
1 ripe banana
2 tbs. honey
1/4 cup milk
1/2 tsp. vanilla

Blend all ingredients together in blender until smooth. Makes 3 cups. (Variation: Substitute 8-oz. can crushed pineapple, undrained, for strawberries.)

Patty Howse
Great Falls

11

Ice Cream Punch

1 (12-oz.) can 7-Up
1 (46-oz.) can pineapple
  juice
1 (46-oz.) can Hawaiian fruit
  punch
1/2 gallon vanilla ice cream

Mix juices and 7-Up together well. Chill. Pour into punch bowl. Scoop balls from ice cream half an hour before serving and float on top of juices. Add more ice cream later if desired. Makes about 15 servings.

Lorelei Winkelman
Great Falls

Hot Chocolate Drink Mix

4 1/2 cups powdered milk
1/2 cup unsweetened
  baking cocoa
1 cup powdered
  non-dairy creamer
1 cup powdered sugar
1/2 cup sugar

Mix all ingredients in a large mixing bowl. Store in glass or plastic container. To serve, mix 2 or 3 heaping spoonfuls into 1 cup of boiling water. Makes 18 cups.

Diane Browder
Great Falls

Hot Holiday Wassail

2 cups water
2 cups sugar
1 tsp. ground ginger
2 sticks cinnamon
10 whole cloves
1 quart apple cider
2/3 cup lemon juice
3 1/2 cups orange juice
1 cup cranberry juice
3 cups strong tea

The day before serving, make syrup of water, sugar, ginger, cinnamon, and cloves by boiling for 5 minutes in saucepan. Cool slightly and pour into jar. Set out overnight.

About 15 minutes before serving, remove cloves and cinnamon sticks. Place syrup along with rest of ingredients in a large pan. Blend well. Heat, but do not allow punch to boil. Serve warm in a punch bowl or pitcher. To garnish, float orange and lemon slices on top of punch. Makes 12 cups.

Isabel Cox
Winston

Colorado Springs Punch

1 (46-oz.) can
   pineapple juice
1 (46-oz.) can apricot nectar
1 (12-oz.) can frozen
   lemonade concentrate
1 (12-oz.) can frozen
   orange juice concentrate
1-1 1/2 cups apricot brandy
1-1 1/2 cups vodka
Squirt, 7-Up, or other mixer

Mix all but last ingredient in very large container. Freeze. Scoop 1/4 to 1/2 cup of slush into 8-oz. glass; add Squirt, 7-Up, or desired mixer. Makes 30-60 servings.

Elsie Clark
Great Falls

13

Elegant Champagne Punch

Lemon ice:
4 cups water
1 3/4 cups sugar
1 egg white
3/4 cup fresh lemon juice

1 pint white Rhine wine
1 bottle (4/5 quart)
   champagne
1 quart soda water

At least a day before serving punch, prepare lemon ice. Combine water and sugar in a saucepan and boil for 5 minutes to make a thin syrup. Cool. Beat egg white until frothy. Add the egg white and lemon juice to cooled syrup. Blend. Place in mold of your choice and freeze well.

When ready to serve punch, combine remaining ingredients in punch bowl. Unmold frozen lemon ice and float on top of punch. Serve in champagne glasses. To garnish, add two sugar cubes tinted with food coloring (red and green for Christmas, for example) to each glass before adding the punch. Makes 20 (4-oz.) servings.

Missy Cox
Winston

Peach Fuzz

3 ripe peaches, unpeeled
1 (6oz.) can pink
   lemonade concentrate
6 oz. vodka
Ice cubes

Cut up peaches and remove pits. Put peaches, lemonade, and vodka into blender. Add ice cubes to fill blender. Blend. Serve slushy or freeze for later use. Serves 4-6.

Pam Johnson
Billings

Chokecherry Wine

1 gallon ripe chokecherries
2 gallons cold water
8-10 pounds sugar
1 cup raisins
1 package dry yeast

Mash berries well with hands. Add water and sugar and stir well. Add raisins and yeast. Do not stir. Cover loosely and set in warm place. Three days later, stir well. Let stand 7-8 more days, stirring 2 or 3 times during this period. Strain and bottle. Do NOT put caps on tight for at least 1 month. Make wine in a crock or plastic container. Never use metal container. Makes about 12 wine-sized bottles.

Marlyse Drogitis
Harrison

Rose Hip Wine

5 pounds rose hips, fresh,
   rehydrated, or ground
12 pints water
2 1/2 cups sugar
1 package yeast
1 orange or lemon,
   thinly sliced

If dried hips are used, soak them in boiling water until soft. Drain. Grind fresh or rehydrated hips coarsely. Add water, sugar, yeast, and orange or lemon. Stir and pour mixture into large container. Cover loosely and allow to ferment for 48 hours. Strain into clean crock. When all fermentation has stopped (no more bubbles will be visible), strain again and bottle. Let age about 2 months, leaving cap loose for at least first month. Makes about 1 1/2 gallons.

Gracene Long
Hamilton

15

Mulled Wine

1/2 gallon apple
   cider or juice
1/2 gallon Burgundy wine
5 sticks cinnamon
4 orange slices
4 lemon slices
10 whole cloves

Mix all ingredients in large pan and simmer at least half an hour to mellow flavors. Makes 15 cups.

Alene Gorecki
Helena

Apple Knockers Hot Punch

3 cinnamon sticks
2 tsp. whole cloves
1/2 tsp. ground nutmeg
1/2 gallon cider
1 cup sugar
2 cups orange juice
1/2 cup lemon juice
1 cup peach brandy

Place spices in cheesecloth bag. Simmer cider, sugar, and spices for 15 minutes. Remove spices. Add juices and peach brandy; heat to bubbling and serve. Keep warm while serving. Makes about 11 cups.

Sue Kaul
Belgrade

Tom and Jerry Batter

1 dozen eggs, separated
1 pinch salt
1 tsp. vanilla
1 lb. butter, melted
3 lbs. powdered sugar

Beat egg yolks and vanilla until thick. In separate bowl, mix melted butter and powdered sugar. Add egg yolks to butter mixture. In another bowl, beat egg whites until foamy. Add pinch of salt and continue beating until whites form stiff peaks. Fold egg whites into yolk mixture. Store in tight container in refrigerator. Stores well. Makes 3 quarts.

Donna Davis
Lewistown

Kahlua

4 cups strong coffee
2 1/4 cups honey
1 fifth vodka
1 cup bourbon
1 vanilla bean, thinly sliced

Bring coffee and honey to a boil. Let simmer 15 minutes. When cool, pour into gallon jar. Add vodka, bourbon, and vanilla bean. Cover and let stand in cool place for about 30 days (the longer in cold storage, the better the flavor). Strain and bottle. Makes 1/2 gallon.

Gracene Long
Hamilton

17

Irish Cream

1 1/2 cups Canadian whiskey
1 pint whipping cream
1 (14-oz.) can sweetened
    condensed milk
2 eggs
4 tbs. chocolate syrup
4 tbs. water

Mix all ingredients in blender and serve.
Makes 6 cups.

Birdie Joers
Augusta

Some like it hot—and strong

The cowboy's recipe for making coffee was "take one pound of
coffee, wet it good with water, boil it over a fire for thirty minutes,
pitch in a horseshoe, and if it sinks, put in some more coffee...." All
joking aside, the standard formula was about one handful of
ground coffee for each cup of water. If the brew was of less
strength, there was apt to be grumbling about the cook's ability as a
coffee maker.

Ramon F. Adams
Come 'an Get It: The Story of the Old Cowboy Cook

Appetizers

Taco Dip

1 (16-oz.) can refried beans

3 ripe avocados, mashed

8 oz. sour cream

2 green onions, chopped

8 oz. taco sauce
(more if desired)

4 oz. Monterey Jack
cheese, shredded

Layer all ingredients in a pie plate or quiche dish in the order given. Mix a little of the sour cream with the avocados, and be sure to cover the avocado layer with sour cream to prevent discoloration. Serve with tortilla chips or crackers. Makes 3 cups.

Leona Henke
Ethridge

Bailey's Famous Quick Bean Dip

1 (16-oz.) can refried beans

1/2 cup salsa

1/4 cup chopped onion

1/4 cup grated sharp
cheddar cheese

1/2 cup cooked pork
sausage (optional)

Combine the refried beans, salsa, onion, sausage, and half the cheese, and heat until cheese begins to melt. Sprinkle the remaining cheese over the top before serving. Serve with tortilla chips. Makes 3 cups.

Malcolm S. Bailey
Billings

Cheesy Chip Dip

14-16 oz. sharp cheddar
    cheese, grated
8 oz. cream cheese
1/2 medium green
    pepper, chopped
1/4 medium onion, chopped
3/4 cup green olives
    (save liquid)
1 hot pepper, ground, OR
    a few drops of hot sauce
Garlic salt to taste
Ground black pepper
    to taste
2 heaping tbs. Miracle Whip
    salad dressing

Bring cheddar cheese and cream cheese to room temperature. Then blend all ingredients in blender or in bowl using electric mixer. Add liquid from olives until mixture reaches proper dipping consistency. Turn into bowl and chill to let flavors blend. Serve with potato chips, pretzels, or fresh vegetable sticks. Makes about 3 cups.

Beverly Hollister
Hamilton

Wonderful Crab Dip

2 (8-oz.) packages cream
    cheese, softened
14 oz. fresh or frozen
    crabmeat
1/2 cup white wine
1 tsp. pepper
2 tsp. onion powder
1 tsp. garlic powder
2 tbs. hot sauce
1 loaf French bread

Mix all ingredients except bread together until well-blended. Hollow out the middle of a baked loaf of French bread. Cube the removed bread and set aside. Put dip into loaf and serve with bread cubes and crackers. Makes 3-4 cups.

Erin Brenteson
Choteau

Low-Calorie Clam Dip

24 oz. lowfat cottage cheese
8 oz. Neufchatel cheese
3 tbs. Durkee's Famous
   sandwich and salad sauce
2 tsp. chopped parsley
1 tbs. Worcestershire sauce
1 tsp. onion powder
1/2 tsp. garlic salt
3 (6 1/2-oz.) cans chopped
   clams, drained (reserve
   liquid from one can)
Pepper to taste

Blend Neufchatel cheese with reserved clam liquid. Mix in all other ingredients in order given. Chill for at least an hour, and then serve with whole-wheat snack crackers. Makes 4-5 cups.

Mary-Anne Sward
Kalispell

Cucumber Dip

1/2 cup mayonnaise
1/2 cup sour cream
1/2 cup grated cucumber,
   drained well
2 tbs. grated onion
1/2 tsp. salt
1/8 tsp. pepper
1 tsp. dill weed

Blend all ingredients together well. Store in a covered container in the refrigerator. Makes 1 1/2 cups.

Gladine Nehus
Great Falls

Hot Curry Dip

1/2 cup sliced black olives
1/2 cup chopped
    green onions
1/2 cup shredded
    cheddar cheese
1 tsp. curry powder
Mayonnaise to moisten

Blend all ingredients in small serving dish. Bake at 350 degrees until browned on top—about 15 minutes. Serve hot with crackers. Makes 1 1/2 cups.

Emily Peck
Billings

Hawaiian Meatballs

1 1/2 lbs. ground beef
2/3 cup oatmeal
1/3 cup minced onion
1 (8 oz.) can chopped
    water chesnuts
1 1/2 tsp. salt
1/2 tsp. minced garlic
1/4 cup milk

Sauce:
1/2 cup brown sugar
2 tbs. cornstarch
1 (8 oz.) can pineapple tidbits
    (drain but save juice)
1/3 cup vinegar
1 tbs. soy sauce
1 cup water
1/3 cup chopped green
    pepper

Mix meatball ingredients together and shape into small balls. Bake or fry until completely browned. Drain off fat. To make sauce, heat all sauce ingredients except pineapple and juice together until thickened. Remove from heat and add pineapple and juice. Pour over meat balls. Heat through. Makes 24-30 small meatballs.

Evelyn R. Dolberg
Great Falls

Oriental-Mex Egg Rolls

1 package (80) won ton
  wrappers
2 cups vegetables (any
  combination of carrots,
  onions, snow peas, celery,
  green peppers, or
  cabbage)
4 fresh jalapeño peppers
2 cups cooked chicken,
  turkey, pork, or beef
2 (7 3/4 oz.) cans shrimp,
  salmon or mackerel,
  drained
1/2 cup soy sauce
4 cups cooking oil

Chop meat, fish, and vegetables until fine, or put through food processor. Mix thoroughly with soy sauce. Heat oil to 380 degrees. Put 1 tbs. mixture in center of each won ton wrapper. Dampen edges with water, roll, and press edges together to seal. Fry in hot oil until lightly browned on both sides. Drain. Serve with hot mustard, chutney, or sweet and sour sauce.

Lillian A. Dove
Missoula

Cantonese Chicken Wings

1 tbs. cooking oil
1 tbs. soy sauce
1/4 cup brown sugar
1/4 cup vinegar
1 (10-3/4 oz.) can condensed
  tomato soup
1 tsp. chili powder
1/2 tsp. salt
1/2 tsp. celery seeds
3 lbs. chicken wings, tips
  removed

Mix together all but last ingredient. Dip chicken wings into sauce and arrange in baking dish in a single layer. Bake 30 minutes at 375 degrees, until browned. Pour remaining sauce over chicken, cover, and bake for 45 more minutes at 350 degrees. Remove cover and baste with juices. Bake covered for 15 more minutes. Makes about 30 pieces.

Gloria Guessen
Missoula

Avocado Crab Puffs

6-8 oz. crabmeat
2 tbs. lemon juice
1/2 avocado, mashed
1 tbs. sour cream
1 tbs. mayonnaise
1 green onion, minced
Slight dash of hot sauce
1/2 - 1 tsp. horseradish
Salt and pepper to taste

For puffs, see a chou pastry recipe in a basic cookbook. Or you can buy the puffs from most bakeries. To make filling: Toss crabmeat with lemon juice and mix in other ingredients. Fill puffs. Makes 1 1/2 cups.

Sherrill Halbe
Girdle Mountain Summer House
Belt

Cheesy Shrimp Canapes

10 slices white bread
2 tbs. butter
1/2 tsp. thyme
4 oz. frozen, shelled,
   deveined shrimp, cooked
   and chopped
1/2 cup shredded
   Swiss cheese
1/3 cup mayonnaise
Fresh dill for garnish

Using a 2-inch-round fluted cookie cutter, cut 2 circles from each slice of bread. Save remaining bread pieces. In a 1-quart saucepan over low heat, melt butter with thyme. With pastry brush, brush bread circles with butter mixture and arrange on cookie sheet. Bake 10 minutes at 375 degrees, or until golden brown. Combine shrimp and remaining ingredients except dill. Shape shrimp mixture into 20 balls. Preheat broiler. Lightly press a shrimp ball onto each bread circle. Broil about 7-9 inches from heat for 10 minutes, or until bubbly. Sprinkle fresh dill sparingly over tops. Makes 20.

LaVonne Brown
Cut Bank

25

Smoked Salmon Cheesecake

Filling:
1/2 lb. smoked salmon, deboned
1 small onion, chopped
1 3/4 lb. cream cheese
1/3 cup half and half
4 eggs
1/3 cup grated Swiss cheese
Salt to taste

Crust:
About 2 cups bread crumbs
1/4 cup grated Parmesan cheese
1/2 tsp. dill weed

Wrap bottom of 10-inch spring-form pan in foil and then assemble pan. Mix together crust ingredients and sprinkle in bottom of pan. Combine filling ingredients in a food processor or blender and blend until all lumps are gone. Pour into prepared pan and place pan in oven. Set pan of hot water on rack below. Bake 1 1/2 hours at 325 degrees. When baked, turn upside-down onto platter and remove spring form. Surround with fresh parsley and serve cold, sliced in pie-shaped wedges, with crackers. Serves 15-20.

Sharon Burgess
Kalispell

A pioneer cure for leanness

Leanness is generally caused by lack of power in the digestive organs to digest and assimilate the fat-producing food. First restore digestion, take plenty of sleep, drink all the water the stomach will bear in the morning on rising, take moderate exercise in the open air, eat oatmeal, cracked wheat, Graham mush, baked sweet apples, roasted and boiled beef. Cultivate jolly people, and bathe daily.

Ethel Reed
Pioneer Kitchen: A Frontier Cookbook

Smoked Salmon Spread

8 oz. lowfat cream cheese
1 1/2 - 2 cups smoked
   salmon
1 tsp. lemon juice
1/4 cup finely chopped onion
1-2 tbs. Worcestershire sauce

Mix all ingredients together and allow to stand for a couple of hours so that flavors can blend. Serve on rye crackers or small pieces of rye bread. To make a dip, add plain yogurt until desired consistency is reached. Makes 2-3 cups.

Maryann Cianca
Butte

Escargot Supreme

1 1/2 cups butter
2 1/2 tsp. garlic powder OR 4
   cloves garlic, minced
2 tbs. shallots, crushed
1 tsp. finely chopped pecan
3/4 cup bread crumbs
3/4 cup sherry
1 (30-oz.) can snails
1 tbs. chopped fresh parsley

Over medium heat, saute garlic and shallots in butter for 3-5 minutes. Add remaining ingredients except snails and parsley, and saute another 3-5 minutes. Remove from heat. Drain and wash snails. Stuff shells with snails and top with butter mixture. Place stuffed snails in a baking pan, shell-side-down, and broil 2 minutes. Serve immediately. Serves 6-8.

Deb Strohmyer
Libby

Caviar Quickie

6 eggs
1/2 cup butter
   (not margarine), melted
2 tsp. garlic salt
1 cup sour cream
1 small jar caviar

Hardboil eggs, remove shells, and mash while still hot with tines of a large fork so that no large pieces of white remain. Add garlic salt and melted butter. Put into decorative dish about 7 inches round or square. Chill thoroughly. When ready to serve, spread sour cream over surface and sprinkle with well-drained caviar. Serve with crackers.

Clarice Robinson Cox
Helena

Cheese Balls

2 (8-oz.) packages cream
   cheese
8-oz. sharp cheddar cheese,
   shredded
1 tbs. finely chopped
   pimiento
1 tbs. finely chopped
   green pepper
1 tbs. finely chopped onion
1 tsp. lemon juice
2 tsp. Worcestershire sauce
Dash salt and pepper
1 cup chopped pecans

Blend cream cheese and cheddar with a mixer. Then stir in remaining ingredients except nuts. Shape into two balls or logs and refrigerate for 24 hours. Roll in nuts and serve. May be prepared in advance and frozen. Makes 2 cheese balls.

Hazel B. Favero
Billings

Cheese Boxes

1/2 lb. butter
3/4 lb. sharp cheddar
   cheese, grated
6 thin slices of bread
2 egg whites

Melt butter and cheese together. In separate bowl, beat egg whites until stiff. Pour cheese mixture into egg whites and blend together. Trim crusts from bread. Spread some cheese mixture on each slice. Stack three slices and cut into quarters. Frost the four sides and top of each quarter with cheese mixture. Repeat for other three slices of bread. Place on cookie sheet and bake 12-15 minutes at 350 degrees. Cheese boxes can be frozen before baking. Makes 24.

Mary A. Van Sice
Silver Star

Cheddar Cheese Carrot Log

2 cups cheddar cheese,
   shredded
3 oz. cream cheese, softened
1/2 cup salted peanuts, finely
   chopped
1/4 cup shredded carrot
1/8 tsp. dill weed
2 tbs. finely chopped red
   onion

Beat cheeses together. Add remaining ingredients. Chill. Shape into a log, tapering at one end to resemble a carrot. Cover and chill. Garnish with a carrot top or fresh dill. Serve at room temperature. Makes one 8-inch log.

Laura Hicks
Troy

Stuffed Mushrooms

24 large mushrooms, stems
   removed
1 cup grated Parmesan
   cheese
1 (4 1/4-oz.) can chopped
   ripe olives
3 tbs. bacon bits
2 tbs. dried onion flakes
1 tsp. horseradish
3/4 cup mayonnaise
1/2 cup chopped walnuts

Mix all ingredients except mushrooms together. Stuff mixture into mushroom caps. Place in shallow pan and bake 12-15 minutes at 350 degrees. Makes 24.

Helen Streblow
Livingston

The bounty of a spring shower

Mushrooms were not a luxury item to the homesteaders and their prairie children. Spring usually came early on the plains and hot sunny days would be interrupted by quick spring showers. A sudden night shower would leave the soil damp and pulsing with growing things. The grass would suddenly seem greener, the strong smell of the earth would rise in the humid air. Mamma would say, "Girls, see if you can find some mushrooms," and mostly we could.

Louise K. Nickey
Cookery of the Prairie Homesteader

Marinated Mushrooms

2 tbs. butter
2 tbs. lemon juice
1/4 tsp. salt
2 lbs. small button
    mushrooms

Marinade:
3/4 cup vegetable oil
1/4 cup red wine vinegar
1/2 cup Worcestershire sauce
1/2 tsp. dry mustard
2 cloves garlic, minced
1 tsp. salt
1 tbs. sugar
1/4 tsp. pepper
1/2 tsp. paprika
Dash cayenne pepper
Dash hot sauce
1-2 bay leaves

Boil first four ingredients in water, covered, for 3-5 minutes. Drain and set aside. Combine marinade ingredients. Add boiled mushrooms and marinate, refrigerated, overnight. Serves 12-15.

Rebecca Smith
Missoula

Stuffed Mushrooms II

12 large mushrooms
1/2 cup crabmeat
1/2 cup grated mozzarella
   cheese
1/4 cup grated Parmesan
   cheese
1 tsp. diced onion
1/2 tsp. dried basil
1/2 tsp. dried oregano

Combine crab and mozzarella cheese. Add basil, oregano, and onion. Wash mushrooms and remove stems. Stuff tightly with crab mixture. Sprinkle with Parmesan cheese. Bake 10 minutes at 400 degrees. Serve warm. Makes 12.

Robin Arbuckle Jones
Great Falls

Spinach Balls

2 (10 oz.) packages frozen
   chopped spinach
2 cups stuffing mix
1/4 cup finely chopped onion
4 eggs, beaten
1/2 cup grated Parmesan
   cheese
3/4 cup butter, melted
1/2 tsp. garlic salt
1 tbs. monosodium
   glutamate (optional)
1/4 tsp. thyme
Pepper to taste

Thaw and drain spinach. Squeeze out excess moisture. Add all remaining ingredients and form into bite-sized balls. Place on cookie sheet and freeze. When frozen, seal in plastic bags and store in freezer. To serve, bake about 20 minutes at 350 degrees. Balls will appear slightly brown at edges when done.

Mrs. Glen Fahlgren
Billings

Soups

Meatball Chowder

2 lbs. lean ground beef
2 tsp. seasoning salt
1/4 tsp. pepper
2 eggs, slightly beaten
1/4 cup chopped parsley
1/3 cup fine cracker crumbs
2 tbs. milk
3-5 tbs. flour
3 medium onions, chopped
1 tbs. cooking oil
3 cups diced celery
3 cups diced potatoes
1/4 cup long grain rice
6 cups tomato juice
6 cups water
1 tbs. sugar
1 tsp. salt
2 bay leaves
1 (7-oz.) can Mexican corn

Combine first 7 ingredients and mix thoroughly. Form meatballs the size of walnuts, roll them in flour, and fry in hot oil in skillet until brown. Place in Dutch oven and add remaining ingredients except corn. Bring to a boil, cover, and simmer for 30 minutes, or until rice is tender. Add corn and cook 10 more minutes. Serves 8-10.

Becky Marsh
Belgrade

Vegetable Beef Soup

2 cups ground roast beef OR
  1 lb. extra-lean ground
  round
4 cups chopped tomato
2 carrots, diced
2 stalks celery, diced
2 cups chopped cabbage
1/2 cup diced pimiento
1/2 cup peas
1/2 cup corn
1/2 cup lima beans
1/2 cup green beans
1 (8-oz.) can tomato sauce
2 cups beef broth or bouillon
2 potatoes, diced
2 onions, diced
Salt and pepper to taste

Mix meat and tomatoes together in large pot and bring to a boil. Simmer until meat is browned. Add remaining ingredients and cook until vegetables are tender, about 2 hours. Serves 10-12.

Donna Davis
Lewistown

Best-Ever Oxtail Soup

3 medium oxtails
3/4 cup pearl barley
1 small onion, diced
1 (28-oz.) can tomatoes
1 cup finely chopped carrot
1 cup diced celery
Parsley to taste
1 bay leaf
Salt and pepper to taste
1 cup finely chopped okra

With scissors, remove fat from oxtails. Place in large kettle, cover with water, and simmer until tender, about 6-8 hours. Long slow cooking is very important. Add more water as needed. When oxtails are tender, add remaining ingredients except okra and cook until vegetables are tender. Add okra near end of cooking time. Serves 6-8.

Olga M. Sheire
Great Falls

35

Taco Soup

1/2 cup chopped onion
1/2 cup chopped celery
4 cups canned whole
   tomatoes (with liquid)
1 (8-oz.) can tomato sauce
1/2 cup salsa
1 package taco seasoning
1 1/2 lbs. ground beef
2 (14-oz.) cans kidney beans
   (with liquid)
1 (17-oz.) can corn
   (with liquid)
1-2 cups water
Grated cheddar cheese

Saute celery and onion together in a little butter. Add ground beef and cook until browned. Drain excess fat. Combine celery, onion, beef, and remaining ingredients except cheese in a kettle. Simmer 1-2 hours, adding water as needed. Ladle into bowls and top with grated cheese. Serves 8.

Ti Dahlseide
Helena

Corned Beef Soup

1 onion, chopped
1 tbs. butter
4 potatoes, peeled
   and cubed
1 (10-oz.) package frozen
   Brussels sprouts
1 can corned beef
1 (5 3/4-oz.) can
   evaporated milk
4 tbs. flour

Saute onion in butter until limp. Cut Brussels sprouts in half. Add potato and Brussels sprouts to onion. Cover with water and cook until tender. Flake corned beef and add to vegetables. Cook gently until hot. Add milk. Thicken soup with flour stirred into some of the cold milk. Serves 6-8.

Chef's note: "Prior to the existence of refrigeration in the Hawaiian Islands, beef was corned in order to preserve it. I got this recipe in Hawaii."

June Stohr
Anaconda

Creamy Chicken Vegetable Soup

7 cups chicken broth
1/2 cup rice
5 mushrooms, sliced
1 medium onion, chopped
3 medium carrots, sliced
   1/8 inch thick
3 stalks celery, sliced
   1/4-inch thick
2 small zucchini, sliced
   1/4-inch thick
1/3 cup butter
1/3 cup flour
2 cups half and half or milk
1/2 tsp. dill weed
4 cups cubed cooked
   chicken
1/2 cup sliced green onion
Salt and pepper to taste
1/4 cup minced parsley

In a kettle, heat 6 cups of broth to boiling. Add rice, cover, and simmer 10 minutes. Add mushrooms, onion, carrot, celery, and zucchini. Simmer covered until just tender, about 10 minutes.

Meanwhile, in another pan, melt butter. Blend in flour and cook until bubbly, stirring constantly. Remove from heat and gradually stir in cream (or milk) and 1 cup broth. Heat and stir sauce until it thickens. Add seasonings, blend, and stir into vegetables in kettle. Add chicken, green onion, and parsley. Heat until warmed through. Serves 8.

Carol Johnson
Missoula

Chicken Taco Soup

1-lb. chicken, skinned,
   deboned, and cut up small
2 (16-oz.) cans tomatoes,
   chopped (with liquid)
2 (10 3/4-oz.) cans
   chicken broth
1 (4-oz.) can green chilies
   (with liquid)
1/4 tsp. salt
4 corn tortillas, halved
1/2 cup chopped
   green onion
1/2 cup shredded Monterey
   Jack cheese
1/4 cup chopped fresh
   cilantro
1/4 cup green taco sauce

Combine chicken, tomatoes, broth, chilies, and salt in a large pot and simmer uncovered for 30 minutes. Lay tortilla half in each of 8 soup bowls. Top each with 1 cup soup, 1 tbs. green onion, 1 tbs. cheese, 1 1/2 tsp. cilantro, and 1 1/2 tsp. taco sauce. Serves 8.

Judy Soiseth
Colstrip

Ana's Romanian Ciorba

1 (3-4 lb.) chicken, skinned, deboned, and cut up small
2 medium carrots, coarsely grated
1 green pepper, cut into strips
1 red bell pepper, cut into 1/4-inch cubes
8 green onions, chopped
2 medium tomatoes, seeded and chopped
1/4 lb. fresh green beans, cut into 2-inch lengths
1 cup cauliflowerets
2 cups chicken stock
3 cups water
1 tsp. salt
1/2 tsp. pepper
1/4 cup chopped fresh parsley
1/4 cup chopped fresh dill OR 1/2 - 1 tsp. dry dill
4-6 oz. dry egg vermicelli
2 egg yolks
2/3 cup sour cream
1/4 cup lemon juice

In a large saucepan, combine chicken, vegetables, stock, salt and pepper, and water. Bring to a boil and simmer, partially covered, until chicken is tender, about 1 hour. Add dill, parsley, and vermicelli and cook about 5 minutes, until noodles are tender. Skim off any fat from surface.

In a small bowl, combine egg yolks and sour cream until blended well. Gradually whisk in 1/4 cup of the hot cooking liquid and then stir egg-sour cream mixture into soup. Stir in lemon juice and serve. Serves 6-8.

Rebecca Smith
Missoula

39

Italian Minestrone Soup

1 lb. dry navy or
   Great Northern beans
3 quarts water
4 tsp. cooking oil
3/4 cup finely chopped
   carrot
1/2 cup finely chopped onion
1/2 cup finely chopped
   celery
1/4 tsp. garlic powder
2 1/2 cups diced zucchini
1 (10-oz.) package frozen cut
   green beans, thawed
1 lb. smoked ham hocks
2 beef bouillon cubes
1 tsp. basil
1/2 tsp. salt
1/2 tsp. oregano
1/2 tsp. pepper
1 (28-oz.) can whole
   tomatoes, cut up
1/2 cup uncooked pastina
   macaroni
Grated Parmesan cheese

Place dried beans in large soup pot with water. Bring to a boil and cook 3 minutes. Remove from heat and let stand 1 hour.

Heat oil in another large soup pot. Add carrots, onion, celery, and half the green beans. Saute until tender. Stir in half the zucchini. Cook, stirring occasionally, about 5 minutes. Stir in navy beans and the liquid in which they are soaking, ham hocks, bouillon, basil, salt, oregano, pepper, and garlic powder. Cover, bring to a boil, and simmer about 2 hours.

Stir in tomatoes and macaroni. Continue to simmer 30 minutes, or until macaroni is done but somewhat firm. Add remaining green beans and zucchini. Remove ham hocks, dice meat, and return to soup. Serve with grated Parmesan cheese. Serves 12-15.

Royce Pearson
Great Falls

Potato Soup with Sausage

1 lb. sausage
1 cup sliced celery
1/2 cup chopped onion
1/2 tsp. thyme
1/2 tsp. salt
2 tbs. flour
1 cup milk
1 (10 3/4-oz.) can chicken
  broth
1/2 cup water
4 cups diced potato
1 cup cooked green beans

If using link sausage, slice thin. In a large kettle, brown sausage and drain off excess fat. Add celery, onion, thyme, and salt and cook until onion is tender. Stir in flour and water and cook 1 minute. Gradually add chicken broth and bring to a boil, stirring. Add potato, cover, and simmer 25 minutes, or until potato is tender.

Pour 2 cups of soup into blender container and whirl until smooth. Return to kettle. Add milk, green beans, and sausage and heat through. Serves 4.

Eve McCauley
Helena

Italian Sausage Soup

1 lb. Italian sausage, broken
  up and removed from skin
1 clove garlic, minced fine
1 stalk celery, minced fine
1 large onion, chopped fine
1 (16-oz.) can tomatoes
  (with liquid)
4 cups chicken broth
1 tbs. basil
1 zucchini, cubed
1/2 cup cooked rice
Grated Parmesan cheese

Brown sausage with garlic, onion, and celery. Drain off excess fat and add remaining ingredients, except zucchini and Parmesan cheese. Simmer several hours in crockpot. Add zucchini during last hour. Sprinkle individual servings with Parmesan cheese. Serves 4.

Zella Hunter
Townsend

41

Lentil and Sausage Soup

1 cup dried lentils
3 cups water
1 carrot, sliced
1 stalk celery, chopped
1/2 onion
1/2 bay leaf
1 clove
1 cup tomato juice
1/8 tsp. cumin
1/4 tsp. savory
1/2 tsp. oregano
Smoked or polish sausage,
  cut into 1-inch pieces

Attach bay leaf and clove to onion for easy removal at end of cooking time. In a large saucepan, combine the first 7 ingredients. Bring to a boil, cover, and cook on low heat for about 2 hours. Add remaining ingredients and simmer for 30 minutes to 1 hour longer. Remove onion, clove, and bay leaf. Serves 4-6.

Renate Lehmann
Helena

Indian Bitterroot Soup

Dig and clean 2 cups or more of the root of the Bitterroot. Place in oven to dry after cutting in small sections. When they become dry and hard, remove and crush roots into pulp. Place in stew pot. Add quart of water. Add small diced pieces of meat. Diced meat can be any cooked wild game. Diced jerky even works well in this soup. Serve hot. Montana's state flower, the Bitterroot was used by the Indians as medicine as well as a food.

Tag Rittel
Recipes and Remedies of the Pioneers

Portuguese Bean Soup

1 ham hock
12 oz. precooked link
  sausage, smoked or spicy
4 cups water
1 (8-oz.) can tomato sauce
1 large onion, chopped
2 medium potatoes, peeled
  and cubed
2 carrots, sliced thin
1/4 head cabbage, chopped
1/4 cup chopped celery
2 (16-oz.) cans red kidney
  beans (with liquid)
1 1/2 tsp. salt
Pepper to taste
Dash of paprika
1 tsp. garlic powder
1 bay leaf

In a large pot, simmer ham hock and sausage in water for 30 minutes. Add remaining ingredients, bring to a boil, and simmer until vegetables are done and soup has thickened. Add more water if necessary. Cook at least 2 hours to blend flavors. Remove bay leaf. Serves 6-8.

Dorothy Hinnergardt
Billings

43

Fish and Vegetable Chowder

1 cup flaked cooked fish
4 slices bacon, cut up
1 onion, chopped
1 small green pepper, chopped
1/3 cup chopped celery
1 (1 lb. 12-oz.) can tomatoes
1 (6-oz.) can tomato paste
1 1/2 cups sliced mushrooms
2 cups fish stock
1/2 cup white wine
1/2 tsp. dried oregano

In a Dutch oven, cook bacon over medium-high heat until crisp. Remove bacon from pot with slotted spoon and drain it on paper towels. To pot, add onion, green pepper, and celery. Cook and stir over medium heat for 6 minutes. Add bacon, tomatoes, tomato paste, mushrooms, fish stock, wine, and oregano. Simmer, stirring occasionally, for 30 minutes. Add cooked fish and heat through. Serves 6-8.

Miriam Hendrickson
Great Falls

Creamy Salmon Broccoli Soup

1 (15 1/2-oz.) can salmon
1 (10-oz.) package frozen chopped broccoli
2/3 cup chopped onion
3 tbs. butter
3 tbs. flour
2 cups half and half
3 cups milk
2 chicken bouillon cubes
1/4 tsp. thyme
1/8 tsp. cayenne pepper

Drain salmon, reserving liquid, and break into chunks with a fork. Cook broccoli according to package directions. Drain. Saute onion in butter until soft. Blend in flour. Add reserved salmon liquid, half and half, and milk; stir and cook until thickened and smooth. Dissolve bouillon cubes in hot soup. Add salmon, broccoli, and seasonings, and heat through. Serves 6.

Pamela K. Rausch
Missoula

44

Boston Clam Chowder

1/2 lb. bacon, diced
1 large onion, diced
3 large potatoes, peeled and
  cubed
4 (7-oz.) cans chopped
  clams
Salt and pepper to taste
4 tbs. flour
1/2 cup butter
Milk

Saute bacon in kettle until crisp. Add onion and continue cooking until onion is limp. Set aside. Drain clams and put juice into separate pot. Add potatoes to juice, and add water to cover potatoes. Salt lightly and cook until potatoes are tender; then add clams. Heat to boiling and turn heat to low.

In first kettle, add butter to bacon and onion and cook lightly. Add flour. Continue cooking until flour loses raw taste, about 5 minutes. Add salt and pepper, and then add clams and potatoes with liquid. Simmer 5 minutes.

This soup base can be refrigerated for 2-3 days. To serve, mix 1 cup soup base with 1 cup milk and heat. Makes 8-10 cups soup base.

Susy Baroch
Great Falls

45

Cream of Snow Pea Soup with Shrimp

1/2 cup butter
1 lb. snow peas (remove stems)
2 cups chicken stock
1 cup whipping cream
1/4 tsp. minced fresh mint
Pinch of sugar
Pinch of nutmeg
Salt and pepper to taste
1/4 lb. bay shrimp, cooked and shelled

Melt 1/4 cup butter in kettle and saute peas until tender. Add stock and bring to a boil. Reduce heat and simmer 20 minutes. Puree in blender, and heat again to a boil. Reduce heat to low and add cream, mint, sugar, and nutmeg. Season with salt and pepper to taste. Stir in remaining butter. Heat thoroughly but do not boil. Place shrimp in soup bowls and pour heated soup over. Serves 4.

Laura Hicks
Troy

Broccoli Crab Bisque

1 cup sliced leeks or green onions
1 lb. mushrooms, sliced
1 lb. broccoli, chopped
1 clove garlic, minced
1/4 cup butter
1/4 cup flour
1/4 tsp. thyme
1 small bay leaf
3 cups chicken broth
2 cups half and half
3/4 cup shredded Swiss cheese
1 lb. imitation crabmeat
Splash of white wine

Cook onion, mushroom, broccoli, and garlic in butter until tender. Blend in flour, thyme, and bay leaf. Add chicken broth and half and half all at once. Cook until thick and bubbly. Add cheese and stir until melted. Add crabmeat. Heat through. Add wine. Serves 6-8.

Karen Sampson
Billings

Cheese Soup

1 cup chopped celery
1 cup chopped onion
4 cups half and half
1 cup grated cheddar
  cheese
2 cups processed cheese
  spread
1 cup diced tomato
3 small jalapeno peppers,
  chopped
Salt to taste

Put onion and celery into large saucepan, cover with water, and cook until tender. Add half and half and heat thoroughly. Add cheese spread and then cheddar cheese, a little at a time. Add peppers and tomatoes, heat through, and serve. Serves 6-8.

Sharon Coffman
Red Lodge

Corn Chowder

1 medium onion, sliced into
  thin rings
3 tbs. butter
1 cup whole kernel corn
1 cup creamed corn
1 cup diced, cooked potato
1 (10 3/4-oz.) can condensed
  cream of chicken soup
2 1/2 cups milk
Salt and pepper to taste

Saute onion in butter. Add remaining ingredients and heat but do not boil. Serves 6-8.

LaVonne Brown
Cut Bank

Asparagus Cream Soup

1 large onion, chopped
1/4 cup butter
2 (10 3/4-oz.) cans
   chicken broth
1 lb. potatoes, peeled
   and sliced
2 lbs. fresh asparagus
1 cup half and half
Salt and white pepper
   to taste

In a large saucepan, saute onion in butter for 2 minutes. Stir in potatoes and chicken broth and bring to a boil. Cover, lower heat, and simmer for 20 minutes, or until potatoes are very tender.

Meanwhile, wash asparagus and cut into 1-inch pieces, discarding tough ends. Add to potato mixture and cook 5 minutes, or until asparagus is tender. Remove from heat. If desired, use a slotted spoon to remove some of asparagus tips to use as garnish.

Stir half and half into soup. Ladle about 1/4 of the soup into the container of a blender or food processor. Cover and whirl until mixture is smooth. Pour into large bowl. Repeat until all soup is smooth. Season with salt and pepper, return to saucepan, and heat through. Garnish individual bowls with asparagus tips. May also be served chilled. Serves 6-8.

Judie Murrill
Corvallis

Curried Broccoli and Cheddar Soup

1 1/2 lbs. fresh broccoli
1/4 cup butter
1 tbs. curry powder
1 medium onion, chopped
6 cups chicken broth
2 large potatoes, cubed
4 carrots, sliced thin
1 cup milk
3 cups shredded sharp
cheddar cheese

Trim flowerets from broccoli and cut into small pieces. Discard tough ends of stems; peel remaining stems and slice thin. In a 6- to 8-quart kettle, melt butter over medium heat. Add curry powder and onion and stir for 5 minutes. Add broth, potatoes, broccoli stems, and carrots. Cover and simmer until potatoes mash easily, about 30 minutes.

Whirl about half the broth and vegetables, a portion at a time, in a blender or food processor until pureed. Return to kettle. Heat soup to boiling and add broccoli flowerets and milk. Simmer, uncovered, until flowerets are tender when pierced. Stir in cheese a little at a time until melted. Serves 8-10.

**Sharon M. Fox
Missoula**

Quick Broccoli Soup

1/4 cup chopped onion
2 tsp. butter
2 (10-oz.) packages frozen
broccoli with cheese sauce
1/8 tsp. pepper
2 cups chicken broth
1/2 cup heavy cream
Pepper to taste

Saute onion in butter until clear but not browned. Add broccoli, chicken broth, cream, and pepper. Cook over medium heat for 5 minutes, or until thoroughly heated. Serves 4-6.

**Mrs. Ron Gilchrist
Shelby**

Cauliflower Cheese Soup

2 tbs. butter
4 oz. cooked sausage or
  ham, diced
1 medium onion, chopped
1/2 tsp. caraway seeds,
  crushed
1 lb. potatoes, peeled
  and diced
2 (14 1/2-oz.) cans
  chicken broth
3 cups cauliflowerets
1 cup heavy cream
4 oz. cheddar cheese, grated
Salt and pepper to taste

Melt butter in medium pan and brown meat, about 4 minutes. Remove meat. Add onion, caraway seeds, and ground black pepper to taste. Cook 5 minutes, stirring occasionally. Add potatoes and broth; simmer until potatoes are tender, about 25 minutes. Break potatoes up with spoon. Add cauliflower and simmer until tender. Stir in cream and meat. Add cheese and mix until melted. Season with salt and pepper. Serves 8-10.

Birdie Joers
Augusta

Watercress Soup

1 (8-inch) bunch watercress
2 tbs. butter
4 potatoes, peeled and
  chopped
4 onions, chopped
4 slices bacon, fried and
  broken up
4 cups chicken broth
1 cup whipping cream
1 cup half and half
Salt and pepper to taste

Remove leaves and tender stems from watercress. Chop fine and saute in butter. Boil onion and potatoes in water until soft. Whirl in blender with bacon. In a large saucepan, add watercress to chicken broth. Mix in potato and onion, cream, and half and half. Season to taste. Serves cold garnished with a dollop of sour cream. Serves 6-8.

Sue Kaul
Belgrade

Cream of Vegetable Soup

1 1/2 cups chicken broth
1/2 cup chopped onion
2 cups fresh vegetables,
  seasoned, cooked, and
  chopped fine
2 tbs. butter
2 tbs. flour
1 cup milk or cream
Salt and pepper to taste

Combine broth, onion, and vegetable in large saucepan. Simmer until tender but crispy. In a separate pan, melt butter and add flour to make a paste. Add milk or cream gradually, stirring to thicken. Stir into vegetable mixture and heat through. Serves 4.

(Suggested vegetables: Asparagus seasoned with lemon juice; broccoli seasoned with thyme, garlic, and bay leaf; cauliflower seasoned with pinch of curry powder; celery seasoned with thyme and nutmeg; 4 cups tomato seasoned with basil; 1 cup potato seasoned with dill weed; or 1 cup mushrooms seasoned with garlic and Worcestershire sauce.)

Dixie Engelhardt
Ulm

Algerian Tomato Soup

3 (28-oz.) cans tomatoes,
  cut up
4 medium onions, sliced thin
1 bay leaf
1 cinnamon stick
Dash of ground cloves
1/4 cup orange juice OR 1
  orange, sliced
1 tsp. salt

Combine all ingredients and simmer 1 hour. Remove bay leaf, cinnamon stick, and orange slices. Serves 8-10.

Phyllis V. Thompson
Belt

51

Gazpacho

1 large cucumber (remove seeds if they are large)

2 green peppers

4 cloves garlic, minced

1 large onion

2 lbs. tomatoes, peeled

2 (1-inch-thick) bread crusts, soaked in a little water

2 tbs. olive oil

3 tbs. vinegar

1 tbs. salt or to taste

2 cups cold water

Cut cucumber, peppers, onion, and tomatoes into 1-inch chunks. Process in a food processor, 1/3 at a time. With the last 1/3, add olive oil, garlic, vinegar, salt, and bread. Mix well and then add water. Refrigerate.

When serving, put into cold bowls and pass the following garnishes if desired: chopped green pepper, chopped onion, chopped cucumber, chopped hard-boiled eggs, toasted bread cubes.

Chef's note: "This is an authentic Spanish recipe, as I lived in Spain for 7 years. One day when my maid was making this soup-salad, I sat down with paper and pencil and wrote up this recipe while watching her. It is delicious any time of the year, but it is especially good when it is hot outside and the tomatoes are homegrown."

Laurette Ryan
Bozeman

Salads
& Dressings

Antipasto Salad

1/4 cup olive oil
2 cloves garlic, minced
1 1/2 cups French
   bread cubes
1/4 lb. Genoa salami
1/4 lb. prosciutto or ham
1/4 lb. cooked turkey breast
1/4 lb. provolone cheese
1 red onion, sliced thin
1 red bell pepper, cut into
   thin strips
1 green bell pepper, cut into
   thin strips
1 cucumber, diced
1/4 cup black olives
1/2 cup garbanzo beans
1 carrot, sliced thin
1 head lettuce, torn

Vinaigrette:
2/3 cup olive oil
3 tbs. red wine vinegar
1/4 tsp. dry mustard
1 clove garlic, minced
1 tbs. dried basil
1 tsp. dried oregano
1/4 tsp. dried tarragon
1 tbs. parsley
1 tbs. minced fresh chives
Pinch of cayenne pepper
1/2 tsp. pepper
1 tbs. grated Parmesan
   cheese

Combine vinaigrette ingredients in a jar and shake well. Set aside so that flavors can blend while making salad.

Heat olive oil with garlic over medium heat. Add bread cubes and saute until lightly browned. Remove and drain on paper towel. Slice meats and cheese into thin 1/4-inch strips and put into large bowl. Add remaining ingredients and toss with vinaigrette. Serves 6.

Penny Rubner
Great Falls

Hot Taco Salad

4 cups bite-sized tortilla chips
2 (15-oz.) cans chili
1/2 lb. ground beef (optional)
1 head lettuce, chopped
1/2 onion, chopped fine
2 cups shredded
   cheddar cheese
Sliced ripe olives (optional)
Chopped fresh tomato
   (optional)

In a skillet, brown ground beef. Drain excess fat. Add chili and cook until heated through. Arrange tortilla chips in a 9 x 13-inch baking pan. Layer with remaining ingredients in this order: chili, lettuce, onion, cheese, olives, tomatoes. Broil for 1-2 minutes, until cheese starts to melt. Overheating will cause lettuce to wilt. Serve immediately. Serves 4-6.

Kathryn Kennedy
Butte

Sausage and Potato Vinaigrette

4-5 large baking potatoes
1 1/2 lbs. kielbasa or garlic
   knockwurst
1 egg yolk
1 tsp. Dijon mustard
1/4 cup white wine vinegar
1 cup olive oil
1/4 tsp. tarragon leaves
2 green onions, chopped
1 tbs. chopped parsley
1 clove garlic, minced
Pinch of sugar
Salt and pepper to taste

To make vinaigrette: Combine egg yolk, mustard, and vinegar and whisk with wire whip. Add olive oil in slow, steady stream until vinaigrette thickens. Stir in seasonings.

Steam potatoes until tender. Cut into 1/4-inch slices. Simmer sausage in 1 inch of water, covered, about 7 minutes. Drain, remove casings if necessary, and cut into 1/4-inch slices. On a serving plate, alternate layers of potato with layers of sausage. Pour vinaigrette over all. Serves 4-6.

Carolyn Lehman
Kalispell

Chicken Salad with Sesame Dressing

3 quarts leaf lettuce, washed

4 large kiwis, peeled and sliced thin

2 cups cubed, cooked chicken

1 large avocado, peeled and sliced

1 cup thinly sliced celery

1/3 cup thinly sliced green onion

Dressing:

3 tbs. sesame seeds

1/3 cup salad oil

1/2 tsp. grated lemon peel

1/2 tsp. dry mustard

1/4 cup lemon juice

1 tbs. sugar

1 tbs. soy sauce

To make dressing: In a 6- to 8-inch skillet, cook sesame seeds in oil until golden, about 5-8 minutes. Stir often. Stir in remaining dressing ingredients, mix well, and remove from heat.

Break lettuce into bite-sized pieces and arrange in large salad bowl. Top with kiwi slices, chicken, avocado, celery, and green onion. Pour dressing over salad and toss gently. Serves 6-8.

LaVonne Brown
Cut Bank

Flying Farmer's Salad

2 cups cooked chicken
  chunks
2 tbs. salad oil
2 tbs. orange juice
1 tsp. salt
3 cups cooked rice
1 1/2 cups seedless green
  grapes, halved
1 1/2 cups sliced celery
1 (20-oz.) can pineapple
  chunks or tidbits, drained
1 (11 oz.) can mandarin
  orange segments, drained
1 cup slivered almonds,
  lightly toasted
1 1/2 cups mayonnaise

Mix all ingredients together and refrigerate several hours or overnight. Serves 9-12.

Melinda Reed Hettick
Stevensville

A dandy spring tonic

Our ancestors brought the dandelion from Europe because they wanted it here. Its yellow flowers reminded them of home. And they ate it. If we didn't have supermarkets with year-round fresh produce we'd be outside in March praying for a little old dandelion. With all that vitamin C to cure our end-of-winter letdown, the dandelion is a spring tonic.

Kim Williams
Cookbook & Commentary

57

Greek Pasta Salad with Chicken

1 lb. boneless chicken
   breasts
1/3 cup olive oil
3 tbs. lemon juice
1 clove garlic, minced
2 tsp. dried oregano
Salt and pepper to taste
1/2 lb. spinach fettucine,
   cooked
1/2 lb. feta cheese, crumbled
3 medium tomatoes,
   chopped
1/2 cup Greek olives
1/2 cup chopped fresh
   parsley
1/4 cup pine nuts, toasted

Vinaigrette:
1/4 cup olive oil
3 tbs. lemon juice
1 clove garlic, minced
1/4 tsp. hot sauce
1 tbs. oregano
Salt and pepper to taste

Mix vinaigrette ingredients together and set aside. Marinate chicken for 20 minutes to 2 hours in a combination of olive oil, lemon juice, garlic, oregano, salt, and pepper. Remove from marinade and bake 30 minutes at 325 degrees. Cool and shred. Combine chicken with remaining salad ingredients. Fold in vinaigrette and serve at room temperature. Serves 6.

Penny Rubner
Great Falls

Salmon Salad

1 (16-oz.) can salmon,
    drained and flaked
6 potatoes, boiled, peeled,
    and sliced
2 dill pickles, chopped fine
3 black olives, chopped
2 stalks celery, chopped
1 small onion, chopped fine
6 hard-boiled eggs, diced
Salt and pepper to taste
Mayonnaise to moisten
    (optional)

Mix all ingredients together, adding eggs last. Refrigerate until ready to serve. Serve on lettuce. Serves 4-6.

Evelyn Dalry
Helena

Oriental Shrimp Salad

2 cups bean sprouts, rinsed
2 (4 1/2-oz.) cans shrimp
1 (8 1/2-oz.) can chow mein
    noodles
1 (5-oz.) can water chesnuts,
    drained and sliced
1/4 cup chopped
    green onion
1/4 cup chopped celery
3/4 cup mayonnaise
1 tbs. lemon juice
1 tbs. soy sauce
3/4 tsp. ground ginger
Salt and pepper to taste

Mix together mayonnaise, lemon juice, soy sauce, ginger, salt, and pepper. Fold in remaining ingredients. Serves 4-6.

Charlotte R. Higbee
Noxon

59

Bowl 'em Over Crab Salad

Bowl:
1/2 cup water
1/4 cup butter
1/2 cup flour
1/8 tsp. salt
1/2 - 1 tsp. caraway seed
2 eggs

Filling:
1 cup chopped crabmeat
1 cup diced celery
1 cup chopped lettuce
1 tsp. lemon juice
1 tsp. minced onion
Salt and pepper to taste
Mayonnaise to moisten

Garnishes:
Tomato wedges
Lemon wedges
Hard-boiled eggs, sliced
Ripe olives

To make bowl: In a saucepan, heat water and butter to boiling. Stir in flour, salt, and caraway seed. Stir vigorously over low heat until mixture leaves the sides of the pan and forms a ball, about 1 minute. Remove from heat and cool slightly, about 10 minutes. Add eggs one at a time, beating until smooth after each addition.

Spread batter evenly in the bottom and up the sides of a greased 9-inch pie plate. Bake 45-50 minutes at 375 degrees. The dough will form a bowl, high on the sides and flat in the center. Cool slowly away from drafts.

Mix all filling ingredients except mayonnaise and chill. Just before serving, toss with mayonnaise to moisten and heap in baked dough bowl. Garnish with tomato wedges, lemon wedges, slices of hard-boiled egg, and olives. Serves 4.

Florence R. Olson
Butte

Spaghetti Shrimp Salad

16 oz. vermicelli spaghetti
2 (4 1/2-oz.) cans small
shrimp
2 cups chopped tomato
1 green pepper, chopped
2 stalks celery, chopped fine

Dressing:
3/4 cup mayonnaise
3/4 cup French dressing
1/2 cup sweet pickle relish
1/2 tsp. celery salt
1/2 tsp. onion salt
1/4 - 1/2 tsp. garlic powder

Cook spaghetti according to package directions and drain. Mix spaghetti with shrimp and dressing ingredients and allow to marinate overnight in the refrigerator. Just before serving, add tomato, green pepper, and celery. Serves 4-6.

Gladine Nehus
Great Falls

Seafood Salad

1 (3-oz.) package lemon
gelatin
1 scant cup boiling water
1 (5-oz.) jar pimiento cheese
spread
1 (4 1/2-oz.) can shrimp
1 cup mayonnaise
1 cup cream
1 cup chopped celery
2 tbs. chopped green pepper
1/2 tbs. grated onion
3 hard-boiled eggs, chopped

Dissolve gelatin in boiling water. Add pimiento cheese spread and stir to melt cheese. Add remaining ingredients. Pour into 7 x 11-inch pan and refrigerate until set. Serve on lettuce with crackers. Serves 8.

Eva Thompson
Butte

61

Chinese Salad

1 1/2 cups cooked rice, cooled
1 (10-oz) package frozen peas, thawed
1 1/2 cups chopped celery
1/4 cup chopped onion
1 (8 oz.) can sliced water chesnuts
1 (5 oz.) can chow mein noodles

Dressing:
1/2 cup salad oil
1 tsp. celery seed
2 tsp. curry powder
1 tbs. vinegar
1/2 tsp. sugar
Soy sauce to taste

Add peas to cooked rice. Fold in celery, onion, and water chesnuts. Chill until ready to serve. Meanwhile, mix together dressing ingredients. Just before serving, add noodles and dressing to salad. Serves 8-10.

Marlys Carpenter
Billings

Molded Tomato Salad

2 cups tomato juice
1 (3-oz.) package lemon gelatin
1 cup shredded cabbage
2 tbs. chopped green pepper
1/4 tsp. salt
3/8 tsp. celery salt
1/2 cup sliced green olives
3 tbs. lemon juice

Heat 1 cup tomato juice to boiling and pour over gelatin in a bowl. Stir until gelatin is dissolved. Add 1 cup cold tomato juice. Cool until slightly thickened. Fold in remaining ingredients and pour into an oiled 6-inch ring mold or 6 small molds. Refrigerate until set. Unmold onto lettuce leaves. Serves 6.

Mildred Gates
Anaconda

62

Perfect Tomato Aspic

2 (3 oz.) packages
   unflavored gelatin
3/4 cup cold water
1 cup boiling water
2 cups tomato juice
1/4 cup sugar
1/2 tsp. salt
2 tbs. lemon juice
Dash of pepper
Dash of hot sauce
Dash of Worcestershire sauce
1 cup diced onion
1 cup diced celery
1 cup diced carrot
1 cup sour cream
Paprika to taste

Soften gelatin in cold water; add hot water and stir until gelatin is dissolved. Stir in next 7 ingredients. Add onion, celery, and carrot. Pour into 8 x 12-inch glass casserole dish. Refrigerate until firm.

Frost with sour cream and sprinkle with paprika. Slice into 2-inch squares. Serve on lettuce leaves. Serves 12.

Mary Whitney
Twin Bridges

Lime Avocado Salad

1 (3-oz.) package lime
   gelatin
1 cup hot grapefruit juice
3/4 cup cold orange juice
2 tbs. lemon juice
1/2 tsp. grated onion
1 cup diced avocado
1 cup grapefruit sections

Dissolve gelatin in hot grapefruit juice. Add next 3 ingredients and refrigerate until slightly thickened. Fold in avocado and grapefruit sections. Refrigerate until firm. Serves 6-8.

Lillian McGinnis
Great Falls

63

Cooper's Molded Vegetable Salad

1 (3-oz.) package lime or
  lemon gelatin
1 cup boiling water
1 cup shredded carrot
1 cup finely chopped celery
2 tbs. finely chopped green
  pepper
2 tbs. diced onion
1 cup mayonnaise
1 cup cottage cheese

Dissolve gelatin in boiling water. Allow to cool and set slightly and then fold in vegetables. Stir in mayonnaise and cottage cheese and refrigerate until completely set. Serves 8.

June Halgren
Great Falls

Three-Bean Salad

1 (16-oz.) can French-cut
  green beans
1 (16-oz.) can yellow wax
  beans
1 (16-oz.) can red kidney
  beans
1/2 cup chopped green
  pepper
1/2 cup chopped onion

Dressing:
1/2 cup salad oil
1/2 cup vinegar
3/4 cup sugar
1 tsp. salt
1/2 tsp. pepper

Drain all beans and mix together in glass bowl or jar. Add green pepper and onion. Mix well. Mix dressing ingredients together, pour over vegetables, toss well, cover, and refrigerate overnight. Serves 6.

Johanna Pearson
Great Falls

Kidney Bean Salad

1 (16-oz.) can kidney beans,
  drained
1 cup diced celery
1 large onion, chopped
4 tbs. sweet pickle relish

Dressing:
1/2 cup white vinegar
1/2 cup sugar
1 egg, beaten
2 tsp. dry mustard

In saucepan, mix dressing ingredients and bring to a boil. Remove from heat. Mix beans, celery, onion, and pickle relish in a salad bowl. Pour dressing over bean mixture. Chill. Serves 4.

Laura Hicks
Troy

Patio Potato Salad

1/2 cup chopped onion
1/2 cup mayonnaise
10 cups cubed cooked
  potato
6 hard-boiled eggs, cut up

Dressing:
1 cup milk
2/3 cup sugar
1/2 cup vinegar
2 eggs
1/2 cup butter
2 tbs. cornstarch
1 tsp. salt
1 1/2 tsp. celery seed
1/2 tsp. dry mustard

Cook dressing ingredients in a saucepan over low heat until thickened. Remove from heat and add onions and mayonnaise. When cool, add potato and egg. Serves 12.

Leona Henke
Ethridge

65

Party Potato Salad

4 large potatoes
1 small onion, diced
2 stalks celery, diced
4 hard-boiled eggs
1 (4-oz.) can sliced ripe
   olives, drained
1 (2-oz.) jar pimiento, drained
2 medium sweet pickles,
   diced
1 large dill pickle, diced
1 tbs. dried parsley
1 cup diced cheddar cheese
1/4 tsp. celery seed
1/4 tsp. garlic salt
1/4 tsp. pepper
1 tbs. prepared mustard
About 2 cups mayonnaise

Boil unpeeled potatoes in water until tender. Cool, peel, and dice. Add remaining ingredients and blend well. Refrigerate at least 2 hours before serving. Serves 8.

Dawn Zimmerman
Kalispell

Sweet Potato Salad

2 (18-oz.) cans sweet
   potatoes, drained
6 hard-boiled eggs
1 cup finely chopped celery
1/2 onion, chopped OR 1/2
   cup chopped green onion
Salt and pepper to taste
1/2 cup mayonnaise
1/2 cup Durkee's Famous
   Sauce

Cut up sweet potatoes and eggs and mix together in a large bowl. Add remaining ingredients. Amounts of mayonnaise and Durkee's may be adjusted so that salad is moistened as desired. Serves about 8.

Joy Fulton
Great Falls

66

German Potato Salad

1 - 1 1/2 lbs. small red
  potatoes
1/2 tsp. celery seeds
1 onion, chopped
Chives or parsley to taste

Dressing:
2 slices bacon
1/2 tsp. dried mustard
1 tbs. flour
1/3 cup vinegar
1/2 cup potato cooking
  water
Salt to taste
1/4 tsp. pepper
3 tsp. sugar

Boil potatoes in skins, chill thoroughly, and then peel and slice. Add celery seed, chives, and onion to potato.

To make dressing: Cook bacon in skillet until crisp. Remove from pan and dice. Add water, vinegar, sugar, salt, and pepper to bacon fat in skillet. Mix flour and mustard with a little water to make a paste. Add to vinegar mixture and boil 2 minutes.

Add diced bacon to potatoes. Then pour hot dressing over salad and shake to distribute, taking care not to crush potatoes. Serves 4-5.

Mrs. Rebe D. Laird
Billings

German Slaw

1 large head cabbage,
  coarsely shredded
1 large onion, shredded
3/4 cup sugar
1 cup vinegar
1 1/2 tbs. dry mustard
1 cup salad oil
1 tsp. celery seeds (optional)

Mix cabbage and onion in large bowl. In a saucepan, mix vinegar, sugar, oil, and mustard, and bring to a boil. Pour hot over cabbage and onion. Let stand overnight. Mix in celery seeds before serving. Serves 10-12.

Ruth Saholt
Whitefish

Mixed Slaw in Sour Cream Dressing

Dressing:
1 cup sour cream
2 tbs. lemon juice
2 tbs. vinegar
2 tbs. sugar
1 tsp. salt
1/8 tsp. pepper
1 tsp. dry mustard

1 cup shredded cabbage
1 cup shredded carrot
1 cup shredded peeled
   apple
Salted peanuts to taste
Pimiento strips to taste

Beat sour cream until smooth. Add other ingredients in order given. Chill until serving time. Garnish with pimiento strips and salted peanuts. Serves 3-4.

Olga M. Sheire
Great Falls

Coleslaw with Grapes and Almonds

1 medium head cabbage,
   coarsely chopped
2 cups seedless green grapes
1 cup slivered blanched
   almonds
1 tsp. salt
1 tsp. sugar
1 tsp. dry mustard
2 tbs. vinegar
1 tsp. grated onion (optional)
1 cup mayonnaise

Combine cabbage, grapes, and almonds in a large serving bowl. Mix remaining ingredients except mayonnaise and pour over cabbage mixture. Toss well and stir in mayonnaise. Serves 12.

Mildred Gates
Anaconda

68

Layered Green Salad

1/2 head lettuce, torn up
1/2 bunch spinach, torn up
12 slices fried bacon,
  crumbled
1 cup fresh mushroom slices
1/2 cup red onion rings
1 (10-oz.) package frozen
  peas, thawed
5 hard-boiled eggs, sliced
1/2 cup grated mild cheddar
  cheese
1/2 cup mayonnaise
1/2 cup sour cream
1 tsp. sugar

In a large, clear-glass bowl, arrange layers as follows: lettuce, spinach, bacon, mushroom, red onion, peas, and eggs. In a small bowl, combine remaining ingredients, mix well, and spread carefully over the top of the salad, much like frosting a cake. Cover with plastic wrap and refrigerate overnight. Serves 4-6.

Katie Burns
Butte

Spinach Orange Toss

8 oz. fresh spinach
1 (11-oz.) can mandarin
  orange segments
1 cup sliced fresh mushrooms
3 tbs. salad oil
1 tbs. lemon juice
1/2 tsp. poppy seed
1/4 tsp. salt
3/4 cup toasted slivered
  almonds

Place torn spinach in a large bowl. Add orange segments and mushrooms. Toss lightly, cover, and chill. Combine remaining ingredients except almonds in a jar, cover, and shake well. Chill. Shake again and pour over salad. Sprinkle salad with toasted almonds. Serves 4.

Robin Arbuckle Jones
Great Falls

69

Sarah's Salad

4 cups torn lettuce
2 tomatoes, chopped
3 green olives, chopped
1 carrot, sliced thin
   diagonally
1 cup torn spinach
1/2 cup sliced cucumber

Dressing:
3 tbs. canola oil
1 tbs. rice vinegar
1/2 tsp. garlic salt
1/2 tsp. curry powder
1 tbs. sugar
1/2 tsp. lemon juice
1/2 tsp. Dijon mustard
Poppy seeds to taste
   (optional)
3 hard-boiled eggs, chopped

Combine dressing ingredients, mix well, and refrigerate 1 hour before using. Toss salad ingredients in large salad bowl. Fold in dressing 5 minutes before serving. Serves 6.

Sarah Leipheimer
Anaconda

Linda's Salad

1 head lettuce, torn up
1 head cauliflower, chopped
1 sweet onion, sliced
1 lb. bacon
2 cups mayonnaise
1/3 cup grated Parmesan
   cheese
1/4 cup sugar

Mix together mayonnaise, Parmesan cheese, and sugar and set aside. Fry bacon until crisp, drain off excess fat, and crumble bacon. Layer lettuce, cauliflower, onion, and bacon in salad bowl. Refrigerate dressing and salad overnight. Mix in dressing before serving. Serves 8-10.

Linda Greaves
Helena

70

Lemon and Mustard Carrot Salad

Dressing:
1/4 cup lemon juice
2 tsp. Dijon mustard
2 tsp. sugar
1/2 cup minced green onion
6 tbs. salad oil
1/2 tsp. salt
1/8 tsp. pepper
2 tsp. dried dill weed

1 lb. carrots, cut in long, thin
    strips
3 cups water
Pinch of salt
1 tsp. sugar

Mix dressing ingredients together in a jar with lid and shake well. Set aside. In a saucepan, combine carrots, water, and salt and sugar. Bring to a boil, lower heat, and cover. Simmer until tender, about 5 minutes. Do not overcook. Drain and cool quickly by holding under running cold water. Pour dressing over carrots and toss well to coat. Serves 6.

Laura Hicks
Troy

Salad for Singles

2 cucumbers, peeled and
    diced
2 medium carrots, chopped
2 cups diced celery
1 bunch green onions, diced
1 large or 2 medium
    tomatoes, diced
1 green pepper, diced
1/4 cup seasoned rice
    vinegar
3 cups cold water
1 tbs. salt

For 30 minutes, soak cucumber in cold water to which salt has been added. Rinse and drain. Add rice vinegar and remaining vegetables to cucumber. Store in a covered bowl in the refrigerator. Mixture keeps well for a week. Makes about 9 cups. To serve, add 1 cup vegetable mix to chopped lettuce. Add dressing.

Chef's note: "Living alone, I find preparing vegetables for 1 serving of salad tedious. This is how I solved the problem."

Madelene Voeller
Helena

Snow Pea Salad

1 (7-oz.) package frozen
  snow peas
2 cups cauliflowerets
1 (5-oz.) can water chesnuts,
  drained and sliced
2 tbs. chopped pimiento

Dressing:
2 tbs. sesame seeds
1/3 cup salad oil
1 tbs. lemon juice
1 tbs. vinegar
1 tbs. sugar
1/2 clove garlic, minced
1/2 tsp. salt

Combine snow peas and 1/2 cup water in saucepan and bring to a boil. About 1 minute after water boils, remove pan from heat and place under running cold water to cool quickly. Drain. Cook cauliflowerets in boiling, salted water for about 3 minutes after water comes to a boil. Drain. Combine peas, cauliflowerets, water chesnuts, and pimiento. Chill.

To make dressing: Arrange sesame seeds in a shallow baking pan and bake 5-8 minutes at 350 degrees, or until browned. Cool. In a jar with cover, combine all dressing ingedients. Shake to blend well and chill. Add dressing to vegetables in amount desired and toss lightly. Serves 6.

Phyllis Reyner
Missoula

Green Pea Salad

1 cup sour cream
1 tbs. seasoned salt
1/4 tsp. lemon pepper
1/4 tsp. garlic powder
1 (20-oz.) package frozen
  peas, thawed
1/2 lb. bacon, cooked
1 tomato, chopped
1/4 cup chopped red onion

Mix sour cream and seasonings. In a large bowl, combine peas, crumbled bacon, tomato, and onion. Blend in seasoned sour cream. Chill several hours or overnight before serving. Serve on lettuce leaves.

Birdie Joers
Augusta

72

Marinated Vegetable Salad

3 medium tomatoes, cut into
  wedges
1 cup sliced cucumber
  (with peel)
1 medium onion, sliced thin
1/2 cup thinly sliced carrot
1/2 cup thinly sliced celery
3/4 cup tarragon vinegar
1/2 cup cold water
1/4 cup sugar
1 tsp. basil
1/2 tsp. salt
1/4 tsp. pepper

Place vegetables in large bowl. Combine other ingredients, mix well, and pour over vegetables. Refrigerate at least 4 hours before serving. Toss well. Serves 8.

Royce Pearson
Great Falls

Parsnip Salad

2 cups grated parsnip
1/2 cup grated carrot
1/2 cup minced celery
2 tbs. minced pimiento
4 tbs. mild horseradish
1/2 cup mayonnaise

Combine all ingredients and serve on lettuce leaves. Serves 4-6.

Ina Gackle
Plentywood

White Corn Salad

1 (16-oz.) can French-cut
   green beans
1 (16-oz.) can tiny
   sweet peas
1 (12-oz.) can white corn
1 (2-oz.) can pimiento
1 cup chopped celery
1 large green pepper,
   chopped
About 10 green onions,
   chopped

Dressing:
3/4 cup vinegar
1/2 cup salad oil
1 tsp. salt
1/2 cup sugar
1 tsp. pepper
1 tbs. water
1/2 tsp. onion powder

Combine dressing ingredients in a saucepan and bring to a boil to dissolve sugar. Cool and pour over vegetables in large bowl. Refrigerate at least 6 hours before serving. Serves 10.

Barbara McPherson
Canyon Creek

Tabbouleh

1 cup bulgur wheat
3/4 cup chopped green
    onion
4 medium tomatoes, peeled
    and diced
1 cup diced, pared
    cucumber
Fresh sprigs of mint to garnish

Dressing:
1 clove garlic, crushed
1 1/2 cups finely chopped
    parsley
3/4 cup olive oil
3 tbs. lemon juice
1 1/2 tsp. salt
1/4 tsp. pepper
3/4 cup chopped mint
Ground red pepper flakes to
    taste

Rinse bulgur in cold water and drain well. Cover with boiling water and soak for 2 hours. Drain and squeeze out excess water. Combine dressing ingredients in a large bowl, and add bulgur, tossing lightly. Layer vegetables on top of bulgur. Refrigerate overnight and toss before serving. Serve on lettuce leaves with mint sprigs for garnish. Serves 10.

Enis Ingold
Great Falls

75

Sunshine Salad

1 head broccoli, cut up
1 cup shelled sunflower
  seeds
1/2 cup raisins
1/2 lb. bacon, fried and
  crumbled
Sliced red onion to taste
  (optional)

Dressing:
1 cup mayonnaise
1/2 cup sugar
2 tbs. vinegar

Toss salad ingredients together in large bowl. Blend dressing ingredients together and pour over salad. Toss to moisten and chill before serving. Serves 6.

Patricia White
Belgrade

Fruit Salad with Lemon Dip

24 fresh strawberries
24 fresh purple grapes
2 medium bananas, sliced
24 cantaloupe balls
1/4 cup orange juice
1/4 cup lemon juice
1/4 cup sugar

Lemon dip:
1 cup sour cream
3 tbs. powdered sugar
1/2 tsp. grated lemon peel

Mix dip ingredients together well to blend flavors. Set aside. Blend juices and sugar together and pour over fruit in large bowl, tossing well, to prevent discoloration. Serve fruit with lemon dip. Serves 4-6.

Johanna Pearson
Great Falls

76

Orange Salad Bowl

1 large head leaf lettuce, torn
1 (11-oz.) can mandarin
   orange segments, drained
1/2 cup toasted slivered
   almonds
1 cucumber, sliced
4-5 green onions, chopped
   (including green part)

Dressing:
1/3 cup sugar
1 tsp. salt
1 tsp. dry mustard
1/3 cup tarragon vinegar
1-2 green onions,
   chopped fine
1 cup salad oil
1 tbs. celery seeds

Combine dressing ingredients and mix well. Chill for at least 30 minutes before using. Toss all salad ingredients together lightly in a large bowl. Top with a small amount of dressing and toss again just to moisten. Serves 6-8.

Mary Ann Bigelow
Missoula

77

Five-Fruit Salad

3 oz. frozen pineapple juice
  concentrate, thawed
2 tbs. creamy peanut butter
1/3 cup salad oil
1 cup pineapple chunks,
  drained
1 cup peach slices
1/4 medium cantaloupe,
  peeled and cut into
  wedges
1/2 cup seedless grapes,
  halved
1/2 cup strawberries, halved

To make dressing: Combine pineapple juice and peanut butter in blender container, cover, and blend until smooth. With blender running on high, gradually add salad oil through opening in lid. Blend well. Transfer to a covered container and refrigerate.

Mix fruits in large bowl and moisten with dressing. Serves 6-8.

Patti Billet
Missoula

Yogurt Honey Waldorf Salad

3 cups diced red apple
  (with peel)
1 tbs. lemon juice
1 cup diced celery
1/2 cup chopped raisins
1/2 cup chopped walnuts
2 tbs. honey
1 cup plain yogurt
Salt and pepper to taste

Combine first 5 ingredients together in a large bowl. Mix together the honey, yogurt, salt, and pepper, and pour over the apple mixture. Toss to mix. Chill. Serves 6.

(Variation: Omit raisins and walnuts, and add 2 cups cooked, chilled wild rice. Replace 2 tbs. honey with 2 tbs. brown sugar. Replace 1 cup plain yogurt with 1/2 cup plain yogurt mixed with 1/4 cup mayonnaise. Laura Hicks, Troy)

Ruthanne Monahan
Butte

Anniversary Fruit Salad

1 (16-oz.) can fruit cocktail
  (with juice)
1 (20-oz.) can pineapple
  chunks (with juice)
1/2 lb. seedless green grapes
4 red apples, diced
  (peel only 2)
2 cups miniature
  marshmallows
2 (3 1/2-oz.) packages
  instant vanilla pudding
12 oz. whipped cream
8 oz. lemon yogurt

Mix together in order listed and chill for at least 2 hours before serving. Serves 18-20.

Pat Lauri
Elliston

Pineapple Wheat Salad

1 cup whole wheat berries
2 cups boiling water
1 1/2 cups crushed
  pineapple, drained
8 oz. cream cheese
2 (3 1/2-oz.) packages
  instant vanilla pudding
3 tbs. lemon juice
12 oz. whipped cream
1 tsp. vanilla

The night before serving salad, pour boiling water over wheat berries and allow to soak overnight. The next day, simmer wheat for 30 minutes. Allow to cool.

To make salad: Add softened cream cheese to pudding mix and lemon juice. Mix well; stir in whipped cream and vanilla. Fold in pineapple and wheat, adding pineapple juice to bring salad to desired consistency. Serves 12-14.

Nancy Morast
Kalispell

79

Pineapple Rice Salad

2 (3-oz.) packages lemon
   gelatin
1 (15 1/2-oz.) can crushed
   pineapple (reserve juice)
3 cups liquid (pineapple
   juice and water)
1 pint pineapple sherbet
1 1/2 cups cooked rice
1/2 cup chopped nuts
1 (6-oz.) jar maraschino
   cherries, cut up

Dissolve gelatin in liquid. Add remaining ingredients and pour into 9 x 13-inch pan. Refrigerate to set. Serves 12.

Toni Rowlison
Laurel

Creamy Pear Salad

1 (29-oz.) can pears
   (reserve juice)
1 (3-oz.) package lemon
   gelatin
8 oz. cream cheese
1 cup whipped cream
1 cup chopped pecans

Boil 1 cup pear juice and add gelatin to dissolve. Chill until almost set. Put pears into blender, add cream cheese, and blend until creamy. Stir in gelatin and fold in nuts and whipped cream. Chill until set. Serves 6.

Becky Marsh
Belgrade

Rhubarb Strawberry Salad

4 cups diced rhubarb
3/4 cup sugar
2/3 cup water
2 (3-oz.) packages
  strawberry gelatin
12 oz. ginger ale

Place rhubarb, sugar, and water in saucepan, and cook until rhubarb is tender. Add gelatin and dissolve. Stir in ginger ale. Pour into mold or pan and refrigerate until set. Serves 8-10.

Mamie Fiers
Hide Away Ranch
Wolf Creek

Raspberry Salad

1 (10-oz.) package frozen
  raspberries, thawed
  (reserve juice)
1 (6-oz.) package raspberry
  gelatin
2 cups boiling water
1 pint vanilla ice cream
1 (6-oz.) can frozen
  lemonade concentrate
1/4 cup chopped pecans

Dissolve gelatin in boiling water. Add ice cream by spoonfuls, stirring to melt. Stir in lemonade and juice from raspberries. Chill until partially set. Add raspberries and nuts, and chill until firm in a 6-cup mold. Serves 6-8.

Patty Howse
Great Falls

Cranberry Relish Mold

2 (3-oz.) packages cherry
   gelatin
1 tsp. unflavored gelatin
2 cups boiling water
1 (16-oz.) can whole
   cranberry sauce
1 (7-oz.) can crushed
   pineapple, drained
1/4 cup chopped celery
Fresh cranberries for garnish
   (optional)
Mayonnaise to garnish

Dissolve gelatins completely in boiling water. Let cool slightly, and then stir in cranberry sauce, pineapple, and celery. Pour into a glass serving bowl or 6-cup mold that has first been rinsed under cold water. Chill until firm.

To serve, dip mold briefly in a pan of hot water to loosen, and unmold onto chilled plate. Garnish with fresh cranberries if desired. Top each serving with a small dollop of mayonnaise. Serves 8-10.

M.J. Hendrickson
Great Falls

Kids' Aquarium Gelatin

1 (3-oz.) package lime
   gelatin
18 "gummy fish" candies
6 clear plastic cocktail
   glasses

Prepare gelatin according to package directions. Pour in equal amounts into plastic glasses, and chill until slightly thickened. Submerge 3 "fish" in each "aquarium." Chill until firm. Serves 6.

Carolyn Lehman
Kalispell

Blender French Dressing

1 cup sugar
1 cup salad oil
1/2 cup catsup
1/2 cup vinegar
2 tbs. lemon juice
1 small onion, chopped
1/2 tsp. salt
1/4 tsp. ground ginger
1/4 tsp. paprika

Blend all ingredients together in blender until creamy. Store in refrigerator. Makes about 3 cups.

Dixie Engelhardt
Ulm

Thousand Island Dressing

2 cups mayonnaise
1/2 cup chili sauce
3 hard-boiled eggs, chopped
1 1/2 medium dill pickles,
    chopped and drained
1/3 cup finely chopped
    celery
Chopped green pepper to
    taste
1 small onion, chopped fine

Combine all ingredients and blend well. Store in refrigerator. Makes 4 cups.

June Halgren
Great Falls

83

Blue Cheese Dressing

1/2 lb. blue cheese,
   cut into small chunks
2 1/2 cups mayonnaise
1/2 cup milk
3/4 tsp. garlic powder
1/4 cup cider vinegar
1/4 tsp. salt
1/2 tsp. dry mustard
1/2 tsp. white pepper

Combine all ingredients and blend well, either in a blender or in a large bowl by hand. Store in refrigerator as long as 2 months. Makes 4 cups.

Deb Strohmyer
Libby

Russian Dressing

1 green pepper
1 small onion
1 (10 3/4-oz.) can condensed
   tomato soup
1/2 cup catsup
1/2 cup salad oil
1/4 cup vinegar
2/3 cup brown sugar
1 tsp. salt
1 tsp. dry mustard
1 tsp. paprika

Grind green pepper and onion together in a food processor. Add remaining ingredients and process. Store in refrigerator. Makes 4 cups.

Gloria Guessen
Missoula

Poppy Seed Dressing

1/4 cup honey
1/2 tsp. salt
1 tsp. dry mustard
1 tsp. paprika
1 tsp. grated lemon peel
6 tbs. lemon juice
1 cup salad oil
1 tbs. poppy seeds

Combine all but salad oil and poppy seeds in blender container, and whirl at high speed to mix well. While blending, slowly pour in oil through opening at top of blender container. Continue whirling until dressing has thickened. Stir in poppy seeds. Put in a jar, cover, and chill for several hours or more before using. Makes 1 1/2 cups.

Lillian McGinnis
Great Falls

Onion Dressing

1 small onion, chopped
1 1/4 cups sugar
3 tsp. prepared mustard
1 tsp. salt
1/2 cup vinegar
2 cups salad oil
1 1/2 tsp. poppy seeds
   (optional)

Mix first 5 ingredients together in blender. Add oil gradually while blending until dressing is thick. Add poppy seed if desired. Makes about 3 cups.

Mary Ellen Olmstead
Cut Bank

85

Mustard Dill Dressing

1/3 cup Dijon mustard
1/3 cup stone-ground
   mustard
1/3 cup tarragon-white wine
   vinegar
1/3 cup raspberry vinegar
1 1/4 tsp. dried dill
1 tsp. dried tarragon
3 3/4 cups corn oil
1/8 cup grated Parmesan
   cheese

Place all ingredients except oil and Parmesan cheese in blender or food processor. Blend. Very slowly, drop by drop, add oil. When all oil is added, mix in cheese. Makes 5 cups.

Chef's note: "This is our house dressing. We get many requests for this recipe."

The Stovetop Restaurant and Deli
Helena

Pink Peppercorn Dressing

4 tbs. pink peppercorns
2 egg yolks
2 tbs. minced garlic
2 tbs. Dijon mustard
2 tbs. dried thyme
2 tbs. parsley
2 1/4 cups fruity olive oil
3/4 cup champagne wine
   vinegar

Mix together peppercorns, egg yolks, garlic, and mustard. Add vinegar and mix well. Pour mixture into food processor, and add oil in a thin stream while blending to thicken. Stir in parsley and thyme. Makes 3 1/2 cups.

The Stovetop Restaurant and Deli
Helena

Entrees

Katie's So Good Meat Loaf

1 1/2 lbs. ground beef
1 cup grated carrot
1 cup grated potato
1 small onion, grated
1 (4-oz.) can mushroom
  pieces (with liquid)
2 slices bread, torn into
  small pieces
1 cup milk
1/4 cup plus 2 tbs.
  white vinegar
1 tsp. salt
1/4 tsp. pepper

Add vinegar to milk and set aside. Combine all other ingredients in large bowl and mix until well blended. Add milk and vinegar and mix again. Pour into 9 x 13-inch baking pan. Bake one hour at 375 degrees. Serves 6.

Katie Burns
Butte

Sicilian Meat Loaf

2 eggs, beaten
1 cup tomato juice
1/2 tsp. oregano
1/4 tsp. pepper
2 lbs. ground beef
3/4 cup soft bread crumbs
2 tbs. parsley
1/4 tsp. salt
1 small clove garlic, minced
1 (3-oz.) package thinly
  sliced ham
2 cups shredded
  mozzarella cheese

Combine eggs, 1/2 cup tomato juice, garlic, and seasonings. Let mixture sit for a few minutes and then mix in ground beef and bread crumbs. Pat this out into a 10 x 12-inch rectangle on foil or cookie sheet. Arrange ham slices on meat, leaving a small margin at edges. Sprinkle cheese over ham and roll up meat loaf. Seal edges and ends. Pour remaining 1/2 cup tomato juice over top of meat loaf. Meat loaf may be covered with a portion of cheese the last few minutes of baking. Bake 1 1/4 hours at 350 degrees. Serves 6.

Gale Anderson
Missoula

88

Muffin Meat Loaf a la Montana

1 egg
1/2 cup milk
1 1/2 tsp. salt
1/4 tsp. paprika
1/4 tsp. ground pepper
3/4 cup whole wheat
   bread crumbs
1 lb. ground chuck or
   ground round

Sauce:
1 (8-oz.) can tomato sauce
   with tomato bits
1 lbs. honey
1 tbs. wine vinegar
1 clove garlic, finely minced
1 green onion, chopped
1 tbs. diced green
   chili pepper

Break egg into large bowl and beat slightly with fork. Add milk, seasonings, and bread crumbs. Blend in ground beef. In separate bowl, combine sauce ingredients and mix well. Place 1 tsp. sauce in bottom of 6-8 muffin cups. Divide meat mixture among muffin cups, shaping slightly. Bake 20-25 minutes at 350 degrees. Heat remaining sauce and serve with meat loaves. Serves 3-4.

Gary M. Monahan
Butte

Meatball Surprise

2 lbs. ground beef
1 cup crushed soda crackers
3 eggs
1 package onion soup mix
1 cup beef broth
1/2 cup whole cranberry
   sauce
1 cup brown sugar
1 (32-oz.) can sauerkraut

Mix first 4 ingredients together and form into balls. Place in 9 x 12-inch pan. Drain sauerkraut, mix with remaining ingredients and pour over meatballs. Bake 1 1/2 - 2 hours at 325 degrees. Serves 6.

Mamie Fiers
Hide Away Ranch
Wolf Creek

89

Montana Tacos

Pancakes:
3 eggs
1 1/2 cups milk
1 cup sifted all-purpose flour
1 tsp. salt
1/2 cup yellow cornmeal
2 tbs. butter, melted

Filling:
2 lbs. ground beef
1 envelope onion soup mix
1 (1 lb. 2-oz.) can tomato
    juice
1 cup catsup
1/4 cup brown sugar, firmly
    packed
2 tbs. vinegar
2 tbs. Worcestershire sauce
2 tsp. salt

Topping:
2 cups dairy sour cream
1 cup grated sharp cheddar
    cheese
1 medium green pepper, cut
    into thin rings
Cherry tomatoes

To make filling: Brown ground beef in large, heavy skillet with cover. Drain fat. Stir in remaining filling ingredients and mix well. Cook covered over low heat, stirring occasionally, for 2 1/2 hours or until mixture is thick.

To make pancakes: Beat egg with milk. Sift in flour and salt. Stir in cornmeal and melted butter. Beat until smooth. Heat a 7-inch skillet over low heat. Lightly grease with butter. Pour in a scant 1/4 cup batter at a time, tipping pan to cover the bottom completely. Fry until pancake top is dry and underside is golden brown. Turn quickly and brown other side. Repeat, lightly greasing pan before each pancake, to make 12 pancakes.

Spoon about 1/4 cup filling onto each pancake; roll pancake up and place seam-side-down in a shallow, buttered baking dish. Save remaining filling to use as topping. Keep pancake rolls warm until all are baked and filled.

Spoon sour cream down the middle of the pancake rows. Sprinkle with cheese. Spoon remaining filling along edges of sour cream. Bake 30 minutes at 325 degrees or until bubbly and pancakes are heated through. Pancakes can be made ahead and chilled or frozen. If chilled, increase baking time to 45 minutes; if frozen, to 60 minutes. Garnish with green pepper rings and cherry tomatoes. Serves 6.

Donna McCulloch
Colstrip

90

Sandy's Taco Pizza

3 cups biscuit mix

3/4 cup water

2 (10 1/2-oz.) cans pizza
  sauce

1 lb. ground beef

1 package taco seasoning

1 (4-oz.) can chopped black
  olives

1-2 tomatoes, chopped

2-3 cups chopped lettuce

24 oz. sour cream

1 lb. mozzarella
  cheese, shredded

1 lb. cheddar
  cheese, shredded

1 cup crushed taco chips

Brown ground beef and mix in taco seasoning. Set aside. Mix together biscuit mix and water. On floured board, knead 20 times. Spread in a lightly greased pizza pan. Spread dough with pizza sauce, then meat, and then other ingredients, ending with cheese. Pizza will be very thick. Bake 15-20 minutes at 450 degrees. Makes 1 large pizza.

Sandy Schlosser
Shepherd

Legendary Christmas dinners

Toiling over an open hearth or a patented hay-burning stove with heavy iron skillets and Dutch ovens characterized the bulk of Christmas Day activities for many a homesteading wife. Stuffing of onions, mashed potatoes, homemade loaves of bread, and jellies made from wild plums and berries served as complements to main dishes of wild fowl, venison, or buffalo in early years.

John H. Monnett
A Rocky Mountain Christmas: Yuletide Stories of the West

Filled Taco Buns

Buns:
10 cups flour
3 tbs. dry yeast
3 3/4 cups warm water
6 tbs. butter
6 tbs. sugar
4 tsp. salt
2 eggs

Filling:
3 lbs. ground beef
2 packages taco seasoning
Salt and pepper to taste
2 tbs. raw onion,
  chopped fine
3 cups shredded American
  or cheddar cheese

To make buns: Mix yeast into warm water. Add butter, sugar, and salt. Whip eggs with fork and then add to yeast mixture. Stir in 4 cups flour and blend well. Add remaining flour gradually to form soft dough. Cover and let rise until doubled in volume. Punch down and let rise again until doubled in volume.

To make filling: Brown ground beef in skillet. Drain excess fat and add taco seasoning, salt, pepper, and onion.

Pinch off enough dough to make a bun. With greased hands, spread dough out flat and thin. Fill with 1 tbs. filling and sprinkle with shredded cheese. Fold dough circle in half to enclose filling. Pinch to seal edges. Place buns in greased baking pan and bake 30 minutes at 375 degrees, or until golden brown. After removing from oven, brush tops with butter.

Marianne Roose
Eureka

Tamale Pie

Filling:
1 lb. ground beef
1 cup chopped onion
1 cup chopped
　green pepper
1 (16-oz.) can tomato sauce
1 (12-oz.) can corn
1/2 cup sliced ripe olives
1 (16-oz.) can kidney or
　pinto beans
1 (4-oz.) can chopped
　green chilies
1 clove garlic, minced
1 tbs. sugar
1/2 tsp. salt
2-3 tbs. chili powder
Dash of pepper
6 oz. cheddar cheese, grated

Topping:
1 cup biscuit mix
1 cup cornmeal
2/3 cup milk

Cook ground beef, onion, and green pepper in large skillet until meat is browned. Drain excess fat. Stir in remaining filling ingredients except grated cheese. Simmer 20-25 minutes until thick. Add cheese and remove from heat.

Mix topping ingredients together. Spoon topping over filling. Cover tightly and simmer until cornmeal is firm, about 10-15 minutes. Serves 6.

Mary Schneider
West Glacier

Gourmet Chili

1 lb. ground beef
1 lb. pork sausage
1 lb. bacon, cut up
1 (4-oz.) can
   mushroom pieces
1 large onion, diced
1 green pepper, diced
4 (15-oz.) cans chili beans
1 quart tomato juice
1 (30-oz.) can tomatoes
1/2 tsp. salt
1 tsp. garlic powder
1 tsp. pepper
1 tsp. oregano
1 tsp. cloves
1 tsp. cinnamon
1 tsp. chili powder
1 tsp. cumin
1 tbs. sugar

Fry beef, sausage, onion, and green pepper together until meat is browned. Fry bacon separately until about half-cooked. Drain bacon and other meat. In 8-quart Dutch oven, mix all ingredients. Simmer 2-3 hours at 325 degrees. Serves 10-15.

Joyce Jensen
Butte

94

Kay's Quick Mexi-Bake

12 flour tortillas
1-2 lbs. ground beef
1 (16-oz.) can refried beans
1 package taco
   seasoning mix
2-3 cups shredded
   cheddar cheese
1 (8-oz.) can tomato sauce
1 (16-oz.) jar salsa
Sour cream (optional)

Brown meat and add seasoning mix, following package directions. Stir in beans and simmer 10 minutes. Spoon about 1/4 cup mixture onto each tortilla and sprinkle with cheddar cheese. Roll tortillas and place in large baking dish. Mix tomato sauce with 1/2 jar salsa and pour over tortillas. Sprinkle remaining cheese on top. Bake at 350 degrees until cheese is melted and bubbly, about 15-20 minutes. Serve with remaining salsa and sour cream if desired. Serves 6-12.

Kayleen Lockwood
Seeley Lake

Montana Yum-Yum

1 1/4 lbs. ground beef
2 (16-oz.) cans stewed
   tomatoes
1 (6 oz.) can tomato paste
1 clove garlic, crushed
1/2 tsp. salt
1/4 tsp. pepper
8 oz. wide egg noodles
1 cup sour cream
8 oz. cream cheese, softened
6-8 green onions with
   tops, diced
1 cup grated sharp
   cheddar cheese

Cook ground beef in nonstick skillet. Drain excess fat. Add tomatoes, tomato paste, garlic, and spices. Cook and drain noodles according to package directions. Add sour cream, cream cheese, and onion. Place meat mixture in 9 x 12-inch baking pan. Cover with noodle mixture. Sprinkle grated cheese on top and bake 30-40 minutes at 350 degrees. Serves 8.

Adeline Kiss
Helena

95

Ground Beef and Wild Rice Casserole

1 cup uncooked wild rice
4 cups boiling water
1 1/2 lbs. ground beef
3/4 cup chopped celery
1/2 cup chopped onion
1/4 tsp. celery salt
1/4 tsp. garlic powder
1/4 tsp. pepper
1 (10 3/4-oz.) can condensed
  cream of mushroom soup
1 (10 3/4-oz.) can condensed
  cream of chicken soup
1 (10 3/4-oz.) can beef
  bouillon broth
1 (4-oz.) can sliced
  mushrooms
1/4 tsp. onion salt
1/4 tsp. paprika
1/2 cup slivered or
  sliced almonds

Wash rice. Pour boiling water over rice in pan and let stand in water 15-20 minutes. In a large, heavy skillet, brown beef with onions; then add celery and cook until celery is limp. Drain excess fat, add soups and broth, seasonings, and mushrooms. Mix well and heat through.

Drain the wild rice and add to meat mixture. Simmer 15 minutes. Pour into large casserole dish, and top with almonds. Bake covered 1 1/2 hours at 350 degrees. Add more beef broth or soup if it becomes too dry while baking. Can be frozen and reheated when needed. Serves 10.

Dolly Rugland
Kalispell

96

Hamburger Cashew Hot Dish

5 oz. egg noodles
1 lb. ground beef
1 medium onion, chopped
1 tbs. butter
1/2 tsp. salt
1/2 lb. cheddar
  cheese, diced
1 (4-oz.) can
  mushrooms, drained
1 (10 3/4-oz.) can condensed
  cream of mushroom soup
1/2 cup milk
2/3 cup chow mein noodles
1/2 cup cashews

Cook noodles according to package directions and drain. Brown meat and onion in butter. To meat, add remaining ingredients except chow mein noodles and cashews. Mix well and bake 20 minutes at 325 degrees. Add chow mein noodles and cashews. Bake another 10 minutes. Serves 4-6.

Betty Stav
Deer Lodge

Joe's Special One-Dish Meal

1 cup fresh mushrooms,
  sliced
1 cup fresh spinach,
  shredded
1/2 lb. ground beef
2 eggs, beaten
Worcestershire sauce to taste
Catsup to taste

In a large skillet, brown the ground beef. Drain off excess fat. Add mushrooms and spinach. When these appear cooked, add eggs and mix thoroughly. Remove from heat when eggs are cooked. Add Worcestershire and/or catsup to taste. Serves 1-2.

Chef's note: "I learned of (this recipe) and grew to love it while living in San Francisco.... It is an excellent source of protein for the hard worker or athlete. And it is so easy to make, even the worst bachelor-chef can perfect it."

Carlo Canty
Butte

97

Beef Stroganoff Sandwiches

1 loaf French bread, cut in
   half lengthwise
1 lb. ground beef
1/4 cup finely chopped onion
1 cup dairy sour cream
1 tbs. milk
1/4 cup chopped parsley
1/2 tsp. salt
1/8 tsp. pepper
1 tsp. Worcestershire sauce
6 oz. cheese, shredded

Brown beef with onion; drain excess fat. Stir in sour cream, milk, parsley, salt, pepper, and Worcestershire sauce. Heat but do not let boil. Wrap bread in foil and heat for 10 minutes in 375-degree oven. Then spread meat mixture over cut side of bread. Sprinkle with cheese, place on baking sheet, and return to oven for 5 minutes, or until cheese melts. Serves 8.

Bonnie Fastje
Wilsall

Cheeseburger Roll

1 7/8 cups unsifted flour
1 tsp. salt
3/4 cup milk
3 tsp. baking powder
5 tbs. shortening

Filling:
1 lb. ground beef
1/4 tsp. pepper
1/4 cup catsup
1/2 tsp. salt
1/2 tsp. garlic powder
1 cup grated sharp
   cheddar cheese
2 tbs. chopped onion

Mix filling ingredients and set aside. Mix together flour, baking powder, and salt. Cut in shortening. Add milk, stirring with fork until all flour is moistened. Turn out onto lightly floured board and knead gently for 20 seconds. Roll out to form a 10 x 12-inch rectangle about 1/4-inch thick. Spread with filling and roll lengthwise. Turn edges as you roll and seal end. Place seam-side-down on a greased baking sheet; bake one hour at 375 degrees. Serve hot in slices with chili sauce or beef gravy. Serves 8-9.

Terry J. McGillis
Deer Lodge

Runzas (German Sandwiches)

Filling:
1 1/2 lbs. ground beef
1 large onion, chopped
4 cups chopped cabbage
Salt and pepper to taste

Dough:
4 1/2 - 5 cups flour
1/2 cup sugar
1 tsp. salt
2 packages dry yeast
3/4 cup milk
1/2 cup water
1/2 cup shortening
2 eggs

To make filling: Brown ground beef, add onion and cabbage and cook until these are wilted. Mix well and season. Set aside.

To make dough: Mix 2 cups flour with sugar, salt, and yeast. In a small saucepan, heat milk, water, and shortening until warm (120-130 degrees). Pour into flour mixture. Add eggs and beat with mixer on low speed 1/2 minute. Beat on high 3 minutes. Stir in rest of flour. Dough should be soft and rather sticky. Knead until smooth (about 3 minutes). Cover dough and let rest for 20 minutes. Then roll dough into 6- or 7-inch squares.

Drop 3 tbs. filling onto each square of dough, bring corners to center, pinch edges together, and place smooth-side-up on greased baking sheets. Let rise 45 minutes and then bake 20 minutes at 350 degrees. Makes about 18 runzas.

Chef's Note: "Runzas freeze well and can be heated in microwave or oven. They also can be eaten cold."

Dixie Engelhardt
Ulm

Pizza Rollups

Dough:
1/2 cup water
1 3/4 cups milk
1 tbs. margarine
2 tbs. sugar
1/2 tsp. salt
1 package dry yeast
5-6 cups flour

Filling:
3 lbs. ground beef
1 medium onion, chopped
1 (8-oz.) can mushrooms
2 cups tomato sauce
1 envelope spaghetti sauce
   seasoning
1 (4-oz.) can chopped ripe
   olives
1 lb. mozzarella
   cheese, grated
Grated Parmesan cheese

To make dough: Warm milk, water, and margarine until latter has melted. Add sugar, salt, and yeast and stir until yeast dissolves. Add 2 cups flour and mix. Add 3-4 more cups flour, 1 cup at a time. Dough should be slightly soft. Knead dough on floured board for about 5 minutes. Let rise in warm place for 20 minutes. Cover and refrigerate for 2-4 hours. When ready to use, let rise at room temperature for 20 minutes.

To make filling: Brown ground beef and onion; drain excess fat. Add mushrooms, tomato sauce, spaghetti sauce seasoning, and olives. Mix thoroughly and heat through.

Divide dough into 4 parts. Pat out 1 part dough on large, greased cookie sheet to form a 7 x 12-inch rectangle. Top with 1/4 the filling, 1/4 the mozzarella and some Parmesan. Roll up, starting with long edge. Cut roll into 4 pieces—do not separate. Make a second roll on same cookie sheet, and then 2 more on second cookie sheet. Bake 25 minutes at 350 degrees, or until crust is browned. Serves 8.

Kathy Borchers
Great Falls

Popup Pizza Casserole

Filling:
2 lbs. ground beef
1 cup chopped onion
1 cup chopped
   green pepper
1/8 tsp. minced garlic
1/2 tsp. oregano
1/2 cup water
1/8 tsp. hot sauce
15 oz. tomato sauce
8 oz. mozzarella
   cheese, sliced
1 envelope spaghetti
   sauce mix

Popover batter:
1 cup milk
1 tbs. oil
2 eggs
1 cup flour
1/2 cup grated Parmesan
   cheese

To make filling: Brown meat and add remaining ingredients except cheese. Cook 10 minutes. Pour into 9 x 13-inch pan. Top with cheese.

To make batter: Beat milk, oil, and eggs for 1 minute at medium speed. Add flour and beat 2 minutes. Pour over meat mixture and top with Parmesan. Bake 25-30 minutes at 400 degrees. Serves 8.

Sue Kaul
Belgrade

101

Spaghetti Pie

6 oz. spaghetti
1/3 cup grated
   Parmesan cheese
1 lb. ground beef
1/2 cup chopped onion
1/4 cup chopped
   green pepper
1 (16-oz.) can tomatoes
1 (6-oz.) can tomato paste
2 tbs. butter
2 eggs, beaten well
1 tsp. sugar
1 tsp. dried oregano
1/2 tsp. salt
1 cup cottage cheese
1/2 cup shredded
   mozzarella cheese

Cook spaghetti according to package directions. Drain. Stir butter into hot spaghetti and allow to cool slightly. Stir in Parmesan and eggs. Press spaghetti mixture against bottom and sides of a lightly greased 10-inch pie plate to form crust.

Cook beef, onion, and green pepper until vegetables are tender and meat browned. Drain off fat. Stir in undrained tomatoes, tomato paste, sugar, oregano, and salt. Heat through. Spread cottage cheese over bottom of crust. Fill pie with meat mixture. Bake, uncovered, for 20 minutes at 350 degrees. Sprinkle top with mozzarella. Bake 5 minutes more, or until cheese melts. Serves 6-8.

Betty Stav
Deer Lodge

102

Alice Tyler's More

3/4 lb. spaghetti, cooked
   and drained
3 lbs. ground beef
1 lb. pork sausage
1/2 cup chopped onion
1 quart canned
   tomatoes, chopped
1 (6-oz.) can tomato paste
1 (8-oz.) can tomato sauce
1/4 tsp. pepper
2 tbs. parsley
2 cups green
   olives, chopped
2 tsp. celery seed
1 cup canned mushrooms
1 cup grated
   cheddar cheese

Brown beef, pork, and onion. Drain off fat. Add remaining ingredients, except noodles and cheese, and simmer 10 minutes. Add cooked spaghetti and stir. Place in casserole, top with grated cheddar cheese, and bake 1 hour at 325 degrees. Serves 6-10.

Chef's note: "I helped my mother double and triple this recipe 30 years ago when we were feeding the haying crew. I don't know where the recipe originates, but it is one of the best of the traditionally Western standby casseroles: it's delicious, hearty enough for the working rancher, interesting enough for company, and kids love it. It freezes well, and the leftovers are delicious!"

Kathy Tyler Jones
Big Timber

103

Greek Rice Casserole

1 1/2 cups cooked white rice
1 lb. ground beef
1 (16-oz.) can tomatoes
   (with liquid)
1/2 tsp. sugar
1/8 tsp. pepper
1/8 tsp. cinnamon
3/4 tsp. salt
4 eggs
2 cups milk
3/4 cup grated
   Parmesan cheese
4 tbs. butter
1/4 cup flour

Brown ground beef and drain fat. Add tomatoes with liquid, sugar, pepper, cinnamon, and 1/2 tsp. salt, stirring to mix well and break up tomatoes. Remove from heat. In medium-sized bowl with wire whip, beat eggs, milk, and cheese until well mixed. Set aside. In 2-quart saucepan over medium heat, melt butter. Stir in flour and 1/4 tsp. salt until smooth and cook 1 minute. Gradually stir in egg mixture and cook until thickened and smooth, stirring constantly. Do not boil or custard will curdle. Remove from heat.

Spoon half of cooked rice into a greased, 2-quart casserole. Add meat mixture and then remaining rice. Pour custard over all. Bake 25-30 minutes at 350 degrees until custard is set.

Caroline Cole
Choteau

Keftethes (Greek Meatballs)

1 lb. ground beef
  (or lamb or veal)
2 eggs
1 cup soft bread crumbs
1 large onion, grated
Juice of 1 lemon
2 tbs. chopped parsley
1-2 tsp. dried mint
  (or 1 tbs. fresh)
1 tsp. salt
Pepper to taste
Olive oil

Beat eggs lightly in deep mixing bowl. Stir in bread crumbs, onion, lemon juice, herbs, and seasonings. Let sit 10 minutes. Add meat and blend thoroughly. Cover and refrigerate for 1 hour.

With moistened hands, shape mixture into balls about the size of small eggs. Roll in flour and flatten to make thick patties. Fry in hot olive oil until browned (3-4 minutes a side). Drain on absorbent paper. Place in serving dish and keep hot until all patties are done. Makes about 24 meatballs.

Chef's note: "These fried meatballs, keftethes, are crisp on the outside and moist on the inside and are equally delicious hot or cold. The mint gives them a very unusual flavor."

Rena Drakos
Butte

Doh-Moh-Dah (Gambian Beef Stew)

2 lbs. stew beef, cut into 1-1
  1/2-inch cubes
1 (28-oz.) can tomatoes,
  chopped (with liquid)
1 large carrot, cut diagonally
  into pieces
1 stalk celery, cut diagonally
  into pieces
1 medium green or red bell
  pepper, chopped
1 medium onion, sliced
1 medium potato, cubed
1 medium sweet
  potato, cubed
6 tbs. tomato paste
1 tsp. salt
1/2 cup creamy
  peanut butter
1/2 tsp. red pepper flakes
1/2 cup frozen peas, thawed

Combine first 10 ingredients in Dutch oven or large frying pan. Add enough water to cover, stir, and bring to a boil. Reduce heat, cover, and simmer for 1 hour, stirring occasionally. Add peanut butter and red pepper flakes; stir well. Simmer covered for 30 minutes to an hour, until beef and vegetables are tender. Add peas during last 5 minutes. If thicker stew is desired, uncover for last 30 minutes. Serve over hot cooked rice and garnish with slices of red, yellow, and green bell peppers. Serves 8.

Chef's note: "This recipe took first place at (a) state cook-off in Billings in 1987, and I cooked it at the national cook-off in Sun Valley the same year."

Laurette Ryan
Bozeman

Butte Pasties

Pastry:
3 3/4 cups flour
1/2 cup butter, softened
3/4 cup shortening
1 egg
1 tbs. vinegar
1/2 cup very cold water

Filling:
2 lbs. chuck roast or boneless
   stew meat, diced
4 cups diced, peeled
   potatoes
1 medium onion, chopped
Salt and pepper to taste

To make pastry: Beat egg and vinegar together. Add cold water and stir. In separate bowl, cut flour into butter and shortening until crumbly. Add liquid and mix to form a ball.

Brown meat and cool. Roll out dough and cut out 6- to 8-inch circles. Layer potatoes, meat, and onion on each circle. Top each one with a dollop of butter. Moisten the crusts around the edge and fold over to form semicircles; press tightly to seal edge. Brush tops with egg yolk mixed with 1 tbs. water to ensure browning. Bake 1 1/4 - 1 1/2 hours at 350 degrees. Some filling will leak out. Serves 6.

Merrie Johnson
Corvallis

A letter from 'ome

Old-timers will tell you the pasty arrived in Butte along with the first Cornish housewives who followed their husbands into the camp direct from Cornwall. Long favored in the miner's lunch bucket, the pastry-wrapped meal of meat and vegetables was an ideal way for the "Cousin Jenny" to provide a hearty meal for the hard-working "Cousin Jack." As the miner unwrapped his lunch, he would fondly refer to the pasty as a "letter from 'ome."

Butte's Heritage Cookbook

Pepper Steak

1 lb. round steak (beef, deer,
  or elk), cut into cubes
  or strips
1 large onion, diced
1 green pepper, chopped
1 1/2 cups chopped celery
2 tbs. cooking oil
2 tbs. cornstarch
6 tbs. soy sauce
1 tsp. salt
1 bay leaf
1/2 tsp. pepper
4 beef bouillon cubes
4 cups water

Saute beef in oil until browned. Remove meat from pan and add vegetables. Cook and stir over high heat for 2 minutes. Mix cornstarch with soy sauce and add it and rest of ingredients to pan. Add meat. Cover, reduce heat, and simmer 30 minutes. If sauce needs additional thickening, add 1-2 tbs. more of cornstarch mixed with a small amount of the gravy.

This recipe can be varied by adding mushrooms and tomatoes to the vegetables before meat is added. One cup of white wine can be substituted for part of the water. Serve over cooked noodles or rice. Serves 4-6.

Lenora M. Bisch
Whitehall

Flank Steak Barbecue

1/4 cup soy sauce
3 tbs. honey
2 tbs. vinegar
1 1/2 tsp. garlic powder
1 1/2 tsp. ground ginger
3/4 cup cooking oil
1 green onion, minced
1 flank steak
  (about 1 1/2 lbs.)

Mix together first 7 ingredients to make marinade. Place meat in 9-inch-square glass baking dish. Pour marinade over and allow meat to marinate 4 hours or longer in refrigerator.

Barbecue over glowing coals, about 5 minutes on each side for medium rare. Or broil in oven, allowing about 4 minutes per side. Baste with marinade as the steak cooks. Slice diagonally to serve. Serves 4.

Courtney Cox
Winston

108

Beef Quesadillas

12 (8-inch) flour tortillas

1 1/2 lbs. Monterey Jack or
   mozzarella cheese,
   shredded

1 green pepper, sliced thin

1 bunch green onions,
   diced small

2 tomatoes, sliced thin

2 lbs. sirloin steak, cut into
   1/4 x 1/2-inch strips

Marinade:

1 cup soy sauce

1/2 cup red wine

1 clove garlic, crushed

1 (4-oz.) can whole
   jalapeno peppers

1 tbs. hot sauce

Mix together marinade ingredients and marinate meat for 4-5 hours. Arrange tortillas on lightly greased baking sheets and top with equally distributed ingredients except sirloin. Saute sirloin in skillet until browned and then arrange on top of tortillas. Bake 5-8 minutes at 400 degrees, or until cheese bubbles and tortillas brown slightly. Serve with guacamole, salsa, sour cream, and corn chips. Serves 6.

Frank Sonnenberg, Chef-Instructor
Missoula Vocational-Technical School

109

Fajitas

1 (12-oz.) jar salsa
1 medium onion, chopped
4 cloves garlic, minced
2 tsp. dried oregano
1 tsp. ground cumin
1/4 cup red wine vinegar
1 lb. beef flank steak
8 (8-inch) flour tortillas
1 (4-oz.) can green chilies
Condiments: shredded
   cheese, sour cream, sliced
   ripe olives, sliced green
   onion, chopped tomatoes

Combine first 6 ingredients in large shallow dish, add steak and turn to coat with marinade. Cover and refrigerate overnight, turning occasionally. Remove meat from marinade and grill 4-6 inches above hot coals, or broil in oven. Slice meat thinly across the grain.

To serve, cover tortillas with moist paper towel and warm them briefly in microwave, or wrap in foil and heat in oven. Arrange meat on tortillas. Sprinkle with green chilies and desired condiments. Roll up tortillas. Serves 4.

Pamela K. Rausch
Missoula

Dell's Cube Steaks

4 large cube steaks
4 slices bacon
4 dill pickle halves
1 medium onion, sliced
Salt and pepper to taste
1 beef bouillon cube
1 cup water

Brown the steaks on both sides. Place a slice of bacon, pickle half, and some sliced onion on each steak. Roll up and use toothpicks to hold in place. Place in a baking dish with water and bouillon cube. Cover and bake about 1 hour at 350 degrees.

Dell Everaert
Great Falls

110

Spicy Swiss Steak

2 lbs. beef round steak
1/4 cup flour
2 tbs. shortening
1 clove garlic, minced
2 bay leaves, chopped
1/8 tsp. ground ginger
1/2 tsp. marjoram
1 1/2 tbs. red wine
1 (10 1/2-oz.) can beef
  bouillon
1/4 cup water

Pound flour into steak to coat on both sides. In a large skillet, heat shortening. Add meat and brown well on both sides. Meanwhile, blend together the remaining ingredients (except bouillon and water); spread evenly over steak. Transfer steak to a baking dish; pour bouillon and water over it. Cover and bake 2 - 2 1/2 hours at 325 degrees. Baste several times with pan drippings while baking. Serves 6.

Robin Arbuckle Jones
Great Falls

Swiss Bliss

1/2 tbs. butter
2 lbs. chuck steak
1 envelope onion soup mix
1/2 lb. mushrooms,
  sliced (optional)
1/2 green pepper, sliced
1 (1-lb.) can tomatoes,
  chopped (with liquid)
1/4 tsp. salt
Pepper to taste
1 tbs. steak sauce
1 tbs. cornstarch
20-inch sheet of
  heavy-duty foil wrap
1 tbs. chopped parsley

Spread center of foil with butter. Cut steak into serving portions. Arrange on foil, slightly overlapping each portion. Sprinkle with onion soup mix, mushrooms, green pepper, and tomatoes. Season. Mix steak sauce, 1/2 cup of reserved tomato liquid, and cornstarch. Pour over meat and vegetables. Wrap in foil, double-folding edges to seal tightly. Bake 2 hours at 375 degrees. Roll back foil and sprinkle with parsley. Serves 4.

Karen Sumersille
Great Falls

Sweet and Sour Short Ribs

1/2 cup flour
1/2 tsp. salt
1/2 tsp. pepper
4 lbs. short ribs
2 medium onions, sliced
1 green pepper, sliced
3/4 cup catsup
2 tbs. vinegar
2 tbs. Worcestershire sauce
1/4 cup soy sauce
1/2 cup brown sugar
3/4 cup water

Mix flour, salt, and pepper together in pie plate. Roll ribs in seasoned flour and arrange in a large casserole dish. Cover with onions and green pepper. Mix remaining ingredients together, heat, and pour over ribs. Cover and bake 3 hours at 300 degrees. Serves 6.

Harry Ness
Butte

Marinated Short Ribs

3 lbs. beef short ribs, cut into
    serving pieces
2 tbs. hot mustard
3 tsp. salt
1/2 tsp. pepper
1/2 tsp. chili powder
1/2 tsp. sugar
1 tbs. lemon juice
6 tbs. olive oil
2 garlic cloves, crushed
1/2 small onion, thickly sliced

Mix together all ingredients except beef and onion to make a marinade. Place ribs in a deep bowl. Wedge a few slices of onion between pieces of beef. Pour marinade over meat, cover, and refrigerate 8-24 hours, turning occasionally. Remove ribs from marinade and place in roasting pan. Bake about 15 minutes at 400 degrees, until ribs are browned. Add onions and marinade to pan, cover, and turn heat down to 350 degrees. Bake 1 hour. Remove cover to brown onions and to crisp any fat on ribs. Serve with pan juices or gravy made from pan drippings. Serves 4 or more.

M.F. McMahon
Great Falls

112

Waldorf Stew

3-lb. pot roast, cut into
  chunks
1 medium onion, chopped
2 cups chopped carrot
1 cup chopped celery
1 chopped
  rutabaga (optional)
4 potatoes, cubed
2 tbs. tapioca
1 tbs. sugar
1 tsp. salt
1/2 tsp. pepper
1 (10 3/4-oz.) can condensed
  tomato soup
1/3 cup water

Place meat and vegetables in roasting pan. Sprinkle with tapioca, sugar, and seasonings. Pour tomato soup over all, along with water. Cover and bake 5 hours at 250 degrees. Do not open lid. Serves 8-10.

Ella K. Scott
Missoula

Pickled Beef Tongue

1 beef tongue, uncooked
1 1/2 cups cider vinegar
1/2 cup water
2-3 tbs. sugar
1 tbs. pickling spice
1 tsp. salt
1 medium onion, sliced

Cook tongue until tender in lightly salted water to cover. Peel tongue while still hot, slice, and place in glass container. Combine remaining ingredients and pour over tongue while tongue is still hot. Refrigerate 5-6 hours. Will keep well in refrigerator for 2-3 weeks.

Agnes Mogan
Hinsdale

113

Pride of the Rockies Pot Roast

Roast:
2 tbs. flour
4-lb. beef pot roast
1 cup canned tomatoes
1 cup water
2 cloves garlic
1 tsp. salt
1/2 tsp. pepper
1 cup sliced onions
1/4 cup vinegar
1/4 cup lemon juice
1/4 cup catsup
2 tbs. brown sugar
1 tbs. Worcestershire sauce
1 tsp. mustard
1/4 tsp. paprika

Dumplings:
3/4 cup sifted flour
1/2 cup cornmeal
1 1/2 tsp. baking powder
1/2 tsp. salt
1/2 cup milk
2 tbs. oil or melted shortening

To make roast: Rub flour onto meat and brown well on all sides in heavy kettle. Slip rack under meat. Add tomatoes, water, garlic, salt, and pepper. Cover and simmer 2 hours. Combine remaining roast ingredients. Pour over meat, cover, and simmer another 1 - 1 1/2 hours. Remove meat to warm platter and keep warm while dumplings steam.

To make dumplings: Sift together dry ingredients. Stir in milk and shortening until dry ingredients are moistened. Drop by large spoonfuls into boiling pot roast sauce. Cook uncovered for 10 minutes over low heat and then 10 more minutes tightly covered. Serve at once. Serves 10-12.

Ida Seidler Bishop
Great Falls

Sauerbraten

3-lb. boneless round roast
1 tbs. salt
1/2 tsp. pepper
2 onions, sliced
1 stalk celery, chopped
1 carrot, sliced
4 cloves
4 peppercorns
2 cups red wine vinegar
2 bay leaves
2 tbs. shortening
6 tbs. butter
5 tbs. flour
1 tbs. sugar
8-10 gingersnaps, crushed

Wipe meat with damp cloth. Season with salt and pepper. Place meat in large casserole dish. Combine onion, carrot, celery, cloves, peppercorns, vinegar, and bay leaves and pour over meat. Cover and refrigerate for 4 days, turning occasionally.

On the 5th day, remove meat from refrigerator. Drain, and saute in shortening and 1 tbs. butter until seared on all sides. Add marinade liquid and bring to boil. Lower heat and let simmer, covered, about 3 hours. Melt remaining 5 tbs. butter in pan. Stir in flour until smooth. Add sugar, blend well, and let brown. Add to simmering meat. Cover and continue cooking until meat is tender, about 1 more hour.

Remove meat to warm serving platter. Add crushed gingersnaps to juices in which meat was cooked and stir until well blended and thickened. Pour this gravy over meat and serve immediately. Serves 8.

Royce Pearson
Great Falls

115

Creamy Liver and Rice

1 lb. beef liver, cubed
1/4 cup flour
2 tbs. shortening
1/4 tsp. salt
Dash of pepper
1/3 cup milk
1 (10 3/4-oz.) can condensed
   cream of chicken soup
2 hard-cooked eggs,
   chopped
2 tbs. snipped parsley
Hot cooked rice

Coat liver with flour. In 10-inch skillet, brown liver in hot shortening, stirring often. Season with salt and pepper. Blend milk into soup and pour over liver. Cover and cook 10 minutes over low heat, stirring occasionally. Add egg, cover, and simmer 5 minutes longer. Stir in parsley and serve over hot rice. Serves 4.

Shirley A. Goldsmith
Great Falls

Corned Beef with Lima Beans

1 (20-oz.) can lima beans
1 (12-oz.) can corned beef
1/4 cup sliced onions
2 tbs. butter
2 tbs. flour
1/2 tsp. salt
1/8 tsp. pepper
3/4 cup milk
3/4 tsp. dry mustard
1 (10 1/2-oz.) can
   tomato puree

Slice corned beef 1/2-inch thick. Arrange beans in alternate layers with corned beef and onions in a well-oiled baking dish. In a saucepan, melt butter and blend in flour, seasonings, and milk. Stir until thickened. Add mustard and tomato puree. Pour over contents of baking dish and bake 30 minutes at 350 degrees. Serves 6-8.

Mildred Gates
Anaconda

116

Peachy Apricot Chicken

3 whole chicken breasts, halved, skinned, and deboned
1/4 cup cooking oil
1/2 cup thinly sliced carrot, cut diagonally
1/2 cup thinly sliced celery, cut diagonally
1/2 large green pepper, cut into small pieces
1/2 large red bell pepper, cut into small pieces
1/2 tsp. salt
2 cups canned sliced peaches, drained

Sauce:
2 tbs. cornstarch
1/3 cup red wine vinegar
1 tbs. soy sauce
1/3 cup honey
1 (12-oz.) can apricot nectar

To make sauce: Combine sauce ingredients in medium saucepan and heat over medium heat, stirring, until thickened.

Pound chicken to 1/4-inch thickness with meat mallet or similar utensil. Heat oil in skillet. Add carrots, celery, green pepper, and red pepper; cook about 5 minutes, until crisp but tender. Remove vegetables and set aside.

To same skillet, add chicken; sprinkle with salt and saute about 10 minutes or until brown on both sides and fork can be inserted into chicken with ease. Return vegetables to skillet. Add sauce and peaches and heat thoroughly. To serve, place chicken on platter, and spoon vegetables and sauce over top. Garnish with parsley. Serves 6.

Chef's note: "This recipe was chosen by the National Broiler Association to represent Montana at the National Cook-Off in Hershey, Pennsylvania, in 1989. I cooked it there."

Laurette Ryan
Bozeman

Honey Mustard Chicken

2 whole chicken breasts,
   halved, skinned, and
   deboned
4 tbs. melted butter
1/2 cup honey
1/4 cup Dijon mustard
1/4 tsp. curry powder

Season chicken breasts with salt and pepper to taste. Combine butter, honey, mustard, and curry powder. Spoon half of sauce into shallow baking dish. Add chicken breasts and turn to coat well. Bake uncovered about 1 hour at 350 degrees. Turn and baste chicken with sauce often during cooking time. Serves 2.

Patti Billet
Missoula

Green Chili Chicken

2 chicken breasts, skinned,
   deboned, and diced
1/4 cup butter
1/3 cup flour
1/2 cup diced onion
2 cups chicken stock
1 (4-oz.) can green chilies,
   cut into strips
2/3 - 3/4 cup creamed or
   frozen corn
1 1/2 tsp. ground cumin
1 tsp. minced garlic

Melt butter in large skillet. Toss chicken with flour to coat well. Saute in butter. Add onions and garlic, chicken stock, chilies, and spices. Simmer 10 minutes. Add corn and cook 10-15 minutes, until chicken is tender. Do not let liquid boil away; mixture should be consistency of a hearty soup or stew. Serve in bowls with warm tortillas or Mexican cornbread. Garnish with avocado slices and/or sour cream. Serves 2-3.

Susie Miller
Bozeman

118

Stuffed Oriental Biscuit

4 chicken breasts
1 (16-oz.) can Chinese
  vegetable mix
1/2 cup chopped onion
1/2 cup chopped celery
3 cups cooked
  Oriental noodles
1/2 tsp. garlic powder
1/2 tsp. celery salt
1/2 tsp. salt
1/2 tsp. pepper
4 cups water
4 tbs. chicken
  bouillon granules
1/3 cup flour
4 tbs. shortening or butter
5 cups biscuit mix
1 1/3 cups milk

In a 6-quart saucepan, boil chicken breasts in water. When meat is done, remove bones, shred meat, and set aside. Boil Oriental noodles according to package directions.

In a large skillet, melt a little butter, and add Oriental vegetables, half the onion, half the celery, garlic powder, celery salt, salt, and pepper. Saute 10 minutes over low heat. Add chicken and noodles to Oriental vegetables. Mix well. Begin heating 4 cups water with bouillon.

Meanwhile, combine biscuit mix and milk. Roll dough on lightly floured surface until 1/4-inch thick. Cut into 6 x 4-inch squares. Remove Oriental mixture from stove. With a slotted spoon, put about 4 tbs. of mixture on half of the dough squares. Place remaining squares on tops of mixture and press all edges together with a fork until well-sealed. Place in pre-heated deep-fat fryer for about 3-5 minutes, or until golden brown.

To make gravy: In large skillet, melt shortening or butter; add flour and a little salt and pepper to make a paste. Add chicken broth and remaining onion and celery. Stir until thickened. Pour over biscuit squares and serve. Serves 4.

Darrell S. Bolton
Butte

Lime Ginger Chicken with Salsa

4 chicken breasts, halved,
   skinned, and deboned
1/3 cup fresh lime juice
2 tsp. grated, peeled
   fresh ginger
3 garlic cloves, chopped
1/2 tsp. dried red
   pepper flakes

Salsa:
8 oz. ripe plum tomatoes,
   diced
1 medium green bell pepper,
   diced
1/4 cup diced red onion
1 tbs. chopped fresh cilantro
1 tbs. olive oil
1 tbs. fresh lime juice
1 small garlic clove, minced
Salt and pepper to taste
1 lime, thinly sliced,
   for garnish

Cut each chicken breast half lengthwise into three 1-inch-wide strips. Set aside. Mix lime juice, ginger, garlic, and pepper flakes in a non-aluminum bowl. Stir in chicken strips. Cover and chill at least 2 hours or overnight.

To make salsa: Combine first 7 salsa ingredients in a non-aluminum bowl. Season to taste with salt and freshly ground pepper.

Heat 1 tsp. oil in large, heavy skillet over high heat. Add chicken (in batches if necessary) and cook until brown, about 2 minutes per side. Transfer to plates. Add lime slices to skillet and brown on both sides. Set 1 on each plate. Garnish with fresh cilantro. Serve immediately with salsa. Serves 4-5.

**Patti Billet
Missoula**

Chicken Breasts with Beef Jerky Sauce

**4 large chicken breasts,
   skinned and deboned**
1 medium onion, sliced
1 tsp. pepper
1/2 tsp. salt
1/4 cup red wine vinegar
2 cups chicken broth
1/2 cup dry white wine
2 cups heavy cream
2 oz. beef jerky
4 tbs. cooking oil

Cut beef jerky into match-sized pieces and soak in chicken broth for 2 hours. Season chicken breasts on both sides with salt and pepper. Heat oil in skillet and saute chicken until browned, about 10 minutes. Remove breasts and place them in 350-degree oven for 5 minutes.

In the meantime, pour fat from pan, add onions, and saute until lightly browned. Deglaze pan with vinegar; let it reduce by about 2/3. Add white wine, jerky, and chicken stock. Reduce to syrupy consistency. Add heavy cream and simmer; reduce gently by about 1/4. The sauce should be thick enough to coat the back of a spoon. Remove from heat, add chicken, and let sit 5 minutes before serving. Serves 4.

Andre Gagnier
Missoula

121

Parmesan Chicken Breast

4 chicken breasts, skinned
   and deboned
1 cup flour
1 egg
1/8 tsp. salt
1/4 tsp. pepper
1/2 tsp. olive oil
1/2 cup grated
   Parmesan cheese
1/2 cup bread crumbs
10 tbs. butter
3 tbs. minced parsley
3 tbs. lemon juice

Flatten chicken breasts and season with pepper. Mix egg, olive oil, and salt in pie plate. Whirl bread crumbs in blender or food processor until fine. Turn out into a separate pie plate and mix in Parmesan cheese. Dip chicken into flour, shaking off excess, then into egg mixture, and then into cheese and crumbs. Lay out on waxed paper and allow to sit 15 minutes to 2 hours in the refrigerator.

Heat 6 tbs. butter in skillet until foamy. Place chicken pieces into skillet, roll in butter, and cover skillet with waxed paper. After 6 minutes, press top of breast with fingers. If springy, chicken is done. If not, continue cooking a few more minutes. Do not overcook. Remove chicken to platter.

Add 4 tbs. butter to skillet. Heat 1-2 minutes. Add lemon juice and parsley and pour over chicken. Serves 4.

Pam Barnes
Great Falls

Baked Chicken and Sauerkraut

4 whole chicken breasts,
  halved and deboned
1/4 tsp. salt
1/8 tsp. pepper
1 (16-oz.) can sauerkraut,
  drained well
4 slices Swiss cheese,
  4 x 6 inches
1 1/4 cups bottled Thousand
  Island salad dressing
1 tbs. chopped parsley

Place the chicken in a greased baking dish and sprinkle with salt and pepper. Spoon sauerkraut over chicken. Top with Swiss cheese and salad dressing. Cover and bake 1 1/2 hours at 325 degrees. Sprinkle with parsley before serving. Serves 4-5.

Gloria Guessen
Missoula

Chicken Cordon Bleu

8 boneless chicken breasts
8 oz. Swiss cheese, sliced
8 oz. cooked ham, sliced
1 cup flour
1 tsp. paprika
1/2 tsp. salt
1/2 tsp. pepper
2 tsp. chicken bouillon
  granules
2 tbs. cornstarch
2 cups whipping cream
1/4 cup butter
1 cup white wine

Pound chicken breasts flat. Place 1 slice each of ham and cheese onto each breast. Roll up breast and secure with toothpicks. Mix together flour, paprika, pepper, and salt. Dredge chicken rolls in this mixture and brown in butter. Add wine and bouillon to skillet and simmer covered for 30 minutes. Remove to platter and place in warm oven. Blend cornstarch and cream and stir into skillet. Spoon gravy over chicken and serve. Serves 8.

Marlys Carpenter
Billings

Chicken Tangier

1 broiler-fryer chicken, cut up and skinned
1 tbs. cooking oil
1 tbs. butter
3/4 cup chopped onion
1 garlic clove, minced
2 large tomatoes, chopped
2 (8-oz.) cans tomato sauce
2 tbs. chopped parsley
1 tsp. salt
1/2 tsp. ground cinnamon
1/2 tsp. ground ginger
1/2 tsp. ground cumin
1/2 tsp. ground turmeric
Hot sauce to taste
2 whole cloves
1 (16-oz.) can small whole onions, drained
1/3 cup sliced almonds
1/3 cup golden raisins

Put oil and butter into Dutch oven and heat. Add chopped onion and garlic. Cook, stirring occasionally, about 5 minutes, or until onion is soft. Add tomatoes, tomato sauce, parsley, salt, cinnamon, ginger, cumin, turmeric, hot sauce, and cloves. Stir to mix well. Add chicken pieces in a single layer to sauce. Bring to a boil, reduce heat to low, and cook covered for 45 minutes.

Uncover and cook 15 minutes longer, or until sauce is slightly thickened and fork can be inserted into chicken with ease. Add whole onions, stir gently, and cook 5 minutes longer. Remove cloves. To serve, pour sauce over chicken and sprinkle with almonds and raisins. Serves 4.

Chef's note: "This recipe was chosen by the National Broiler Association to represent the state of Montana at the National Cook-Off in Dallas in 1982. I cooked it there."

Laurette Ryan
Bozeman

Craig's Adobo (Filipino Chicken)

3 tbs. olive oil
3 cloves garlic, chopped
1/4 cup soy sauce
1/4 cup white vinegar
1/4 cup water
1/4 cup chopped onion
1/4 cup chopped green
  pepper
1 tbs. pickling spice
1 whole fryer, cut up and
  skinned

In a large skillet, heat olive oil to 300 degrees. Stir in chopped garlic and add chicken pieces. Brown chicken on both sides. Add soy sauce, vinegar, and water and bring to boil. Add onion and pepper, and sprinkle in pickling spice. Reduce heat and simmer, covered, for 35-45 minutes, stirring occasionally. Serve with steamed white rice. Serves 4-6.

Craig Barton
Kalispell

Indonesian Baked Chicken

1 cup almonds
1/2 cup orange marmalade
1/4 cup soy sauce
1 tbs. Dijon mustard
2 tsp. grated gingerroot
1 clove garlic, minced
1/2 tsp. curry powder
1/4 tsp. red pepper flakes
1 whole chicken, cut up and
  skinned

Toast almonds in a single layer on baking sheet by baking 5-8 minutes at 350 degrees. Stir occasionally. Cool and grind in food processor or chop fine. Combine almonds with remaining ingredients except chicken. Dip chicken pieces into almond mixture and place on foil-lined baking sheet. Bake 45-60 minutes at 350 degrees. Serve warm or cold. Serves 6.

Phyllis Reyner
Missoula

Sweet and Pungent Chicken

2 broiler-fryer chickens,
   cut up and skinned
1/3 cup vinegar
1/3 cup prepared mustard
1/3 cup molasses
1 tsp. soy sauce
2 tsp. cornstarch
1/2 tsp. salt
1/4 tsp. ground ginger
1 (13 1/4-oz.) can pineapple
   tidbits (with juice)
1 (11-oz.) can Mandarin
   oranges, drained

Place chicken in single layer in large, shallow baking dish. In saucepan, make sauce by mixing together vinegar, mustard, molasses, soy sauce, cornstarch, salt, ginger, and pineapple juice. Simmer, stirring, over low heat for 5 minutes. Brush sauce on all sides of chicken. Cover and bake 30 minutes at 350 degrees, brushing with sauce frequently. Add pineapple tidbits and oranges to remaining sauce and heat about 3 minutes, or until warm. Pour over chicken. Serves 8.

Chef's note: "This recipe was chosen by the National Broiler Association to represent the state of Montana at the National Cook-Off in Ocean City, Maryland, in 1981. I cooked it there."

Laurette Ryan
Bozeman

126

Paella

1 (3-lb.) fryer chicken
1/2 lb. sausage links, chorizo,
    or pork tenderloin, cubed
1/2 lb. fish
1/2 lb. shrimp or lobster
1/4 lb. squid (optional)
1 green pepper, sliced
1 cup long-grain rice
1/4 cup cooking oil
2 large ripe tomatoes, cut up
1 onion, chopped
1/2 tsp. cinnamon
1 tsp. paprika
1 bay leaf
1 tsp. salt
1/2 tsp. dark red
    ground saffron
2 cups boiling water
1/2 (10-oz.) package
    frozen peas
2 sliced canned pimientos
2 cloves garlic, crushed
1 tsp. chopped parsley

Garnish:
Cooked clams
Lemon wedges

Heat cooking oil. Add chopped tomatoes, onion, cinnamon, salt, paprika, bay leaf, saffron, and two cups boiling water. Cook 10 minutes and set aside.

Place chicken in large skillet, salt it, and add a little water. Cover and steam for 30 minutes. Remove skin from chicken and debone, leaving some pieces of meat the size of an egg.

Lightly grease a paella pan or skillet with cooking oil. Add chicken and pork, chorizo, or sausage and cook 15 minutes. Add green pepper, fish, shrimp, and squid and fry with meats for about 5 minutes. Add additional cooking oil if needed to avoid sticking. Add rice. Mix well with meats. Then add tomato mixture. Add pimientos and peas and cook until rice is tender and all liquid is absorbed. Add paste made by mixing garlic and chopped parsley.

Garnish with cooked clams in the shell—either fresh or canned—and lemon wedges. Serves 6.

Chef's note: "This recipe, the national dish of Spain, may sound complicated, but it is worth the effort. We lived in Spain for seven years, and this is an authentic recipe. In 1981, the Planter's Oil Co. picked this recipe as one of 35 runners-up in its Great Cuisines of the World recipe contest."

Laurette Ryan
Bozeman

127

Chicken Supreme

1/2 cup cooking oil
1/4 cup vinegar
2 tbs. Worcestershire sauce
1 tbs. hot sauce
1 tbs. curry powder
1/2 tsp. onion powder
1/2 tsp. garlic powder
1/2 tsp. seasoning salt
Dash salt and pepper
2 fryer chickens, halved or
   cut up
1 tbs. parsley flakes
Paprika to taste

Mix first 9 ingredients in bowl. Place chicken skin-side-up in large, greased baking pan. Pour sauce over chicken and rub it into meat with fingers. Sprinkle with parsley flakes and paprika. Bake 1 hour at 375 degrees, basting occasionally.

Barbara McPherson
Canyon Creek

Oven-Barbecued Chicken

1 (8-oz.) can tomato sauce
1/2 cup water
1/4 cup molasses
2 tbs. butter
2 tbs. vinegar
2 tbs. minced onion
1 tbs. Worcestershire sauce
1 tsp. salt
2 tsp. dry mustard
1/4 tsp. chili powder
Dash of pepper
2 1/2 - 3-lb. broiler-fryer
   chicken, cut up

In saucepan, combine all ingredients except chicken; simmer 15-20 minutes. Place chicken in shallow baking pan. Brush with the barbecue sauce. Bake about 1 hour at 375 degrees, basting occasionally with additional sauce. Simmer remaining sauce 10 minutes longer and serve with the chicken. Serves 4.

Gloria Broksle
Twin Bridges

Okra Gumbo

1 (16-oz.) package frozen
   okra, cooked and drained
3 tbs. butter
1 cup finely chopped
   green onion
1 medium green
   pepper, chopped
1/2 cup chopped parsley
2 cloves garlic, minced
1 (16-oz.) can stewed
   tomatoes
1 (16-oz.) can tomato sauce
1 (10 3/4-oz.) can
   chicken bouillon
1/8 tsp. cayenne pepper
1/8 tsp. thyme
1/8 tsp. oregano
1/8 tsp. basil
1/8 tsp. hot sauce
1 tsp. Worcestershire sauce
2 bay leaves
1/2 tsp. salt
1/8 tsp. pepper
1 cup cooked sausage,
   broken up
1 cup cooked
chicken, diced

Melt butter in 4-quart pan. Add onion, pepper, parsley, and garlic and saute until onion and garlic are softened. Add tomatoes, tomato sauce, and chicken bouillon. Bring to a boil, reduce heat, and add seasonings, okra, chicken, and sausage. Simmer 30-40 minutes. Serve over rice. Serves 4.

Debra Cruce
Missoula

129

South of the Border Chicken Hot Dish

4 cups cooked rice
1 (16-oz.) can tomatoes,
  drained and chopped
1/2 cup chopped onion
2 (12-oz.) cans cooked
chicken or 3-4 cups diced
  cooked chicken
2 (4-oz.) cans green
  chilies, chopped
1 (6-oz.) can ripe
  olives, drained
Salt and pepper to taste
1 cup sour cream
1 lb. Monterey Jack
  cheese, shredded

In a bowl, stir together rice, tomatoes, onion, chicken, chilies, and olives. Season with salt and pepper. Spoon half of this mixture into greased 2 1/2-quart casserole dish. Cover with half the sour cream and then half the cheese. Spoon remaining chicken mixture on top and then layer with rest of sour cream and cheese. Bake 40-45 minutes at 350 degrees. Serves 4-6.

Rosie Endean
Bozeman

Garlic Chicken

8 chicken thighs, skinned
1/2 cup soy sauce
1/2 cup dry white wine
6 cloves garlic, pressed

Marinate chicken thighs in wine, soy sauce, and garlic for at least 20 minutes or up to 2 hours. Arrange thighs in greased baking dish and pour marinade over top. Cover with foil and bake 45 minutes at 350 degrees, turning once. Serve with rice. Marinade may be poured over rice. Serves 4.

Alene Gorecki
Helena

Chicken Loaf

6 cups diced
  cooked chicken
2 cups cooked rice
4 cups soft bread crumbs
2/3 cup diced celery
1/2 cup chopped pimientos
8 eggs, beaten
2 tsp. salt
1/2 tsp. poultry seasoning
4 cups chicken broth
2 (10 3/4-oz.) cans
  condensed cream of
  chicken soup
2/3 cup milk

Mix chicken, rice, bread crumbs, celery, and pimientos and add to beaten eggs, seasonings, and broth. Bake about 1 hour at 350 degrees in a large loaf pan. When ready to serve, add milk to cream of chicken soup, heat, and pour over top. Serves 8-10.

Lillian Stundahl
Circle

Chicken Broccoli Casserole

1 (10 3/4-oz.) can condensed
  cream of chicken soup
1/3 cup half and half
1/2 cup mayonnaise
1 (10-oz.) package frozen cut
  broccoli, thawed and
  drained
2 1/2 cups cubed,
  cooked chicken
1 cup stuffing mix, prepared
  as package directs
Slivered almonds

Mix soup, half and half, and mayonnaise and set aside. Place alternate layers of broccoli, chicken, and stuffing in casserole dish. Pour soup mixture over top. Dot with butter and sprinkle with almonds. Bake 30-45 minutes at 350 degrees. Serves 3-4.

Kathy Dwyer
Butte

131

e5e55e5e5e

Chicken Almond Bake

3/4 cup mayonnaise
1/3 cup flour
2 tbs. dried minced onion
1 tsp. chicken bouillon granules
1 tsp. garlic powder
2 1/4 cups milk
1 cup shredded Swiss cheese
7 oz. spaghetti, cooked and drained
2 cups chopped cooked chicken
2 cups broccoli, cooked and drained
1/2 cup almond slices
1 (4-oz.) can mushrooms, drained
1/4 cup chopped pimiento
Parmesan cheese, grated
Salt and pepper to taste

In saucepan, combine mayonnaise, flour, onion, chicken bouillon, and seasonings. Gradually add milk; cook, stirring constantly, over low heat until thickened. Add cheese and stir until melted. Combine sauce, spaghetti, chicken, broccoli, mushrooms, and pimiento; mix lightly. Spoon into 9 x 12-inch baking dish, top with nuts, and sprinkle with Parmesan cheese. Bake 40-45 minutes at 350 degrees or until heated through. Serve with grated Parmesan cheese. Serves 6-8.

Debbie Ziesman
Helena

132

Chicken Enchilada Casserole

4 cups chopped
  cooked chicken
12 soft corn tortillas
1/4 cup cooking oil
1 lb. cheddar or Monterey
  Jack cheese, shredded
1 (10 3/4-oz.) can condensed
  cream of chicken soup
1 (10 3/4-oz.) can condensed
  cream of celery soup
2/3 cup evaporated milk
1 medium onion, chopped
1 (4-oz.) can chopped green
  chilies, drained

Heat oil in skillet. Dip tortillas, one at a time, in hot oil to soften, about 5 seconds. Drain and set aside. Put both cans of soup in blender. Add evaporated milk and chopped onion. Blend until smooth. Stir in green chilies.

In 9 x 13-inch baking dish, spread half the soup mixture. Cover soup mixture with 6 tortillas. Spread 2 cups chicken over tortillas. Spread half of grated cheese over chicken. Drizzle half of remaining soup mixture over chicken and cheese. Repeat layers of tortillas, chicken, cheese, and soup. Bake 30 minutes at 350 degrees. Serve hot. May be garnished with guacamole, chopped ripe olives, shredded lettuce, and chopped tomato. Serves 8.

Colette Cook
Butte

Cooking Gary Cooper's goose

Helena native and film star Gary Cooper allowed his recipe for English stuffing for goose to be included in a booklet on food and fashions published by the Fox Theatre of Billings in 1936: One-fourth cupful chopped salt pork, 1 onion chopped, cook 10 minutes then add 1 1/2 cupfuls mashed potatoes, 1 1/2 cupfuls bread crumbs, 1 1/2 cupfuls English walnuts, 1 egg, salt, pepper, sage to taste.

Foods and Fashions of 1936

Turkey Tetrazzini

2 tbs. shortening or butter
3/4 cup diced celery
1/2 cup diced green pepper
1/4 cup chopped onion
1 (10 3/4-oz.) can condensed
cream of mushroom soup
1 cup milk
1/4 lb. medium or sharp
cheddar cheese, grated
1/2 tsp. salt
1/8 tsp. pepper
1 tbs. Worcestershire sauce
1 1/2 cups diced cooked
turkey
4 oz. spaghetti, cooked
Parmesan cheese to taste

Cook onions, celery, and green pepper in shortening or butter until limp. Add milk, mushroom soup, salt, pepper, cheese, Worcestershire, and turkey. Top with cooked spaghetti and grated Parmesan cheese to taste. This can be made entirely in a large skillet or heated in a casserole dish in the oven until bubbly. Serves 6-8.

Chef's note: "I have used this recipe many times for 35 years. It is always gobbled up. It's a great way to use up leftover turkey or chicken."

Doris M. Velde
Missoula

Turkey Loaf

1 1/2 lbs. ground
uncooked turkey
1 cup herb-seasoned
stuffing mix
1 (8-oz.) can tomato sauce
1 egg
1/2 tsp. salt (optional)
1/4 tsp. pepper

Combine all ingredients and mix well. Shape into loaf. Bake in shallow pan for 1 hour at 350 degrees. Can be served with a cream sauce and is good cold for sandwiches. Serves 6.

Juliette W. Hoffmann
Bozeman

134

Mock French Veal

1 1/4 cups ground
　　uncooked turkey
1/4 cup flour
1/2 tsp. salt
1/8 tsp. pepper
3 tbs. butter or cooking oil
1 cup chicken broth
1 tbs. lemon juice

Combine flour, salt, and pepper. Pat turkey into 5 thin patties between waxed paper and dip in the flour mixture. Shake off excess flour. In large skillet, heat oil or butter and brown patties on each side. Remove from skillet and keep warm. Stir remaining flour mixture into skillet; add broth and lemon juice. Stir until thickened, scraping browned pieces from bottom of pan. Return patties to pan, cover, and simmer about 3 minutes. Serve garnished with parsley and lemon slices. Serves 3-5.

Juliette W. Hoffmann
Bozeman

Party Pork Chops

6 large loin pork chops, cut
　　about 1 1/4-inch thick
Salt and pepper to taste
Flour
6 tbs. uncooked rice
6 slices tomato
6 thin slices onion
6 generous tbs. shredded
　　carrot
6 slices green pepper
1 1/2 cups tomato juice

Season chops with salt and pepper. Flour lightly and saute in a little oil until browned on both sides. Drain off excess fat and remove pan from heat. Arrange chops in casserole dish. On each chop, place 1 tbs. rice, slice of tomato, 1 tbs. carrot, slice of onion, and slice of green pepper. Spoon some of the tomato juice over each chop and pour remaining juice into bottom of casserole. Cover tightly and bake 1 - 1 1/2 hours at 350 degrees, or until chops are tender and rice is cooked. Serves 6.

Ruth Saholt
Whitefish

135

Pork Chop and Potato Bake

6 pork chops
1/2 cup milk
1 (10 3/4-oz.) can condensed
  cream of celery soup
1/2 cup sour cream
Salt and pepper to taste
1 (32-oz.) package frozen
  hash browns, thawed
1 cup shredded cheddar
  cheese
1 (2.8-oz.) can
  Durkee's French-fried
  onions

In skillet, brown chops lightly. Sprinkle with salt and pepper and set aside. In same skillet, combine soup, milk, and sour cream. Stir in potatoes, 1/2 cup cheese, and 1/2 onions. Spoon mixture into 9 x 13-inch baking dish. Arrange pork chops over potatoes. Bake covered 40-50 minutes at 350 degrees. Top with remaining cheese and onions. Bake uncovered 5-10 minutes longer. Serves 6.

Julie Nielsen
Billings

Pork Creole

4-6 pork chops, cut into
  1-inch cubes
1/2 cup chopped celery
1 medium onion, chopped
1 green pepper, chopped
1 (16-oz.) can tomato sauce
2 cups water
2 tbs. brown sugar or honey
Salt to taste
1/2 tsp. basil
1 tbs. parsley
1/2 tsp. garlic powder
3-4 cups cooked rice

In large skillet, brown pork and drain off fat. Add remaining ingredients except rice and bring to a boil. Cover and simmer about 1 hour. Serve over cooked rice. Serves 4.

Alice McGinnis
Missoula

136

Pork Chop, Yam, and Apple Skillet

4 pork chops
2 tbs. honey
1 tsp. Kitchen Bouquet
4 medium yams
2 medium tart apples
1/2 cup apple juice or cider
1/2 tsp. salt
1/8 tsp. pepper
1/8 tsp. ground cinnamon
1/8 tsp. ground nutmeg

Trim excess fat from pork chops. In a large skillet, combine honey and Kitchen Bouquet; place over low heat. Place chops in skillet, turning to coat with honey mixture. Increase heat to medium and brown chops. Meanwhile, pare yams and cut into 1/4-inch rounds. Pare, core, and quarter apples and cut into thick slices.

Remove chops from skillet and add a little apple juice to pan, stirring to loosen browned bits. Arrange yams and apples in skillet and top with chops. Combine remaining apple juice and seasonings and pour over chops. Bring to boil, cover, and cook over low to medium heat until chops and yams are tender, about 45 minutes. Baste chops with apple juice occasionally. Garnish with chopped parsley. Serves 4.

Ruthanne Monahan
Butte

137

Nancy's Cranberry Pork Chop Broil

6 pork loin or rib chops,
   about 3/4-inch thick
Salt to taste
1 (8-oz.) can jellied
   cranberry sauce
1 tsp. lemon juice
1/2 tsp. almond extract
1/4 tsp. ground nutmeg
1 (29-oz.) can peach halves,
   drained

Broil pork chops for 5 minutes. Sprinkle with salt. Heat cranberry sauce, lemon juice, almond extract, and nutmeg over low heat. Brush pork chops with sauce. Continue broiling, turning and brushing with sauce occasionally, for 10-15 minutes, or until done. Transfer chops to serving platter and brush with sauce. Fill each peach half with about 1 tsp. sauce; serve with pork chops. Serves 6.

Diane Browder
Great Falls

Pork, Sauerkraut, and Dumplings

1 lb. pork chops
1 lb. pork ribs
1 lb. bacon, cut up
2 quarts sauerkraut

Dumplings:
4 cups flour
2 tsp. salt
2 eggs
1-2 cups water

In large kettle, cover meat with water and boil 30 minutes, skimming fat off during cooking. Add sauerkraut and its liquid to meat and cook another 30 minutes.

To make dumplings: Mix flour, salt, and eggs together until well-blended. Add water slowly until mixture forms a soft dough. Roll into medium-sized balls. Add to meat and sauerkraut and cook covered for 30 minutes. Serves 10.

Jerry Zwetow
Lolo

Calabacitas (Zucchini with Pork)

1 (16-oz.) can tomatoes

1/4 cup olive oil

2 lbs. pork butt, deboned and cut into 1/2-inch cubes

3 slices bacon, finely chopped

12 mushrooms, sliced

1 large onion, finely chopped

2 green onions, finely chopped

1 red chili pepper, peeled and chopped

1 green pepper, finely chopped

4 cloves garlic

1/4 cup parsley flakes

1/2 tsp. dried oregano

1/2 tsp. salt

1 tsp. pepper

1/2 tsp. soy sauce

1 cup sherry (or beef bouillon)

1 (10-oz.) package frozen corn

10 small zucchini, cubed

Blend or crush tomatoes to sauce consistency. Set aside. Heat oil in Dutch oven over medium heat. Add pork, bacon, and mushrooms and cook until meat is browned. Add onions, chili, and green pepper. Squeeze in garlic through a press. Add parsley, oregano, salt, pepper, and soy sauce. Cook and stir until green pepper and onions are tender. Add tomatoes and sherry (or bouillon). Simmer, uncovered, until sauce becomes thick and meat is tender, stirring often. Stir in corn and zucchini. Cover and simmer until zucchini is tender, about 10 minutes. Serves 6-8.

Chef's note: "I only make this dish once or twice during the zucchini season, but it is well worth the effort."

Jonne Shearman
Baxter Creek

Sarma (Pork and Beef Cabbage Rolls)

1 head cabbage
2 lbs. sauerkraut
2-4 kielbasa sausages, cut
   into chunks

Filling:
2 lbs. ground pork
1 lb. ground beef
1 cup uncooked rice
6 cloves garlic, finely
   chopped
2 large eggs
Salt and pepper to taste

Cut out center core of cabbage and put into large kettle. Pour boiling water over to loosen leaves. Let sit for 10-15 minutes. Then pour cold water in the core cavity and the leaves will come apart. Dry leaves well, and cut the back vein off each leaf.

Mix ground pork and beef together until well-blended. Lightly mix in other filling ingredients. Place about 2 tbs. filling onto each cabbage leaf and roll up, tucking in ends.

Place a layer of sauerkraut in a large pan, then add cabbage rolls and another layer of sauerkraut. Fill the pan no more than half full, as cabbage rolls will swell as rice cooks. Completely cover with water. Bring to a small boil and simmer for 2 hours. Top cabbage rolls with kielbasa pieces about 30 minutes before finished cooking.

Chef's note: "This is a Croation recipe that I got from my grandmother, Rose Sulentic."

Sue Heffron
Helena

Sweet and Sour Ribs

2 1/2 - 3 lbs. country-style
  pork ribs
2 cups catsup
2 tsp. dry mustard
1/2 cup vinegar
4 tbs. smoked barbecue
  sauce
1 cup brown sugar

Boil ribs in water until tender. Drain and pat dry. Prepare sauce by combining remaining ingredients. Dip ribs in sauce and arrange in large roasting pan. Pour remaining sauce over ribs and bake covered for 1 hour at 350 degrees. Remove cover and bake another 15 minutes. Serves 6.

Pam Johnson
Billings

Luau Ribs

1 (13 1/2-oz.) can crushed
  pineapple
1/4 cup molasses
1/4 cup prepared mustard
1 tsp. monosodium
  glutamate (optional)
3 tbs. lemon juice
3 tbs. soy sauce
2 tbs. Worcestershire sauce
Dash of pepper
4 lbs. spareribs or loin back
  ribs

Combine all but meat and set aside. Place ribs bone-side-down in a baking dish and bake at 350 degrees until browned, about 15 minutes. Turn and brown other side. Turn again and brush with pineapple glaze. Continue baking until meat is well done, about 1 1/2 - 2 hours. Cut ribs apart and serve. Serves 6.

Ina Gackle
Plentywood

141

Mandarin Pork Roast

4-lb. boneless pork loin
1/2 tsp. salt
1/4 tsp. garlic powder
2 tbs. Dijon mustard
1 (11-oz.) can mandarin
   oranges
1/4 cup brown sugar
1/4 cup vinegar
1 chicken bouillon cube
1 tbs. soy sauce
2 tbs. cornstarch
1/2 cup water
1 medium onion, chopped
1/3 cup chopped green
   pepper

Trim excess fat from roast. Sprinkle roast with salt, pepper, and garlic powder. Spread mustard over roast and place it in large Dutch oven. Cover and bake 2 1/2 hours at 325 degrees, or until meat thermometer reads 170 degrees.

Drain mandarin oranges, reserving liquid. Set oranges aside. Combine liquid, brown sugar, vinegar, bouillon cube, soy sauce, cornstarch, and water in a saucepan. Cook over medium heat, stirring constantly, until smooth and thickened. Remove from heat; stir in onion, green pepper, and oranges.

Spoon sauce over roast. Bake, uncovered, for 30 minutes at 400 degrees, basting occasionally. Slice pork and serve with warm pan drippings. Serves 12-14.

Pam Johnson
Billings

Ham Royale

6-8 lb. ham with bone
12 oz. 7-Up or ginger ale
2 tbs. bottled barbecue
  sauce
1/2 cup brown sugar
1/2 cup pineapple juice
Pineapple slices
Maraschino cherries

Place ham in baking dish deep enough to hold soda pop, and pour 7-Up or ginger ale over it. Bake according to directions that come with ham, basting a few times with the pop. During last half hour of baking, baste ham with mixture of barbecue sauce, brown sugar, and pineapple juice. Garnish with pineapple slices and cherries secured to meat with toothpicks. Serves 12-14.

Audrey M. Vandeventer
Helena

Ham Loaf and Raisin Sauce

2 cups ground cooked ham
2 tbs. butter
2 eggs, beaten well
1 small onion, chopped
1/2 cup bread crumbs
2 tbs. catsup
2 tbs. Worcestershire sauce
1/4 tsp. prepared mustard
Salt and pepper to taste

Sauce:
1 cup apple cider
2 tbs. flour
2 tbs. butter
1/4 cup seedless raisins
Pinch salt

Melt 2 tbs. butter in large skillet. When hot, add chopped onion and saute until not quite brown. Add to ham and mix in remaining ingredients. Shape into a loaf. Bake 40 minutes at 350 degrees in well-greased loaf pan. Turn out onto platter and serve with sauce.

To make sauce: Melt 2 tbs. butter in saucepan. Add flour and salt and brown slightly. Add cider gradually, stirring to make a smooth sauce. Add raisins and serve hot. Serves 4-6.

Mildred Gates
Anaconda

143

Ham Loaf with Horseradish

2 lbs. ground ham
1 lb. ground pork
1/2 cup cracker crumbs
2 eggs, beaten
3/4 cup milk
Pepper to taste
1/4 cup spicy tomato juice

Topping:
2 tbs. horseradish, drained
1 tsp. prepared mustard
3 tbs. mayonnaise
1/2 tsp. salt
1/2 cup cream, whipped stiff
Dash of cayenne pepper

Mix first 7 ingredients and form into 2 loaves. Bake 1 hour at 350 degrees. To make topping: Mix all remaining ingredients, folding in cream last. Serve over ham loaf. Serves 12.

June Halgren
Great Falls

Tass Kebab (Armenian Lamb Stew)

2 lbs. cubed lamb, leg or
  shoulder
1 medium onion, sliced
1 green pepper, cut into 1-
  inch squares
1 (4-oz.) can mushrooms
  (optional)
2 tbs. butter
1 (28-oz.) can whole
  tomatoes (with liquid)
2 tsp. oregano

Brown lamb in butter. Add onion, green pepper, and mushrooms. Saute briefly until onion wilts. Break up tomatoes and add with oregano to meat and vegetables. Simmer until done, about 30-45 minutes. Serve over rice pilaf. Serves 6-8.

Aimee Hachigian
Ulm

144

Fish
& Game

Venison Stew

2 1/2 lbs. venison stew
 meat, cubed
1 (28-oz.) can tomatoes
 (with liquid)
1 (10-oz.) package
 frozen peas
3-4 tbs. quick tapioca
4 beef bouillon cubes
1 cup chopped celery
4 medium carrots, sliced
3 medium onions, chopped
1 tsp. salt
1 tsp. seasoning salt
1 tsp. sugar
Pepper to taste
1/8 tsp. ground thyme
1/8 tsp. rosemary
1/8 tsp. marjoram
1/4 cup red cooking wine
1/2 tsp. garlic powder
1/2 tsp. onion powder

Combine all ingredients in 5-quart Dutch oven.
Cook covered for 5 hours at 250 degrees; stir
after 3 1/2 hours. Serves 6-8.

Barbara McPherson
Canyon Creek

146

Venison Jerky

3 lbs. lean venison, cut into
4-inch strips
1 tbs. salt
1 tsp. onion powder
1 tsp. garlic powder
1 tsp. pepper
1/3 cup Worcestershire sauce
1/4 cup soy sauce
1 tbs. prepared mustard

Arrange venison strips in glass or pottery dish. Mix remaining ingredients and pour over meat. Marinate overnight in refrigerator. Then remove meat from marinade and place on paper towels to dry. To oven-dry: arrange on cookie sheets and bake 6-8 hours at 200 degrees. Or use a dehydrator, following jerky instructions that come with it.

Eve McCauley
Helena

Layered Venison Braciole

1 lb. boneless venison steaks
1/4 cup Parmesan cheese
2 tsp. parsley
1 tsp. dried basil
1 tsp. chopped garlic
2 tsp. finely chopped onion
Pepper to taste
Dash of salt
Olive oil
2-3 strips bacon, halved
1 cup shredded mozzarella
cheese
1 cup tomato sauce
1/2 cup red wine

Arrange half the venison in a 2-quart casserole dish. In food processor, whirl the next 7 ingredients, adding a little olive oil to make a paste. Spread paste over steaks. Lay bacon strips over meat and then sprinkle with cheese. Cover with remaining venison. Pour tomato sauce over top and then gently pour wine over all. Bake covered for 45 minutes at 350 degrees. Uncover and bake another 30 minutes. Serves 3-4.

Jackie Kieser
Kila

147

Oriental Stuffed Game Loin

1 (2 - 2 1/2-lb.) antelope,
  deer, or elk loin roast
1 medium green
  pepper, sliced
8-10 green onions, chopped
1/2 lb. fresh white
  mushrooms, sliced
1/2 - 3/4 lb. thick-sliced
  lean bacon

Marinade:
1/2 cup brown sugar
1/2 cup white vinegar
1 1/2 cups soy sauce
2 tbs. sesame seed oil
4 slices fresh gingerroot,
  minced
2-3 cloves garlic, minced
1 cup chopped green onion
1 cup dry white wine or beer

Mix all marinade ingredients together in pan large enough to hold venison roast. Cut loin lengthwise 3/4 of the way through. Lay open on wooden cutting board. With large meat-tenderizing mallet, pound entire loin to half its original thickness.

Spread green pepper, green onion, and mushrooms over low 1/3 of meat. Carefully roll meat, tucking in stuffing at ends. Wrap bacon strips around rolled meat, securing with toothpicks. Marinate covered roast 2 1/2 - 3 hours in refrigerator. Remove from marinade and broil 1 hour in 400-degree oven on middle rack. Close oven door while broiling meat. Turn meat frequently and baste with marinade. Lower oven temperature if roast gets too brown. Remove toothpicks and let roast stand a few minutes before slicing. Serves 6-8.

Sandra Hanson
Helena

Marinated Steak

2 cups apple juice
1/4 cup soy sauce
1 tsp. garlic powder
2 beef bouillon cubes,
    dissolved in a little hot
    water
4-6 deer, antelope, elk, or
    buffalo steaks
Cornstarch or flour
1 (4-oz.) can mushrooms
    (optional)

Mix first 4 ingredients together in large bowl. Add steaks to marinate. Refrigerate 4-6 hours, depending upon toughness of cut. After removing steaks from marinade, quick-sear them to desired doneness. Set steaks aside. Pour marinade into skillet. Mix in enough cornstarch or flour to thicken into a sauce. Add seasoning to taste. If desired, mix in drained mushrooms. Pour sauce over steaks and serve with rice. Serves 4-6.

Chef's note: "If you cook for a hunter, you may be looking for a tasty new way in which to prepare the latest of whatever kind of meat he decides to drag home. Here's a versatile dish that can be fixed using antelope, deer, elk, or buffalo. I have used all of these, and they are all good in this recipe. You can also use beef if that is all you have."

Karen Cameron
Helena

149

Venison Pepper Steak

1/4 cup butter
1-2 lbs. venison steak, cubed
2 cloves garlic, minced
1 cup diced onion
2 beef bouillon cubes
1 1/2 cups boiling water
2-3 tbs. soy sauce
1 (4-oz.) can sliced
  mushrooms
1 (4-oz.) can button
  mushrooms
1 green pepper, cut into
  1-inch chunks
1 red bell pepper, cut into
  1-inch chunks
1 (4-oz.) can sliced water
  chesnuts
2 tbs. cornstarch
1/4 cup cold water
2 tomatoes, peeled and cut
  into chunks
4 cups hot cooked rice
Pepper to taste

In large skillet, saute onions and garlic in butter until onions are tender. Push them to one side and saute mushrooms. Push them to side with onions. Brown venison cubes on one side, pepper to taste, and finish browning on other side. Stir in beef broth made by combining bouillon cubes with 1 1/2 cups boiling water. Stir in soy sauce. Cover and simmer for 20 minutes.

Add pepper chunks, cover, and simmer 5 minutes more. Stir in the water chesnuts. Mix cornstarch in 1/4 cup cold water and pour over meat. Cook, stirring constantly, until mixture thickens and boils. Boil and stir several minutes, add chopped tomatoes, heat through, and serve over rice. Serves 4-6.

Mary Anne Sward
Kalispell

150

Barbecued Venison Strips

1 medium onion, finely
   chopped
2 cups cooked venison, cut
   into strips
1 (8-oz.) can tomato sauce
1/2 cup catsup
1/4 cup brown sugar
1 tbs. Worcestershire sauce
1/2 tsp. dry mustard
1/2 tsp. chili powder
1/2 tsp. salt
1/8 tsp. pepper

Combine all ingredients in 1 1/2-quart casserole dish. Microwave on high for 10-12 minutes, or until hot and bubbly. Stir 2-3 times during cooking. Serve in hamburger buns. Serves 4-6.

Barbara Wolfe
Lewistown

Venison Lunch Meat

2 lbs. ground deer or other
   game meat
1 cup water
1 1/2 tbs. meat tenderizer
1 tsp. garlic powder
1 tsp. onion powder
2 tsp. liquid smoke
1 1/2 tsp. pepper

Mix all ingredients together well and chill in refrigerator for 24 hours. Shape into 2 loaves and wrap in foil, with foil dull-side-out. Poke holes in bottom of foil so that juices can escape. Place in loaf pans and bake 1 1/2 hours at 325 degrees. Chill and slice for lunch meat. Makes 2 small loaves.

Dixie Engelhardt
Ulm

Coffee Venison Roast

2 onions, thinly sliced
3-5 lb. venison roast
1/3 cup vinegar
4 slices bacon
2 cups brewed coffee
2 cups water
Salt and pepper to taste

Make slits in meat and insert an onion slice in each one. Add enough water to vinegar to make 1 cup, and pour over meat in large bowl. Refrigerate overnight. Remove meat from marinade, and brown in bacon fat. Remove meat to baking pan, top with cooked bacon strips and season. Pour coffee and water into pan and bake covered 1 1/2 - 2 hours at 350 degrees. Serves 6-8.

Evelyn Dalry
Helena

Campfire Steak and Beans

1 lb. venison or elk
1 (15-oz.) can baked beans
1 medium onion, chopped
1/4 tsp. dry tarragon leaves
1/4 cup dry red or white wine

Cut meat into serving-size pieces and arrange in skillet. Add remaining ingredients. Cover and simmer 20-30 minutes. Serve with potatoes or pasta. Serves 3-4.

Birdie Joers
Augusta

Venison Liver and Onions

2 lbs. venison or elk liver
1 lb. bacon
2 large onions, sliced
Flour

Clean liver by removing all membranes and blood vessels. Slice 1/2-inch thick and wash to remove blood. Fry bacon until crisp, remove from pan, and saute onion in bacon grease. Remove onion and set aside with bacon. Coat liver in flour and fry in bacon grease. Return onion and bacon to pan and heat through. Serves 8.

Chef's note: "This is a traditional hunting-camp dish at our outfit. The successful hunter gets the first plate and doesn't have to wash the dishes. I hate washing dishes, so I try to be successful."

Aimee Hachigian
Ulm

Tuesday's Fast Food

2 lbs. venison or elk
  meat, diced
1 cup chopped
  green pepper
1 cup chopped mushrooms
1 cup chopped onion
1 cup grated carrot
1 cup chopped celery
1 (15-oz.) can stewed
  tomatoes, chopped
2 tbs. seasoning salt

Place all ingredients in crockpot or casserole dish. Cook in 250-degree oven or on low temperature for 8 hours. Serve over rice or alone. Serves 5-6.

Gayle Carpenter
Helena

153

Breaded Chops

4 trimmed game chops
Cooking oil
1 clove garlic, chopped
1 cup cracker crumbs
1/2 cup grated
 Parmesan cheese
1/4 cup flour
1 tbs. parsley flakes
1-2 eggs, beaten

Combine cracker crumbs, cheese, flour, and parsley in pie plate. In skillet, heat about 1/4-inch oil. Add garlic. Dip chops in beaten egg and then in cheese and flour mixture. Fry in hot oil until browned on both sides. Turn only once. Serves 4.

Emily Peck
Billings

Elk Pin Steak

5-6 lb. elk roast
1/2 lb. salt pork
Water or broth

Remove elk roast from freezer and allow to thaw just enough to be able to shave thin slivers with sharp knife. (Or use food processor to slice frozen meat into very thin slices.) Chop salt pork into small pieces. Stir-fry elk and salt pork together, and then simmer several hours until tender, adding broth or water as needed to keep meats moist. Serves 8-12.

Chef's note: "This recipe is one that was very popular with the 'old-timers' in Elliston. My mother-in-law, Ceil Pierce, passed this recipe on to me as one of the family favorites."

Nancy Pierce
Elliston

Montana Stir-Fry

3 lbs. elk meat
Cooking oil
1 tsp. salt
2 tsp. cornstarch
2 tsp. soy sauce
1 large onion, cut into
   1-inch chunks
1 green pepper, cut into
   1-inch chunks
1 (9-inch) zucchini, cut into
   1-inch chunks
2 handfuls edible pea pods
1 cup fresh bean sprouts
3 stalks bok choy
2 cloves garlic, crushed

Sauce:
1/2 cup brown sugar
2 tbs. cornstarch
1/2 cup cider vinegar
1 1/2 cups pineapple juice
2 tbs. soy sauce

While meat is still partially frozen, slice into finger-length strips about 1/8-inch thick. Heat a small amount of oil in a wok or deep skillet. While oil is heating, put meat, salt, cornstarch, and soy sauce into a bowl and mix thoroughly. In wok or skillet, cook garlic until golden. Remove garlic and stir-fry each vegetable separately. Stir-fry meat and add to vegetables and garlic.

Combine sauce ingredients and cook over high heat until clear. Pour over meat and vegetables. Serves 8.

Enis Ingold
Great Falls

155

Hearty Elk Chili and Beans

2 lbs. ground elk
1 lb. red or pinto beans
2 medium cloves garlic,
 finely chopped
1 large onion, chopped
1 medium green pepper,
 chopped
1 (28-oz) can tomatoes
 (including liquid)
1 (16-oz.) can tomato sauce
1 cup water
1/4 tsp. salt
1/4 tsp. pepper
2 tbs. ground cumin
2 tbs. unsweetened
 baking cocoa
2-4 tbs. chili powder
2 tbs. flour

Bring beans to a boil in 1 quart water. Turn off heat and soak 3 hours covered. Drain, cover beans with water and bring to a boil, then turn to simmer and continue cooking.

In a skillet, saute elk until almost done. Add onion, garlic, and green pepper. Saute until onion is clear. Add flour and stir until flour forms a paste. Add tomatoes, tomato sauce, and water. Stir until well-mixed. Add remaining spices and cocoa. Bring mixture to a boil and simmer 15 minutes. Add to cooking beans and continue cooking until beans are tender. Add water as needed during cooking. Stir often. Serves 5-6.

Dawn Zimmerman
Kalispell

Humps, tongues, and marrowbones

My fare is really sumptuous this evening; buffaloe's humps, tongues and marrowbones, fine trout parched meal pepper and salt, and a good appetite; the last is not considered the least of the luxuries.

Meriwether Lewis
Journal entry, June 13, 1805, at the Great Falls of the Missouri

156

Elk Stroganoff

2 lbs. elk meat, cubed
   or sliced
2 tbs. butter
1 envelope onion-mushroom
   soup mix
1 medium onion, sliced
8 oz. mushrooms, sliced
2 cups milk
2-4 tbs. cornstarch
1/4 cup cold water
1/2 - 1 cup sour cream
1/2 tsp. garlic powder
   (optional)

Brown meat in butter and saute with onion. Set aside in a separate dish. Add milk to pan and scrape browned bits from pan bottom over low heat. Stir in soup mix, mushrooms, and garlic powder. Dissolve cornstarch in cold water (the amount of cornstarch used will determine thickness of gravy). Stir into milk mixture and heat until thickened. Add sour cream to taste and add meat. Heat gently; do not boil. Serve over rice or noodles. Serves 5-6.

Aimee Hachigian
Ulm

Wild Game Roast

3-4 lb. roast (deer, moose,
   bear, etc.)
1 cup vinegar
1 medium onion, sliced
4 bay leaves
6 cups water
2 tsp. salt
1 tsp. pepper
3 cloves garlic
3 tbs. butter, melted

Clean, wash, and dry meat. Combine remaining ingredients, except garlic and butter, in a large bowl. Insert garlic cloves into slits in meat and add to bowl. Marinate meat overnight in refrigerator. Remove meat from marinade and pat dry. Add meat and butter to open pan and roast 1 1/2 - 2 hours at 325 degrees, turning and basting often with marinade. Serves 6-8.

Dorothy Christianson
Great Falls

157

Black Bean Buffalo Chili

3/4 cup dried black
   turtle beans
1/2 cup dried red
   kidney beans
2 cups water
1 lb. ground buffalo meat
1 small onion, diced
1 small green pepper, diced
1 dried red chili pepper,
   crumbled into small pieces
2 tsp. chili powder
1/2 tsp. garlic powder
1/2 cup fresh
   mushrooms, sliced
2 (28-oz.) cans whole
   tomatoes (including liquid)
1 (15-oz.) can tomato sauce

Rinse beans thoroughly in cold water. In a large heavy saucepan, heat the beans and water to boiling and boil 3 minutes. Remove from heat, cover, and let stand 1 hour. Add enough water, if necessary, to cover beans and heat to boiling again. Reduce heat, cover, and simmer for 1 1/2 hours. Beans should be tender.

Remove beans and liquid from saucepan and set aside, reserving the liquid. Brown the buffalo and onion in the saucepan. Add green pepper, red chili, chili powder, and garlic powder. Add tomatoes and liquid, crushing each tomato as it is added. Add tomato sauce and mushrooms.

Add beans and liquid in which they were cooked to meat mixture. Heat chili to boiling, reduce heat, and simmer about 2 hours, stirring occasionally. Serves 6-8.

Mary Dry
Bozeman

Buffalo Roast

4-6 lb. buffalo haunch
1 1/2 cups burgundy wine
2 bay leaves
1 cup finely minced onion
1/2 cup finely minced celery
2 tbs. parsley flakes
2 tbs. oregano
3/4 cup flour
1/2 tsp. salt (optional)
1/8 tsp. pepper
4 tbs. oil
1 (8-oz.) can tomato sauce
4 strips bacon, fried until crisp
1 small onion, sliced and
   separated into rings

Combine wine, bay leaves, minced onion, celery, parsley and oregano. Pour over meat, cover, and marinate overnight. Take meat from marinade and reserve liquid. Dredge meat in seasoned flour. Heat oil in Dutch oven and brown meat on all sides. Combine marinade and tomato sauce and pour over meat. Bake 3-4 hours at 300 degrees, or until meat is tender. (Note: When using beef, increase oven temperature to 325 degrees.)

Remove roast from oven and slice, laying slices in a shallow baking dish. Spoon sauce from Dutch oven over meat. Crumble bacon and sprinkle over top; arrange onion rings over all. Return to oven for 15 minutes. Serves 8-10.

Elaine Kyriss
Billings

159

Rabbit Stew

1 (3-lb.) rabbit
1 cup vinegar
Olive oil
2 (15-oz.) cans Italian
   tomatoes, chopped
   (including liquid)
1 medium onion, chopped
6 cloves garlic, crushed
2-3 bay leaves
1/4 tsp. dried rosemary
1/2 tsp. sugar
1/2 tsp. cinnamon
Salt and pepper to taste

Wash the rabbit and cut it into serving pieces. Sprinkle with 1/2 cup vinegar and let stand 2 hours. Heat enough olive oil in a skillet to brown the rabbit pieces, and then transfer pieces to a larger pan. Add more olive oil to skillet if necessary and saute the onion and garlic until light brown. Transfer them to the pan of rabbit pieces, along with any remaining olive oil.

Add tomatoes, reserved tomato liquid plus enough water to make 1 cup, the rest of the vinegar, bay leaves, rosemary, salt, and pepper. Cover and cook over medium-low heat until rabbit is done, about 1 hour. When done, transfer rabbit pieces to a serving plate and keep warm.

Bring sauce to a boil, stirring to keep it from sticking to the bottom of the pan. Boil until sauce has thickened. Add sugar and cinnamon. Pour sauce over rabbit or serve sauce on the side. Serves 4.

Cynthia Haumberger
Billings

160

Montana Pheasant in Wine Sauce

1 pheasant, quartered
1/2 cup sour cream
3 tbs. plus 2 tsp. butter
1 tsp. rosemary
1/2 tsp. salt
1/2 tsp. pepper
1 tsp. sage
3 cups chicken broth
1 tsp. chopped parsley
1 bay leaf
1 1/2 cups port or rosé wine
3 cloves garlic, minced
2 cups sliced mushrooms
1 cup diced onion
1/4 cup milk
1/2 cup flour

In a large skillet, brown pheasant back, wings, legs, and breasts in 3 tbs. butter over medium heat. Remove pheasant pieces to baking dish. To skillet, add wine and stir well. Add spices, sour cream, and broth. In a separate pan, make a paste with the flour and milk. With a wire whisk, stir the paste into the skillet, whisking sauce until smooth.

In a separate pan, saute onions, mushrooms, and garlic in 2 tsp. butter over low heat. Add to wine sauce. Pour sauce over pheasant pieces, cover baking dish with foil or lid, and bake 1 1/2 hours at 325 degrees. Serves 4.

Deb Strohmyer
Libby

A 'delicacy' spurned

For one Yuletide festival at Fort Union, Montana, James Kipp, a grizzled veteran of the fur trade, planned to give his trappers and their Indian allies a real "Eastern" delicacy for Christmas dinner.... Kipp fattened a large heifer, a rare commodity at that time in the mountains.... (But) after eating only a small portion of the beef the diners fell silent, and shortly, throwing all pretense of propriety aside, the men adamantly refused the meat. Returning to their familiar buffalo roast, the trappers unanimously condemned the "tame beef" as being "too fat and downright sickening."

John H. Monnett
A Rocky Mountain Christmas: Yuletide Stories of the West

161

Roast Mallard Ducks with Stuffing

3-4 mallard ducks, plucked
  and cleaned
1 cup brown rice
1 tsp. salt
1 cup coarse dry
  bread crumbs
1/2 tsp. pepper
1 tsp. poultry seasoning
2 tbs. chopped parsley
1 small onion, chopped
3 tbs. chopped celery heart
3 tbs. butter
Juice of 3 oranges, strained

Place washed rice in flat-bottomed pan; cover to twice its own depth with boiling water. Add 1/2 tsp. salt and bring to a boil; then reduce heat, cover, and cook until tender, about 20-25 minutes.

To the cooked rice, add bread crumbs, 1/2 tsp. salt, pepper, poultry seasoning, and parsley. Fry onion and celery in butter until yellow and tender. Add to dry ingredients; toss lightly but mix well. Stuff the ducks lightly, sew up, and place in roaster. Pour in 1 cup boiling water, cover, and bake 30 minutes at 500 degrees. Reduce heat to 375 degrees and continue baking for 1 1/2 hours. Remove cover for last 3/4 hour. Baste every 15 minutes.

Remove duck to hot platter, discarding excess fat. Add orange juice to glaze in pan. Bring to a boil, stirring, and pour over ducks. Serves 3-4.

Mildred Gates
Anaconda

162

Kwik Kiwi Trout or Salmon

2 (2-3 lb.) trout fillets OR
   1 (3-5 lb.) salmon fillet
2 green onions, finely sliced
Juice of 1/2 orange
Juice of 1/2 lemon
Lemon slices
1/2 tsp. soy sauce
2 kiwis
Pepper to taste
Paprika to taste
Garlic powder to taste

Arrange fillets in shallow, foil-lined baking dish. Peel and mash kiwis and mix with onion, soy sauce, and orange and lemon juice. Pour over fish and sprinkle with seasonings. Bake 30 minutes at 400 degrees. Remove fish to serving platter. Garnish with fresh parsley and lemon slices. Serves 8-10.

Lynne Egan
Clancy

Trout-A-Rudies (Trout Omelet)

1 large cooked trout
1/2 large onion, diced
1/4 lb. bacon, diced
1 clove garlic, minced
1 large tomato, diced
6 eggs
1/4 cup half and half
1 tsp. hot sauce
Salt and pepper to taste
2 cups grated
   hot-pepper cheese

Flake fish from bones and set aside. Saute onion and bacon in skillet until onion is soft; add garlic and tomato and saute briefly. Set aside.

Mix together eggs, half and half, hot sauce, and salt and pepper. Add to large, lightly oiled skillet. Cook over low heat until eggs are slightly set. Add onion mixture and fish flakes to one side of egg. Cover and cook about 5 minutes over very low heat. Fold egg mixture in half to cover fish and onion. Cover with cheese, cover skillet, and cook until cheese melts. Serves 6.

Gracene Long
Hamilton

163

Low-Calorie Trout Sandwich Spread

1 cup flaked cooked trout
1/3 cup low-calorie
  ranch dressing
2 green onions, minced
1 tsp. pickle relish
1 small tomato, diced
1/2 small stalk celery, diced

Combine ingredients and mix well. Spread between two slices of bread along with cream cheese and sliced cucumber. Makes about 1 1/2 cups.

Gracene Long
Hamilton

Missouri River Grilled Trout

1 large trout, cleaned
  and rinsed
Lemon pepper to taste
1 cup cooked rice
Corn husks
2 tbs. butter
1/4 tsp. parsley
1/4 tsp. garlic powder
1/4 tsp. onion powder
1/2 tsp. lemon juice
1 drop liquid smoke
1 tsp. Worcestershire sauce

Sprinkle inside of trout with lemon pepper and stuff belly with rice. Wrap trout in corn husks and place on large sheet of aluminum foil.

Melt butter and season with remaining ingredients. Mix well and pour over corn husks. Wrap foil around fish loosely but so that sauce cannot escape. Place wrapped trout over red-hot barbecue coals or campfire and grill 10 minutes on each side. Trout should flake easily when done.

Mr. and Mrs. R.S. Yaeger
Helena

164

Frontier Town Featured Trout

6 (8-oz.) boneless trout
6 slices bacon, cooked
   and drained
2 cups cooked brown rice
1/4 lb. butter
2 tbs. finely diced celery
2 tbs. finely diced
   green onion
4 tbs. cooked or canned
   small whole shrimp
4 tbs. crabmeat,
   chopped small
2 tbs. finely diced
   green pepper
1 tbs. soy sauce
Lemon pepper to taste
Flour

In a large pan, melt butter and add soy sauce, vegetables, and seafood. Saute over low heat until vegetables are tender. Blend in cooked rice and continue cooking over low heat, stirring often.

Mix lemon pepper with flour and coat trout in this mixture. Grill on barbecue or saute in a small amount of butter until done. Place trout skin-side-down on individual serving plates. Cover half with seafood-rice mixture, and fold other half over the mixture. Place a slice of fried bacon on top. Garnish with parsley and lemon. Serves 6.

Chic Beals, Chef
Frontier Town Restaurant
Helena

Fresh Trout a la Creole

4 medium trout
1 (16-oz.) can tomatoes, chopped (including liquid)
1 (6-oz.) can tomato paste
4-5 green onions, chopped (including green part)
1/2 green pepper, chopped
2 cloves garlic, minced
1 stalk celery, finely chopped
2 tbs. chopped fresh parsley
2 bay leaves
1 tsp. thyme
1 tsp. tarragon
1/4 - 1/2 tsp. cayenne pepper
Juice of 1/2 lemon
1/2 cup dry white wine
Salt and pepper to taste
1/4 cup butter
2 tbs. flour

Melt butter in saucepan and add onion, garlic, green pepper, and celery; saute until onions are transparent and tender. Add the flour to make a paste. Add the chopped tomatoes, including liquid, and tomato paste. Add enough water to make a sauce. Add parsley, bay leaves, thyme, cayenne, tarragon, lemon juice, and wine. Simmer for at least 30 minutes. Add salt and pepper to taste.

Place trout in a buttered casserole dish. Pour creole sauce over fish to cover. Bake 30-45 minutes at 350 degrees. Serve with rice. Salmon may be used in place of trout. Serves 4.

Mary Ann Bigelow
Missoula

Creamed Poached Montana Trout

4 cups heavy cream
1 cup finely diced carrot
1/2 cup finely diced celery
1/2 cup finely diced
   green onion
1 tbs. minced parsley
6 (6-8 oz.) trout, cleaned

In a large skillet, bring cream to a simmer. Add vegetables and cook 5 minutes. Lay trout in sauce and poach for 5-7 minutes, or until fish flakes easily from the bone. Keep each trout warm in oven until all are cooked. Serves 6.

Frank L. Sonnenberg, Chef-Instructor
Missoula Vocational-Technical School

Pickled Montana Trout

20 medium trout
3 cups white vinegar
1 cup water
3/4 cup sugar
1 1/2 tbs. plain or pickling salt
   (non-iodized)
2 cloves garlic
2 tbs. pickling spices
2 large onions, sliced

Clean, skin, and cut up trout into 2-inch pieces. Put in large pan and cover with water. Bring to a boil and cook 3 minutes. Drain. Pack fish with sliced onion into sterilized quart jars. Combine vinegar, water, sugar, salt, garlic, and spices in saucepan and boil together 15 minutes. Pour hot syrup over fish in jars and seal. Let stand in jars 2-3 days or longer before using. Makes about 10 quarts.

Ann Harding
Philipsburg

167

Montana Canned Trout

6 (2-6 lb.) trout
7 tsp. vinegar
7 tsp. canning salt

While fish are partially frozen, scale and cut off fins, heads, and tails. Slice into 1 - 1 1/2-inch pieces. Pack into hot, sterilized pint jars. Add 1 tsp. salt and 1 tsp. vinegar to each jar. Seal jars and put in boiling water bath to cover jars. Boil 4 hours. Age 30 days before using. Fish also can be cooked for 1 hour 40 minutes in a pressure cooker at 10 lbs. pressure. Makes 7 pints.

(Variation: Place in each jar along with fish, 1 tsp. canning salt, 3 tbs. spicy tomato juice, 4 tbs. vinegar, 1/4 tsp. Worcestershire sauce, and 1 tsp. cooking oil. Cook as above. Judy Kuhl, Helena.)

Gertrude Thornton
Helena

Suckers for a good meal

Once the homesteaders got their farming operations underway, the men of the families would be gone part of the time harvesting on other farms. This left the women to fend for themselves, which was not all bad. For example, the women and kids had fun catching as many as they could of the small but tasty suckers that lived in the river. "Ah, they were good to eat," Mrs. Kindzerski said. "I'd rather eat a fried sucker than anything.... We'd dry them partly in the oven and partly in the sun. Then we'd put them in a bag and keep them in a dry place."

Daniel N. Vichorek
Montana's Homestead Era

168

Pickled Paddlefish

Paddlefish, cleaned and cut
  into 1 1/2 - 2-inch chunks
Salt water
White vinegar
2-3 large onions, sliced
1/2 large lemon, sliced

Brine:
3 cups white vinegar
3 cups sugar
1 1/2 cups white wine
4 dried red chili peppers
1/3 cup pickling spice
1/4 tsp. mustard seed
1/4 tsp. celery seed

Pack fish chunks into a gallon jar, filling almost to top. Pour in salt water strong enough to float an egg and soak 24 hours. Drain but do not rinse. Soak another 24 hours in white vinegar. Drain again but do not rinse.

Put all brine ingredients into a kettle, stirring to dissolve the sugar. Bring to a boil, remove from heat, and let cool. Remove fish from jar. Layer fish, onion slices, and lemon slices in jar until jar is full. Press fish down gently and cover with brine. Refrigerate 20 days. Trout may be used in place of paddlefish. Makes 1 gallon.

Marlyse Drogitis
Harrison

Curry of Fresh Salmon

4 (8-oz.) salmon steaks
4 tbs. butter
1/4 lb. mushrooms, sliced
2 tbs. minced green pepper
1/2 tsp. ground coriander
1 tsp. turmeric
2 tsp. ground cumin
1 1/4 tsp. ground ginger
1/2 tsp. finely minced
   chili pepper
3 tbs. flour
2 cups hot milk
8 green onions, sliced
Salt to taste

Poach salmon in 1 cup salted water for 7-10 minutes, until tender. Drain, remove all skin and bones, and cut salmon into 1-inch cubes. Set aside. Melt butter in heavy saucepan over low flame, add mushrooms, green pepper, coriander, turmeric, cumin, ginger, and chili pepper, mix well, and saute until mushrooms are tender. Stir in flour, mixing very well, and then slowly stir in hot milk. Bring sauce to a boil, reduce heat, and simmer 5 minutes. Add salmon, green onions, and salt to taste, simmer 5 minutes, and serve with rice. Serves 4-6.

Judy Reed
Missoula

Salmon Cakes

1 (15 1/2 oz.) can red
   salmon, drained
2 eggs
2 tbs. milk
1 cup bread crumbs
1 tbs. mayonnaise or
   salad dressing
1 tbs. prepared mustard
2 tbs. seafood seasoning

In large mixing bowl, beat eggs and milk together. Add mustard, mayonnaise or salad dressing, and salmon. Then add bread crumbs and seasoning. Form into patties and fry in skillet with oil. Serves 4-6.

Carol Sue Kehs
Stevensville

Salmon Pie

1/2 lb. mushrooms, sauteed
1 (15 1/2-oz.) can red salmon
3-4 green onions, chopped
3 eggs, beaten
1 cup sour cream
1/2 cup grated sharp
   cheddar cheese
1/4 cup mayonnaise
1 tbs. grated onion
3 drops hot sauce
1/4 tsp. dill weed

Crust:
1 1/2 cups whole-wheat flour
1 cup grated cheddar
   cheese
1/2 tsp. salt
1/2 tsp. paprika
1/2 cup butter
1/3 cup chopped almonds

To make crust: Mix flour, cheese, salt, and paprika in bowl. Cut in butter until crumbly. Add almonds. Set 1 cup of crust aside for topping. Press remaining crust into a 9-inch pie plate.

Drain and flake salmon, removing bones. Save liquid. Add liquid, beaten eggs, sour cream, cheese, mayonnaise, and seasonings to salmon, mixing thoroughly. Fold in mushrooms and green onions. Turn into crust. Sprinkle with reserved crumbs. Bake about 45 minutes at 400 degrees. Serves 6.

Ruth Saholt
Whitefish

171

Cod with Cheese Sauce

1 lb. cod fillet
3 tbs. flour
1/4 cup plus 1 tbs. butter
1 cup milk
1/2 tsp. Dijon mustard
1 tsp. lemon juice
1/3 cup cheddar cheese
1/2 cup sliced mushrooms
1/4 cup chopped onion
1/2 cup green
  pepper chunks
Pepper to taste
1/4 tsp. dried parsley
Dash of paprika
2 tbs. white wine (optional)

In saucepan, melt 1 tbs. butter. Saute onion, green pepper, and mushroom until onion is golden brown. Set aside. In separate saucepan, melt 1/4 cup butter and blend in flour to make a paste. Mix milk into flour paste slowly and stir until sauce has thickened. Add wine, mustard, lemon juice, and cheese. Blend until cheese is melted and stir until smooth. Season with pepper, parsley, and paprika. Bake cod until flaky. Serve cod over rice, topped with cheese sauce. Spoon cooked vegetables over cheese sauce. Serves 4.

Deborah L. Cox
Billings

Baked Fish Fillet

3 lbs. sole or ocean
  perch fillets
1/2 cup finely chopped onion
1 (4 1/2-oz.) can baby shrimp
  or pieces, drained
1/2 cup crumbled croutons
6 tbs. butter, melted
Lemon pepper to taste
1/2 cup finely chopped
  green pepper
1/2 tsp. garlic salt

Arrange fish in baking dish. Scatter onion, green pepper, shrimp, and crumbled croutons over fish. Sprinkle with garlic salt and lemon pepper. Drizzle with melted butter. Bake about 30 minutes at 350 degrees, or until fish is flaky and topping is slightly browned. Serves 6.

Lillian A. Dove
Missoula

172

Sole au Gratin

4 (1/2-lb.) sole fillets
6-12 tbs. butter
4 tbs. chopped fresh parsley
4 green onions, chopped
   (white part only)
2 cups chopped fresh
   mushrooms
Salt and white pepper
   to taste
4 tbs. toasted bread crumbs
1/2 cup dry white wine

Lightly butter a large casserole dish and sprinkle the bottom with half the parsley, green onions, and mushrooms. Season with salt and white pepper. Lay the fish on top. Cover with the rest of the chopped ingredients and top with bread crumbs. Add wine. Melt remaining butter and drizzle over top. Bake 15 minutes at 425 degrees, or until fish is cooked and topping is crisp and golden. At the end of cooking, the dish may be broiled briefly, if necessary, to brown top. Serves 4.

Karen L. L. Stevens
Billings

Montana-Style Snapper

1 cup thinly sliced
   mushrooms
1 small onion, cut into
   thin rings
1 yellow bell pepper, cut
   into strips
1 (14 1/2-oz.) can tomato
   wedges, drained
1 1/2 tsp. dried whole thyme
1 1/2 tsp. garlic powder
1 tsp. parsley
1 lb. red snapper fillets
2 tbs. white wine or
   lemon juice

Lightly oil a large skillet. Heat over medium heat. In skillet, arrange mushrooms, onion, pepper, and tomato wedges in layers. Mix thyme and garlic powder, and sprinkle half the mixture over the vegetables. Place fillets on top of vegetables and sprinkle with wine and remaining seasoning. Bring to a boil, cover, reduce heat, and simmer 10-15 minutes, or until fish flakes easily with a fork. Serves 4.

Pamela K. Rausch
Missoula

173

Red Snapper Los Cruces

4 (8-10 oz.) red snapper fillets
2 tbs. butter, melted
1 tbs. lemon juice
1/2 tsp. garlic powder
2 (15-oz.) cans stewed
  tomatoes, crushed
1-2 jalapeno peppers,
  chopped
1 (15-oz.) can pitted black
  olives, drained and
  chopped
1 small onion, chopped
2 cloves garlic, minced
1/2 tsp. salt
1/4 tsp. cayenne pepper

Arrange fish in a large baking pan. Combine butter, lemon juice, and garlic powder, and baste fish. In a separate pan, combine tomatoes, peppers, olives, onion, garlic, salt, and cayenne pepper. Simmer 10-15 minutes over low heat until onions are transparent. Pour over fish. Place fish in oven and bake uncovered 30 minutes at 350 degrees. Serves 4-6.

Deb Strohmyer
Libby

Pounding pemmican

This is a famous food which is very characteristic of the Blackfeet. Buffalo cut in thin slices was dried for winter. They crushed the dried meat on a flat rock for a variety of foods; some took part of this dried meat, crushed or mashed it by using a flat rock to pound on using a pounder such as a stone hammer. When the dried meat was finely crushed, this was what was called pemmican. This pemmican was sometimes used in soups, mixed with mashed cherries, added to serviceberries to use as flavoring, or packed in little pouches and used for lunches. A more modern practice is to add a little cinnamon and sugar to the meat.

Kiowahkie Bear Woman
Blackfeet Cookbook

Stuffed Baked Bass

1 (3-4 lb.) bass, cleaned
Salt and pepper to taste
4 cups coarse dry bread
  crumbs
1/2 cup finely chopped onion
1 tsp. salt (optional)
1/8 tsp. pepper
2 eggs, beaten
1/2 cup butter, melted
1/2 tsp. ground cloves
4 tbs. port wine
4 tbs. catsup
2 tbs. water
2 tbs. lemon juice
1 cup fine bread crumbs
Lemon slices
Parsley

Wash fish and dry well. Remove head and tail if desired. Sprinkle cavity with salt and pepper and lay fish in buttered baking dish. In a large bowl, combine next 7 ingredients, tossing lightly. Stuff the fish cavity with this mixture; use small skewers to hold cavity closed.

Combine wine, catsup, water, and lemon juice. Pour half of this over the fish. Bake at 375 degrees, 12 minutes per pound or until fish flakes easily with a fork. Remove fish from oven. Combine fine bread crumbs and 2 tbs. melted butter and sprinkle over fish. Return fish to 400-degree oven and bake until crumbs are lightly browned, about 5 minutes. Garnish with lemon slices and parsley. Serves 6-8.

Elaine Kyriss
Billings

Turbot en Casserole

4 turbot fillets
Lemon pepper to taste
1 (6-oz.) can crabmeat,
  drained
1 (6-oz.) can medium
  shrimp, drained
1/4 cup flour
1/4 cup butter
Pinch of salt
2 cups milk
1/4 cup sherry
4 oz. Swiss cheese, grated
4 oz. mozzarella cheese,
  grated
Grated Parmesan cheese

Bake fish sprinkled with lemon pepper on foil for 20 minutes at 325 degrees, or until fish flakes easily with fork. Cool. Melt butter in saucepan and add flour to make a paste. Gradually add milk, stirring constantly until sauce is thickened. Season with salt. Add sherry to white sauce slowly. Add Swiss and mozzarella cheeses. Add broken pieces of baked turbot, crab, and shrimp. Mix thoroughly. Divide mixture among 4 greased individual au gratin dishes. Sprinkle with Parmesan and lemon pepper. Bake 25-30 minutes at 325 degrees. Serves 4.

Phyllis Nord
Missoula

Shrimp Creole

2 tbs. cooking oil
2 onions, sliced
4 stalks celery, chopped
1 tbs. flour
1 tsp. salt
2 cups canned tomatoes
  (including liquid)
1 tbs. vinegar
1 tsp. sugar
2 tsp. chili powder
1 cup water
1 1/2 cups cooked shrimp
Cooked rice

Saute onion and celery in oil until brown. Add flour and seasonings, then slowly add the water. Cook 15 minutes. Add tomatoes, tomato liquid, vinegar, and sugar and cook 10 more minutes. Add shrimp and cook until shrimp are thoroughly heated. Serve over cooked rice. Serves 4.

Lynn Pennebaker Strate
Missoula

Ginger Shrimp and Scallops

1 1/2 cups instant rice
2 tbs. butter
1/2 lb. shrimp
1/2 lb. scallops
2 cups snow peas
1/2 cup chicken broth
2 tsp. cornstarch
1 tbs. shredded fresh ginger
1/4 cup chopped green
  onion

Cook rice according to package directions. Set aside. Melt 1 tbs. butter in skillet. Cook seafood about 3 minutes in butter. Set aside. Melt remaining butter in skillet and add peas. Saute about 2 minutes. Add peas to seafood. Combine broth and cornstarch in skillet and add ginger. Cook until thick, about 1 minute. Return seafood mixture to skillet and heat thoroughly. Stir in onion. Serve over cooked rice. Serves 6.

Laura Hicks
Troy

Shrimp with Cheese and Peppers

1/4 cup olive oil

2 tbs. butter

24 large shrimp, shelled and
  deveined

3 large red bell peppers

3 large green bell peppers

2 large onions

3 yellow jalapeno peppers

1/2 lb. oaxaco or mozzarella
  cheese

Salt, pepper, and garlic
  to taste

6 cups cooked rice

4 large red cherry peppers
  (optional garnish)

Slice vegetables and cheese into long, thin strips. In a large skillet or wok, heat oil and butter and brown onion. Add peppers and cook over low heat for 15 minutes. Season with salt, pepper, and garlic.

Stir in shrimp and toss until shrimp are pink and curled, about 5-8 minutes. Divide rice among 4 large oven-proof bowls. Spoon shrimp mixture over rice, arranging 6 shrimp around the edges of each bowl. Add thin slices of cheese between the shrimp, place in oven, and bake 20 minutes at 350 degrees, until mixture is hot and cheese is melted. Remove from oven and garnish with cherry peppers. Serves 4.

Rose's Cantina
Helena

Hot Shrimp

2 lbs. large shrimp
1/4 cup cooking oil
2 tbs. butter
3 heaping tbs. flour
1 large onion, minced
1-2 cloves garlic, minced
1 (6-oz.) can tomato paste
3 green peppers, chopped
2 tsp. salt
2 tsp. pepper
1/8 lb. sliced pepperoni

Boil cleaned shrimp 5 minutes in water; save stock. Make a paste by heating oil and butter in a separate saucepan and mixing in flour. Stir constantly until browned. Add onion and garlic and brown these slightly. Add shrimp, salt, and pepper, and stir until the shrimp are coated with the paste. Add tomato paste and green pepper and stir for 5-10 minutes over moderate heat. Add 1 cup shrimp stock and pepperoni slices and cook, stirring occasionally, for another hour. Serves 4-6.

Nancy Allard
Malta

Crab Portuguese

1 onion, chopped
1 green pepper, sliced
2 tbs. cooking oil
1 (6-oz.) can tomato paste
3/4 cup orange juice
1/2 cup water
2 tbs. sliced pimientos
1 tbs. brown sugar
1/2 tsp. salt
12 oz. cooked crabmeat
Cooked rice
Orange sections

Cook onion and pepper in oil until tender. Stir in tomato paste, orange juice, water, pimiento, sugar, and salt. Simmer 10 minutes. Stir in crabmeat. Simmer only until crab is heated. Serve over rice and garnish with orange sections. Serves 6.

Laura Hicks
Troy

179

Scallops and Mushrooms

1/2 lb. sliced mushrooms
1 medium onion, sliced
4 tbs. butter
1 lb. fresh scallops
1/4 cup dry sherry
1 cup half and half
1/2 tsp. salt
1/8 tsp. white pepper
Flour as needed

Saute mushrooms and onions in 1 tbs. butter. Add scallops and sherry and bring to a boil. Reduce heat and simmer uncovered for 6 minutes. In separate saucepan, melt 3 tbs. butter. Add flour and stir to form smooth paste. Cook 1 minute, stirring constantly. Gradually add half and half, and cook over medium heat, stirring constantly, until sauce is thick and bubbly. Stir in salt and pepper. Add sauce to scallops, heat through, and serve. Serves 4.

Judy Reed
Missoula

Baked Oysters and Corn

1 (20 oz.) can creamed corn
1 cup crushed soda crackers
1 egg, beaten
1 tsp. sugar
1/2 tsp. salt
1/4 tsp. pepper
1/2 cup heavy cream
1 cup small fresh shucked
  oysters (or canned)

Combine all ingredients and bake in a greased baking dish for 25 minutes at 375 degrees. Do not overbake. Serves 2-4.

Barbara McPherson
Canyon Creek

Seafood Gumbo

1 - 1 1/2 lbs. medium shrimp
1/2 lb. king crab legs OR
   1 (6-oz.) can crabmeat
1/2 lb. scallops
5-6 green onions, chopped
   (including green part)
2-3 cloves garlic, minced
3 stalks celery, chopped fine
1 small green pepper,
   chopped
1/2 cup fresh parsley,
   chopped
1 (14 1/2-oz.) can peeled
   tomatoes (with liquid)
4 tbs. butter
2-3 tbs. flour
8-10 cups stock
1/2 tsp. cayenne pepper
2 bay leaves
1 tsp. dried thyme
1 tsp. pepper
3/4 tsp. dried basil
1/2 lb. okra
3/4 cup uncooked rice

Peel shrimp and set aside; remove crabmeat from shells. Add shrimp shells and crab shells to 8-10 cups of water. Bring to a boil and then simmer, covered, for at least 30 minutes. Set stock aside.

Melt butter in a large pot. Saute onions and garlic until transparent. Add celery and green pepper and saute another 5 minutes. Add the flour to make a paste. (Add additional butter if necessary). Add chopped tomatoes and liquid, okra if desired, parsley, bay leaves, cayenne, thyme, basil, and pepper. Strain stock and add gradually to the paste, stirring to blend well and thicken. Add seafood.

Bring gumbo to a boil and simmer 1 hour or more. Add uncooked rice about 30 minutes before serving. Salt to taste and cook until rice is tender. Add a couple of drops of hot sauce if spicier gumbo is desired. Serves 6.

Mary Ann Bigelow
Missoula

Tuna Ring with Cheese Sauce

1 egg
2 (7-oz.) cans tuna, drained
1/2 cup chopped onion
1/2 cup shredded sharp
   cheddar cheese
1 tbs. chopped parsley
1 tsp. celery salt
1/4 tsp. pepper
2 cups biscuit mix
1/2 cup cold water

Cheese sauce:
1/4 cup butter
1/4 cup biscuit mix
1/4 tsp. salt
1/4 tsp. pepper
2 cups milk
1 cup shredded cheddar
   cheese OR
   1/2 cup crumbled blue
   cheese

To make tuna ring: Beat egg slightly and stir in tuna, onion, cheese, parsley, celery salt, and pepper. Set aside. Stir biscuit mix and water together to form a dough. Knead 5 times on a floured board. Roll into a 15 x 10-inch rectangle. Spread with tuna mixture and roll up, beginning at long side.

Place roll on baking sheet and pinch ends together. With scissors, cut 2/3 of the way through the ring at 1-inch intervals. Turn each section on its side to show filling. Bake 25-30 minutes at 375 degrees.

To make cheese sauce: Melt butter over low heat; blend in biscuit mix, salt, and pepper. Add milk gradually and cook over low heat, stirring until thickened. Blend in cheese and heat until cheese is melted. Serve hot with tuna ring. Serves 6.

Marian Dunbar
Great Falls

Potatoes, Pasta & Rice

Gourmet Potatoes

6 medium potatoes,
  unpeeled
1/4 cup plus 2 tbs. butter
2 cups shredded cheddar
  cheese
1/2 cup sour cream
1 tbs. minced onion
1/4 tsp. pepper
Paprika to taste

Cook potatoes until tender. Cool, peel, and shred coarsely. Melt 1/4 cup butter in saucepan. Add cheese and stir to partially melt. Blend in remaining ingredients except potatoes and paprika and 2 tbs. butter. Fold cheese mixture into potatoes. Spoon into greased 2-quart casserole dish, dot with 2 tbs. butter, and sprinkle with paprika. Bake uncovered for 30 minutes at 350 degrees. Serves 10-12.

Sue Kaul
Belgrade

French-Fried Potato Balls

1 1/2 cups mashed potato,
  warm and unseasoned
2 eggs, beaten
Small amount of milk
1 tsp. grated onion
1/2 tsp. salt
1 tsp. parsley flakes
3/4 cup dry bread crumbs
3-4 cups cooking oil

Combine potato, eggs beaten with a little milk, onion, salt, and parsley. Mix in 1/4 cup bread crumbs. Shape mixture into small balls, about 1 tbs. each. Roll in remaining bread crumbs. Fry in hot oil (380 degrees) for 1 minute or until golden brown. Makes 18-24 balls.

Patty Howse
Great Falls

Lacy Potato Pancakes

3 medium uncooked
   potatoes, peeled
   and quartered
1/4 small onion
1 egg
1 tbs. flour
Pinch of salt
Cooking oil

Combine onion, egg, flour, and salt in blender. Add potatoes 2-3 chunks at a time. Blend well. Heat oil in a large skillet or electric frying pan. Pour 1/4 cup batter for each pancake, spreading batter thin in hot oil. Fry pancakes until golden brown on both sides, turning once. Serve with applesauce or sour cream Serves 3-4.

Patty Howse
Great Falls

Golden-Flaked Potatoes

4 baked potatoes
1/4 cup cream
4 tbs. butter
1 tsp. salt
1/8 tsp. pepper
1 cup finely grated carrot

Cut baked potatoes in half; scoop out insides and reserve skins. Mash insides of potatoes with cream and butter, and season with salt and pepper. Add grated carrot. Pile potato-carrot mixture into potato skins and bake 5-10 minutes at 450 degrees. Serves 8.

Mildred Gates
Anaconda

Spinach-Stuffed Potatoes

6 medium baked potatoes
1/4 cup butter
8 oz. sour cream
1/2 (10-oz.) package frozen
  chopped spinach
Grated Romano cheese
  to taste
Garlic powder to taste
Salt and pepper to taste

Cut a slit in each baked potato and scoop out insides, being careful not to break skins. Mash insides with butter and sour cream until smooth. Season to taste with salt and pepper.

Cook 1/2 package of spinach according to package directions. Drain thoroughly, and season to taste with garlic powder. Fold into mashed potato. Stuff potato skins, and top with grated cheese. Bake at 350 degrees until heated through and cheese melts, about 15 minutes. Serves 6.

Lynn Pennebaker Strate
Missoula

Creamed Potatoes Country-Style

3 cups diced boiled potatoes
2/3 cup evaporated milk
1/3 cup water
3/4 tsp. salt
2 tbs. flour
2 tbs. butter
1 tbs. chopped chives or
  green onions

Place diced potato in cast-iron skillet. Add evaporated milk and water. Sprinkle with salt and flour, add butter, and stir lightly to mix. Heat slowly for about 15 minutes until thick and creamy, stirring 2-3 times. Just before serving, sprinkle with chopped chives. Serves 4-6.

Priscilla Little
Shelby

Cheesy Potato Casserole

1 (2-lb.) bag frozen hash browns
1/4 cup diced onion
2 (10 3/4-oz.) cans condensed cream of potato soup
2 cups sour cream
1 cup shredded cheddar cheese
1/2 cup grated Parmesan cheese

Thaw potatoes and mix with next 4 ingredients. Spread in a greased 9 x 13-inch baking pan. Sprinkle with Parmesan cheese and bake 45-60 minutes at 350 degrees. Serves 12.

(Variation: Sprinkle top of casserole with 2 cups crushed cornflakes. Drizzle 1/4 cup melted butter over crumbs. Bake as above. Debby DeMott, Great Falls)

Gayle Keith
Belt

Sweet Potato Balls in Walnuts

2 1/2 cups mashed sweet potato
1/4 tsp. salt (optional)
1/2 tsp. cinnamon
2 tbs. melted butter
1/3 cup honey
1 cup chopped walnuts

Combine mashed sweet potato with salt, cinnamon, and butter. Chill. Shape into 2-inch balls, using about 1/4 cup potato per ball. In a small skillet, heat honey. When hot, use fork to dip each potato ball in honey glaze, turning to coat completely. Then dip in chopped nuts. Place potato balls so they are not touching in a shallow, buttered baking dish. Bake 20-25 minutes at 350 degrees. Serves 6-8.

Elaine Kyriss
Billings

Hula Sweet Potatoes

6 medium sweet potatoes
1 cup canned crushed
   pineapple
1/4 cup pecan halves or
   blanched almonds
2 tsp. salt
2 tbs. butter

Bake potatoes in skins about 30 minutes, or until tender. Remove skins and mash insides well, adding salt and butter. Drain pineapple and stir into potato. Pour into buttered baking dish. Arrange nuts on top. Bake 15 minutes at 325 degrees. Then place under broiler for a few minutes to brown. Serves 4.

Mildred Gates
Anaconda

Sweet Potato Souffle

3 eggs
1/4 cup milk
2 cups mashed sweet potato
1/4 cup plus 3 tbs. butter
Sugar to taste
1/2 cup raisins
1/2 cup flaked coconut
1/2 cup chopped pecans

In large bowl, combine mashed potato, 3 tbs. butter, and milk. Blend well. Add eggs and blend well again. Stir in raisins, coconut, and nuts, and mix thoroughly. Sweeten to taste.

Melt 1/4 cup butter in baking dish and allow to cool slightly. Pour potato mixture into dish. Bake 30-45 minutes at 350 degrees. Serves 4-6.

Chef's note: "This recipe is also good using butternut squash in place of sweet potatoes."

Bonnie Harwood
Helena

188

Yam Saute

2 tbs. butter
1 large yam, unpeeled and
    cut into 1/4-inch slices
3 large carrots, unpeeled and
    cut into 1/4-inch slices
1/4 tsp. cinnamon

Melt butter in large skillet over medium-high heat. Add yam and carrot slices, and saute until yam is lightly browned, about 10 minutes. Reduce heat to low, cover, and let vegetables steam until tender, about 10 minutes. Transfer to serving platter and sprinkle with cinnamon. Serves 4-6.

Kathy Borchers
Great Falls

Homemade Noodles

1 large egg
1/4 cup cold water
2 tbs. melted butter
1 1/2 cups sifted flour
1/4 tsp. salt
1/8 tsp. baking powder

Beat together egg and water, and add melted butter. Sift together flour, salt, and baking powder. Add dry ingredients to egg mixture, stirring with fork to form soft dough. Add flour if necessary.

Roll out half of dough at a time on a floured pastry cloth or board until paper-thin. Cut into desired widths. Cook about 1-2 minutes in boiling water to which a little salt has been added. Noodles may be dried well and then frozen.

Agnes Van Oosten
Livingston

189

Mexican Stuffed Shells

12 jumbo pasta shells,
    cooked and drained
1 lb. ground beef
1 (12-oz.) jar medium or mild
    picante sauce
1/2 cup water
1 (8-oz.) can tomato sauce
1 (4-oz.) can chopped green
    chilies, drained
1 cup shredded Monterey
    Jack cheese
1 (2.8-oz.) can Durkee's
French-fried onions

Brown ground beef and drain excess fat. Combine picante sauce, water, and tomato sauce. Stir 1/2 cup into ground beef, along with chilies, 1/2 cup cheese, and 1/2 French-fried onions. Mix well. Pour half of remaining sauce mixture onto bottom of 10-inch-round or 8 x 12-inch baking dish. Stuff cooked shells with ground beef mixture.

Arrange stuffed shells in baking dish and top with remaining sauce. Bake covered for 30 minutes at 350 degrees. Top with remaining cheese and onions and bake uncovered for 5 minutes longer. Serves 4-6.

Rhonda Obergfell
Billings

Scrubbing spuds

A good way to clean new potatoes is to place them in a large dishpan with water enough to cover them. Then take an old broom, worn quite short, and kept clean for this purpose; take the potatoes to the well, and scrub them round and round, crosswide, and up and down, until the peeling is all loose. Pour off the dirty water, and pour on more clean water; give them a second scrubbing and they will be clean.

Ethel Reed
Pioneer Kitchen: A Frontier Cookbook

Turkey-Stuffed Shells

36 jumbo macaroni shells
2 tbs. cooking oil
1 lb. ground turkey
1 medium onion, chopped
1 (10-oz.) package frozen
   chopped spinach, thawed
   and drained
8 oz. cottage or ricotta
   cheese
3/4 cup grated Parmesan
   cheese
1/2 tsp. salt
1/8 tsp. pepper
1 tsp. fennel seed
1 clove garlic, minced
1 (32-oz.) jar spaghetti sauce
6 oz. shredded mozzarella
   cheese

Cook shells according to package directions and drain. Brown turkey, onion, fennel, garlic, salt, and pepper in cooking oil. Drain and cool. Add spinach, cottage or ricotta cheese, and Parmesan cheese to meat. Stuff shells with spinach-meat mixture. Arrange in 9 x 13-inch baking dish. Cover with spaghetti sauce and sprinkle with grated mozzarella. Bake 30 minutes at 350 degrees. Serves 6-8.

Judy Kuhl
Helena

191

Red Pepper Pasta with Salmon Sauce

Pasta:
2 tbs. boiling water
2 tsp. red pepper flakes
1 cup semolina flour
1 cup all-purpose flour
1/2 tsp. salt
1 tbs. corn oil
1 tbs. tomato paste
2 eggs, slightly beaten
1 tbs. olive oil

Sauce:
2 cups champagne
2 cups water
1 tsp. whole allspice
1 bay leaf
1 lb. salmon fillets
2 1/2 cups whipping cream
Salt and pepper to taste

Garnish:
1/2 cup minced green onions

To make pasta: Combine red pepper flakes and boiling water in small bowl. Let steep for 15 minutes. Combine flours and salt. Add corn oil, pepper flakes, tomato paste, and eggs, beating constantly until mixture forms a ball. Let rest, wrapped in plastic wrap, for 20 minutes. Roll out; cut into strips by hand or with pasta machine. In a large saucepan filled with boiling water to which 1 tbs. olive oil has been added, cook noodles for 2 minutes; drain.

To make sauce: In a skillet, bring champagne, water, allspice, and bay leaf to a boil. Add salmon. Simmer, covered, for 7-10 minutes, or until salmon is opaque at its thickest part. Lift out salmon and flake. Strain liquid and return it to skillet. Add cream. Boil rapidly until reduced to 2 1/2 cups, stirring occasionally. Add salmon flakes to reduced sauce; season with salt and pepper to taste. Serve hot over red pepper pasta, and garnish with minced green onions. Serves 4.

Pamela K. Rausch
Missoula

Fettucine with Crab and Vegetables

1/2 lb. crabmeat
Juice of 1/4 lemon
3 cloves garlic, minced
1 medium leek, chopped fine
   (including pale green part)
2 tbs. minced shallot
3 green onions, chopped fine
2 tbs. minced chives
1 tbs. olive oil
1 tbs. butter (preferably
   unsalted)
Salt and pepper to taste
1 tsp. dried tarragon
1 small bay leaf
1 cup white wine
2 medium tomatoes, peeled,
   seeded, and diced
Small pinch of baking soda
1/4 cup sherry
About 1 cup whipping cream
1 tbs. minced parsley
8-12 oz. fettucine

In a shallow bowl, break the crabmeat into bite-sized pieces and sprinkle with lemon juice. Heat olive oil in a non-reactive saucepan over medium heat. Add butter and heat until bubbling but not brown. Add garlic, leek, and shallots. Crumble tarragon and add to saucepan along with bay leaf and pepper to taste. Cook, stirring occasionally, until vegetables are soft.

Add white wine and increase heat. Reduce the sauce by about half. Add diced tomato and salt lightly. Add pinch of baking soda. Heat, stirring, for 1-2 minutes. Add sherry and bring to a boil. Add cream and continue to boil for a few minutes until sauce has reached desired consistency. Add crabmeat and chives, blend, and heat to a simmer.

Cook pasta according to package directions; drain. Place on individual plates, top with sauce, and sprinkle with parsley. Serves 4.

Gerald Askevold
Bigfork

193

Jones' Seafood Pasta

1 (4 1/2-oz.) can light tuna in water (reserve liquid)
1 (4 1/2-oz.) can small shrimp (reserve liquid)
1/2 medium onion, chopped
1/2 green pepper, chopped
3 tbs. butter
3 tbs. flour
Chicken broth as needed
2 tbs. dried parsley
1/2 tsp. fennel seeds, crushed
1/2 tsp. celery seeds
1/4 tsp. pepper
2-3 drops hot sauce
8 oz. shell macaroni, cooked and drained
1/4 cup grated Parmesan cheese
1 tbs. sherry (optional)

Saute onion and green pepper in butter until limp. Add flour and cook over low heat for 5 minutes. Stir in 1 1/2 cups liquid made by combining liquids reserved from tuna and shrimp and adding chicken broth as needed. Bring to a boil and thicken.

Remove sauce from heat and add remaining ingredients. Pour into casserole dish and top with more grated Parmesan. Bake about 45 minutes at 300 degrees, or until casserole is bubbly. Serves 4-6.

Chef's note: "In the middle of February, when the temperature is below zero and the lambs are coming at 3 in the morning, I begin dreaming of warm, sunny beaches, palm trees, and unlimited seafood. This casserole is as close as I have gotten so far."

Kathy Tyler Jones
Big Timber

Pasta with Clams and Vegetables

5 cloves garlic, crushed
5 tbs. olive oil
4 stalks celery, chopped fine
2 small zucchini, sliced
1/4 lb. mushrooms, sliced
4 green onions, chopped
2 small tomatoes, chopped
1/4 cup white wine
1 (6 1/2-oz.) can chopped clams (with liquid)
Salt and pepper to taste
1 lb. fettucine, cooked and drained
Grated Parmesan cheese to taste

Saute garlic in oil for a few minutes; do not brown. Add vegetables and saute until all are just tender. Add clams, clam liquid, wine, salt, and pepper. Simmer for a few minutes and serve over hot pasta. Sprinkle with grated Parmesan. Serves 6-8.

Lillian A. Dove
Missoula

Noodles Romanoff

8 oz. fettucine noodles
3 cups large-curd cottage cheese
2 cloves garlic, crushed
2 tsp. Worcestershire sauce
2 cups sour cream
6-8 green onions, chopped
1/2 tsp. hot sauce
1 cup grated Parmesan cheese

Cook noodles according to package directions; drain. Mix remaining ingredients into noodles and pour into buttered 2- to 3-quart casserole dish. Bake 25 minutes at 350 degrees. Serves 6.

Judy Reed
Missoula

Two-Cheese Cannelloni

8 manicotti shells, parboiled
1 (10-oz.) package frozen
 spinach, thawed and
drained
2 cups small-curd cottage
 cheese
1/4 cup instant minced onion
1/2 tsp. basil, crumbled
1/2 tsp. salt
1/4 tsp. nutmeg
1/8 tsp. pepper
2 tbs. lemon juice
1 (8-oz.) can tomato sauce
1/2 cup grated Monterey
 Jack cheese

Herb sauce:
1/4 cup butter
3 tbs. flour
1 clove garlic, minced
1 tsp. basil
1 tsp. salt
2 cups milk
2 tbs. parsley

To make herb sauce: In saucepan, melt butter and blend in flour, garlic, basil, and salt. Stir in milk gradually. Cook, stirring, over medium heat until mixture thickens and boils. Stir in parsley. Set aside.

Mix spinach, cottage cheese, minced onion, basil, salt, nutmeg, pepper, and lemon juice. Stuff into parboiled shells. Pour half of herb sauce into baking dish. Arrange filled shells in a single layer over sauce. Cover with remaining herb sauce. Pour tomato sauce over shells and sprinkle with grated cheese. Cover with foil and bake 45 minutes at 375 degrees, or until heated through. Serves 4.

Laura Hicks
Troy

Spinach-Pasta Bake

2 cups large pasta shells, cooked
1 large onion, chopped
2 tbs. butter
2 cloves garlic, minced
4 cups chopped fresh spinach OR 1 (10-oz.) package frozen chopped spinach
2 tsp. basil
Pinch of nutmeg
1 cup sliced mushrooms

Cheese sauce:
4 tbs. butter
1/4 cup flour
1-2 bay leaves
1 1/2 cups milk
1 tsp. stone-ground mustard
Salt and pepper to taste
8 oz. cheddar cheese, grated

To make sauce: Melt butter in saucepan. Add flour and bay leaves. Stir. Slowly add milk, stirring constantly. After sauce has thickened, add mustard, pepper, salt, and cheese. Allow cheese to melt, remove from heat, and set aside.

In a separate saucepan, saute onion and garlic in butter for 5 minutes, or until transparent. Add spinach, basil, and nutmeg, and simmer until spinach is hot but not wilted. Add mushrooms and cheese sauce. Fold in cooked pasta. Pour mixture into greased baking dish. Bake uncovered 20-25 minutes at 350 degrees. Serves 4-6.

Rebecca Joyce
Missoula

Chinese Fried Rice

2 cups water
1 cup uncooked long-grain
  white rice
1 tsp. butter
8-10 green onions, chopped
  fine
8 slices bacon, cut small
2 eggs, beaten
2 tbs. cooking oil
2 tbs. soy sauce
1 tsp. monosodium
  glutamate (optional)
1 tsp. salt

In the top of a double boiler, bring rice, water, and butter to a boil. Cover and steam for 25 minutes. Remove from heat and chill. Brown bacon until crisp. Scramble eggs and break into small pieces.

Add cooking oil to skillet, heat to high, and add chilled rice, soy sauce, salt, and monosodium glutamate if desired. Toss rice in sauce for 5 minutes, or until thoroughly warmed and coated. Add onion, egg, and bacon and heat 1 more minute. Serves 4-6.

Myrtle Johnston
Boulder

Spanish Rice

6 tbs. butter
1/2 cup brown rice
1/2 cup chopped green
  pepper
1/2 cup chopped onion
1/2 cup diced carrot
2 tbs. canned chopped
  green chilies
1 (1-lb.) can stewed
  tomatoes
1/3 cup water
1/4 tsp. basil
1/4 tsp. oregano
Salt and pepper to taste

Heat butter in saucepan. Add rice, green pepper, onion, and carrot. Cook over medium heat, stirring occasionally, until peppers and onion are tender. Add remaining ingredients. Cover and simmer until rice is tender and all liquid is absorbed about 15-20 minutes. Serves 4-6.

Mary Schneider
West Glacier

Spanish-Rice Burritos

Burritos:
2 tbs. cooking oil
1/2 cup chopped onion
1/2 cup chopped green
  pepper
2 cloves garlic, minced
1 (8-oz.) can whole
  tomatoes, chopped
  (reserve liquid)
About 1 cup chicken broth
1 cup uncooked long-grain
  white rice
3/4 tsp. ground cumin
1/2 tsp. chili powder
1/2 tsp. salt
1/4 tsp. pepper
8 flour tortillas

Cheese-egg sauce:
8 hard-boiled eggs
3 tbs. butter
3 tbs. flour
1/2 tsp. chili powder
1/2 tsp. ground cumin
1 cup milk
1 cup shredded cheddar
  cheese
1/2 cup plain yogurt

To make burritos: Heat oil in large skillet over medium heat. Add onion and green pepper. Saute, stirring occasionally, for 3 minutes. Add garlic and saute another 3 minutes. Drain tomatoes; add enough chicken broth to tomato liquid to make 1 1/4 cups. Add to skillet along with rice, tomatoes, cumin, chili powder, salt, and pepper. Bring to a boil, reduce heat to low, cover, and cook 10 minutes, or until liquid is absorbed.

Wrap tortillas in aluminum foil. Heat 5-10 minutes in 350-degree oven. Spread generous 1/4 cup rice mixture down center of each tortilla. Roll tortillas to enclose filling. Place seam-side-down in greased 9 x 13-inch baking dish. Cover and bake 10 minutes at 350 degrees.

To make sauce: Peel and quarter eggs. Melt butter in medium saucepan over medium heat. Gradually beat in flour, chili powder, and cumin. Cook, stirring, about 3 minutes. Gradually whisk in milk and cook, stirring, until thickened. Stir in cheese until smooth. Stir in yogurt and egg. Cook until heated through, but do not boil. Pour sauce over baked burritos. Serves 8.

Laura Hicks
Troy

199

Zucchini Rice Casserole

1 cup uncooked rice
3 medium zucchini, sliced thin
1 (7 1/2-oz.) can chopped green chilies
12 oz. Monterey Jack cheese, grated
2 large tomatoes, sliced thin
Salt to taste
1 tsp. oregano
2 cups sour cream
1 tsp. garlic powder
1/4 cup chopped green onion
2 tbs. parsley

Cook rice according to package directions. Place in 3-quart, buttered casserole dish. Cover with chopped chilies and sprinkle with half the cheese. Add zucchini and tomatoes. Sprinkle with salt.

Combine sour cream, oregano, garlic powder, and green onions. Spoon evenly over tomato layer, and scatter remaining cheese over all. Bake 45-50 minutes at 350 degrees, or until bubbly. Sprinkle with parsley and serve. Serves 8-10.

Ruth Saholt
Whitefish

Wild Rice Casserole

1 cup grated American cheese
1 cup chopped ripe olives
1 (28-oz.) can tomatoes
1 cup fresh mushrooms, sauteed
1/2 cup chopped onion
1 cup wild rice
1/4 cup olive oil
1 1/2 cups boiling water
Salt and pepper to taste

Combine all ingredients in a large casserole dish and bake 1 1/2 hours at 350 degrees. Serves 6-8.

Dorothy Bradley
Bozeman

Artichoke Risotto with Walnuts

2 (6-oz.) jars marinated
   artichoke hearts
1 cup coarsely chopped
   walnuts
1 cup uncooked white rice
2 cubes chicken bouillon
2 cups water
1 (2-oz.) jar chopped
   pimientos, drained
1/4 cup grated Parmesan
   cheese

Drain about 2 tbs. artichoke marinade into a saucepan. Add walnuts and stir over medium heat about 5 minutes, or until lightly toasted. Spoon out nuts and set aside. Pour remaining marinade into pan. Add rice and cook over medium heat, stirring, until grains become opaque, about 5 minutes. Stir in water and bouillon cubes and bring to a boil. Reduce heat and simmer, covered, for about 20 minutes, or until rice is tender.

Stir 1 jar of artichokes into rice. Stir in pimiento and cheese. Spoon rice into a serving dish and top with remaining artichokes and the walnuts. Garnish with parsley. Serves 4-6.

Rebecca Smith
Missoula

Groceries by the wagonful

My father often told me of his two-day trips to Big Timber (Mont.) twice a year to buy groceries. He would buy a one-hundred-pound barrel of salt for the stock, a second barrel for the house, a one-hundred-pound sack of oatmeal, five hundred pounds of sugar, a thousand pounds of flour, one hundred pounds of dried beans, one hundred pounds of green coffee beans (which we roasted in the oven and ground as we needed it), a few pound cans of smoking tobacco, and many pounds of "Star" and "Horseshoe" plug tobacco.

Christine Green
Five Centuries of Pioneering

201

Montana-Style Rice Pilaf

1 cup uncooked brown rice
1 large bunch fresh spinach, washed and chopped
2 stalks celery, chopped
2 carrots, chopped
6 green onions, chopped
1 cup chopped fresh mushrooms
Juice of 1 lemon
1/2 cup butter
1 tsp. pepper
1 tsp. garlic powder
1 tsp. salt
2 cups plain yogurt
1 1/2 cups grated Parmesan cheese
1 tbs. tarragon
1 tbs. chopped parsley

Cook rice according to package directions. Melt butter in skillet and saute vegetables for 5 minutes over low heat. Add remaining ingredients except lemon juice and parsley. Simmer 30 minutes over low heat, and stir in lemon juice. Top with parsley. Serves 6.

Deb Strohmyer
Libby

The pioneers' staff of life

Potatoes were a staple food for our family and other families on the prairies. Many ate potatoes three times a day—fried for breakfast, boiled for dinner, warmed up for supper.

Louise K. Nickey
Cookery of the Prairie Homesteader

202

Vegetables

Scalloped Asparagus

3 cups cut asparagus
1 1/2 cups milk
2 tbs. flour
2 tbs. butter
1 1/2 tsp. salt
1/8 tsp. pepper
1/2 cup grated cheese
1 cup bread crumbs

Cut asparagus into small pieces and steam until tender in a little water. Thicken milk with flour and add salt, pepper, and butter. Add grated cheese and cooked asparagus to milk mixture. Arrange in alternating layers with bread crumbs in an oiled baking dish. Bake 20 minutes at 350 degrees, or until cheese is melted and dish is heated through.

Judy Reed
Missoula

Easy Baked Beans

1 (15 1/2-oz.) can small red
  beans
1 (15-oz.) can lima beans
1 (15-oz.) can Great Northern
  beans
1 (16-oz.) can baked beans
1/2 lb. bacon, cut up
1 medium onion, chopped
1/2 tsp. garlic powder
1/2 tsp. dry mustard
1/2 cup catsup
3/4 cup brown sugar

Brown bacon and onion in skillet. Add garlic powder, mustard, catsup, and brown sugar. Simmer 20 minutes.

Partially drain liquid from all beans except baked beans. Combine all ingredients in crock-pot. Cook 2 hours on low, or bake 2 hours at 300 degrees in an ovenproof dish. Serves 8-10.

Julie Van Dyke
East Helena

Bob's Baked Beans

2 lbs. navy beans
1 tsp. salt
3 tbs. brown sugar
1/3 cup molasses
2 tsp. dry mustard
2 (1-lb.) cans tomatoes
1 medium onion, sliced
3/4 lb. salt pork OR 1 large
  smoked ham hock

In a large kettle, cover beans with cold water and soak overnight. Drain, add cold water to cover, and simmer until skins burst, about 1 - 1 1/2 hours. Turn into heavy casserole or bean pot without draining.

Combine salt, brown sugar, molasses, mustard, tomatoes, and onion. Add to beans. If liquid does not cover beans, add hot water to cover.

If using salt pork, scrape rind and cut deep gashes in fat 1/2-inch apart. Press pork into beans, leaving only rind exposed. Cover and bake 6-8 hours at 275 degrees, adding more water as necessary to keep beans covered. Remove cover during last half hour of baking. Serve with catsup or chili sauce. Serves 8-12.

Robert H. Lehman
Kalispell

205

Buckaroo Beans

2 1/3 cups dried pinto or red
  beans
6 cups water
1 large onion, chopped
2 cloves garlic, minced
1 bay leaf
2 cups canned tomatoes
1/2 cup chopped green
  pepper
2 tsp. chili powder
2 tbs. brown sugar
1/2 tsp. dry mustard
1/4 tsp. crushed oregano
1/2 lb. smoked ham, bacon,
  or salt pork
Salt to taste

Wash beans. Cover with water and let stand overnight. To cook, cover and bring to boil; cook 2 minutes. Remove from heat and let stand 1 hour. Add onion, garlic, and bay leaf and return to boiling. Turn down heat and simmer 1 1/2 hours, or until beans are almost tender. Add tomatoes, green pepper, chili powder, brown sugar, mustard, oregano, meat, and salt. Bring to a boil again, reduce heat, and let cook slowly for 2 hours, or until liquid resembles a medium-thick gravy. Serves 6.

Laura Hicks
Troy

Bean Burritos

1 (8-oz.) can garbanzo beans
1 (8-oz.) can kidney beans
1/2 cup sliced ripe olives
1/2 small onion, cut into rings
1/2 cup cooking oil
3 tbs. vinegar
3 tbs. packaged taco
  seasoning
1/2 tsp. sugar
Flour tortillas

Mix all ingredients together and let stand several hours before using. Makes 3 cups filling.

To use, spoon filling onto flour tortilla, and add shredded cheese, lettuce, and chopped green chilies. Roll filling inside tortilla.

Emily Peck
Billings

206

Baked Four-Bean Casserole

1 (16-oz.) can kidney beans
1 (16-oz.) can lima beans
1 (16-oz.) can pork and
  beans
1 (16-oz.) can green beans
1 lb. bulk sausage, browned
1 (15 1/2 - oz.) can crushed
  pineapple
1 medium onion, chopped
1 apple, diced
1/2 cup molasses
1/2 cup catsup
1 tbs. lemon juice
2 tbs. brown sugar

Mix all ingredients together well, and turn into a large baking dish. Bake 2 hours at 300 degrees. Serves 14-16.

Charlotte R. Higbee
Noxon

Green Beans with Ham Hocks

3 quarts cleaned and
  snapped green beans
2 ham hocks, cut into 1-inch
  lengths
1/2 tsp. minced garlic
1/2 cup diced onion
1/4 cup chopped green
  pepper
2 cups white wine
1/4 tsp. pepper
1 tsp. salt
2 large potatoes, cubed

Place beans and ham hocks in a large pot and cover with water. Add remaining ingredients and simmer until beans are tender and meat is loosened from bones, about 1 - 1 1/2 hours. Serves 8-10.

(Variation: Add 2 cups cooked black-eyed peas.)

Donna Davis
Lewistown

207

Hot Bean Dish

1 (53-oz.) can pork and
  beans
2 (15-oz.) cans kidney beans
1 (24-oz.) can lima beans
  and ham
1 cup chopped bacon
1 cup chopped onion
1/2 cup chopped green
  pepper
1 (2-oz.) jar pimiento, drained
1/2 cup brown sugar
1 cup catsup
2 tsp. dry mustard
2 tbs. Worcestershire sauce
8 oz. cream cheese

Fry bacon until crisp and remove from skillet. Drain all but a little bacon fat in which to brown onion and green pepper. Drain the cans of beans and put into a 8 x 12-inch baking dish. Add bacon, onion, green pepper, and remaining ingredients except cream cheese. Cube cream cheese and sprinkle over top of beans. Bake 30-45 minutes at 350 degrees. Serves 14-16.

M. Chris Imhoff
Missoula

Cheesy Baked Lima Beans

6 strips bacon, diced
1 small onion, chopped
1 small green pepper,
  chopped
1 tsp. dried basil
2 tbs. flour
3/4 cup chicken bouillon
2 cups shredded cheddar
  cheese
2 (10-oz.) packages frozen
  baby lima beans, thawed
3/4 cup seasoned croutons

In skillet, fry bacon until crisp; remove from pan, leaving about 2 tbs. drippings. Add chopped onion and green pepper and saute until limp. Stir in basil and flour and cook, stirring, until bubbly. Gradually stir in broth. Add grated cheese and stir until melted. Add lima beans and bacon. Turn into a shallow 2-quart casserole. Sprinkle with croutons and bake uncovered for 30-45 minutes at 350 degrees, or until hot and bubbly. Serves 4-6.

Martha Broderson
Cascade

Spicy Chickpeas

2 tbs. cooking oil
1/2 tsp. cumin seeds
1 small onion, chopped fine
1/2 tsp. ground turmeric
1/2 tsp. salt
Pinch of pepper
2 (15-oz.) cans garbanzo
   beans
2 tbs. fresh lemon juice
1/2 tsp. whole black mustard
   seeds
1 tbs. ground coriander
1/2 tsp. paprika
Pinch of ground cinnamon
Pinch of ground cloves
1/2 cup tomato sauce
1-2 tbs. chopped cilantro
   (optional)

Heat oil in large pot and saute mustard seeds until they pop. Stir in cumin and onion; cook until onion is lightly browned. Add coriander, turmeric, paprika, salt, cinnamon, pepper, and cloves, and stir over medium heat until thoroughly blended. Stir in garbanzo beans, including liquid, and continue cooking until desired consistency. Blend in tomato sauce, lemon juice, and cilantro. Heat thoroughly. Serves 6-8.

Dorothy Boulton
Bozeman

Mail-order meals

In 1897, a cook on the wild frontier could order anything she needed from the good old Sears Roebuck catalog. A sample of what was available: Boneless ham, 10 cents a pound; string beans, 7 cents a can; corn, 6 cents a can; tomatoes, 23 cents a can; premium catsup, 50 cents a gallon; an Upright Acme Refrigerator, $10.40; a cook stove, $9.54 - $13.80; a 2-quart saucepan, 41 cents.

1897 Sears Roebuck Catalog

Beets with Mustard Sauce

1 (16-oz.) can beets, drained
2 tsp. dry mustard
2 tsp. sugar
1/2 tsp. salt
1 tbs. flour
Dash of ground cloves
3/4 cup water
1/4 cup vinegar
2 egg yolks, slightly beaten
1 tbs. butter

In top of double boiler, mix mustard, sugar, salt, flour, and cloves. Add water, vinegar, egg yolks, and butter, and cook until thickened. Pour over cooked beets. Serves 6-8.

Mildred Gates
Anaconda

Broccoli with Salmon Sauce

1 cup buttermilk
1/4 cup chopped onion
1 cube chicken bouillon
1 tbs. butter
1/2 tsp. grated lemon peel
1 (12-oz.) can salmon,
    drained
1 (10-oz.) package frozen
    broccoli spears
Lemon wedges to garnish

Cook and drain broccoli. Combine buttermilk, onion, and bouillon cube in saucepan. Heat until bouillon is dissolved. Add butter, lemon peel, and salmon. Heat through. Pour sauce over hot broccoli. Garnish with lemon wedges. Serves 4-6.

Laura Hicks
Troy

210

Sesame Broccoli

2-3 stalks fresh broccoli
1 tbs. cooking oil
1 tbs. vinegar
1 tbs. soy sauce
4 tsp. sugar
1 tbs. sesame seeds, toasted

Clean broccoli and cut into spears. Cook in boiling water until tender and drain. In a small saucepan, combine remaining ingredients and heat to boiling. Pour over hot broccoli and turn spears to coat. Serves 4.

Kathy Borchers
Great Falls

Best Broccoli Casserole

2 (10-oz.) packages frozen
  broccoli OR 1 bunch fresh
  broccoli
1 large onion, chopped
1/2 cup butter
1 (10 3/4-oz.) can condensed
  mushroom soup
1 (4-oz.) can mushroom
  pieces
1 cup processed cheese
  spread
1/2 cup slivered almonds
1 cup toasted bread crumbs

Cook broccoli until almost tender. Drain. Saute onion in butter. Add soup, mushroom, cheese spread, and almonds. Cook over low heat, stirring, until cheese melts. Arrange broccoli in baking dish. Top with sauce and sprinkle with bread crumbs. Bake 30 minutes at 350 degrees. Serves 8-10.

Oma B. Ahrens
Harlowton

211

Sweet Tangy Winter Cabbage

2 tbs. butter
2 cups thinly sliced onion
8 cups thinly sliced cabbage
1 1/2 tsp. salt
1 tsp. caraway seeds
4 green apples, cored and
　　sliced
1/4 cup frozen orange juice
　　concentrate
Pepper to taste

Saute onion in butter until transparent. Add cabbage and salt, and continue to saute until cabbage is tender. Add remaining ingredients. Stir until thoroughly mixed. Cover and simmer for 20-25 minutes. Serves 8-10.

Rebecca Joyce
Missoula

Mexican Cabbage

2 lbs. cabbage, shredded
2 tbs. butter
1/2 cup chopped onion
2 tbs. chopped green pepper
2 whole cloves
1/2 bay leaf
2 tbs. brown sugar
1 1/2 cups canned tomatoes
1 tsp. salt
Dash of pepper

Cook cabbage in water for 10 minutes. Drain and set aside. Saute onion in butter until tender. Add remaining ingredients except cabbage. Simmer 15 minutes. Remove cloves and bay leaf. Add cabbage and heat thoroughly. Serves 6.

Laura Hicks
Troy

Cabbage Casserole

1 medium head cabbage, chopped
2 cups shredded cheddar cheese
1 (10 3/4-oz.) can condensed cream of chicken soup
1/2 cup milk
2 cups cubed bread
3 tbs. butter

Cook cabbage in salt water until tender. Drain. Arrange half the cooked cabbage in a 9 x 13-inch baking dish. Top with half the shredded cheese. Add another layer of cabbage and then cheese. Mix together soup and milk. Pour over cabbage.

Melt butter in skillet and add bread cubes, stirring until all butter is absorbed. Pour over top of cabbage. Bake 30 minutes at 350 degrees, or until bubbly.

Mary Burdette
Great Falls

Carrots au Gratin

1/2 cup crushed seasoned croutons
3 tbs. butter
1/3 cup chopped onion
3 tbs. flour
1 tsp. salt
1 1/2 cups milk
1/8 tsp. pepper
1 tbs. dried parsley flakes
1 cup grated processed cheese
4 cups cooked, sliced carrots

In a saucepan over low heat, melt butter and saute onion until just tender. Stir in flour, salt, and pepper. Remove from heat. Add milk gradually, and stir until smooth. Return to medium heat and cook until bubbly and thickened. Stir constantly. Add cheese and stir to melt. Remove from heat and stir in carrot and parsley.

Spread mixture into greased 1 1/2-quart baking dish. Sprinkle crouton crumbs over top and bake 20 minutes at 350 degrees. Serves 6.

Alice B. Gunlock
Helena

213

Glazed Carrots and Onions

2 tbs. butter
8 medium carrots, cut into
  1/4-inch slices
2 medium onions, cut into
  thin wedges
1/4 tsp. ground ginger
1/4 cup orange juice
1/4 cup red currant jelly
1/4 tsp. salt

Melt butter in medium skillet. Add carrot, onion, and ginger. Cover and cook 5-7 minutes, stirring occasionally. Stir in orange juice, jelly, and salt. Cook uncovered 3-4 minutes, stirring frequently, until vegetables are tender and glazed with jelly mixture. Serves 4.

Laura Hicks
Troy

Cheesy Cauliflower Casserole

3 cups chopped cauliflower
2 tbs. chopped green pepper
8 oz. sliced water chesnuts
1 cup grated cheddar
  cheese
4 tbs. butter, melted
1 cup cubed American
  cheese
2 cups crushed cheese
  crackers
1 (2-oz.) jar pimiento
2 hard-boiled eggs, sliced
1 small onion, chopped
3 tbs. flour
2 cups milk
3 tbs. grated Parmesan
  cheese

Layer cauliflower, pimiento, green pepper, water chesnuts, eggs, onion, and cheddar cheese in 2 1/2-quart casserole. In a saucepan, stir flour into melted butter and cook 1 minute. Add milk gradually. Add American cheese and cook until thick. Pour over vegetables. Sprinkle cracker crumbs and Parmesan cheese on top. Bake 30 minutes at 350 degrees. Serves 6-8.

Sue Kaul
Belgrade

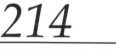

214

Scalloped Celery

3 cups diced celery
1/4 cup slivered almonds
1/2 cup sliced water
  chesnuts
3 tbs. butter
3 tbs. flour
1 cup chicken broth
3/4 cup half and half
1 (4-oz.) can mushrooms
1/2 cup shredded sharp
  cheddar cheese
1/2 cup bread crumbs
Salt and pepper to taste

Parboil celery in salted water for 5 minutes; drain well. Combine celery, almonds, and water chesnuts in 1 1/2-quart casserole dish. In a saucepan, melt butter and stir in flour to make a smooth paste. Stir in chicken broth and half and half gradually. Simmer over low heat until thickened, stirring constantly. Stir in mushrooms, salt, and pepper. Pour over celery. Top with cheese. Bake 30 minutes at 350 degrees. Serves 6.

Lillian McGinnis
Great Falls

Celery Almondine

1/3 cup slivered almonds
2 tbs. butter
4 cups diagonally cut celery
1 chicken bouillon cube
1/2 tsp. instant onion
1/2 tsp. sugar
1/8 tsp. ginger
1/8 tsp. garlic salt

Saute almonds in butter until lightly browned. Add celery. Crumble bouillon cube over celery and add remaining ingredients. Cook 10 minutes, stirring to mix. Serves 6.

Betty Stav
Deer Lodge

215

Mexican Corn Pie

3 large eggs
1 (8 3/4-oz.) can creamed
  corn
1 (10-oz.) package frozen
  corn, thawed and drained
1/2 cup butter, melted
1/2 cup yellow cornmeal
1 cup sour cream
4 oz. Monterey Jack cheese,
  cut into 1/2-inch cubes
4 oz. sharp cheddar cheese,
cut into 1/2-inch cubes
1 (4-oz.) can chopped green
  chilies
1/2 tsp. salt
1/4 tsp. Worcestershire sauce

Grease a 10-inch pie plate generously with shortening. In a large bowl, beat eggs. Add remaining ingredients and stir until thoroughly mixed. Pour into pie plate and bake uncovered for 1 hour at 350 degrees. Serves 8.

Melinda Reed Hettick
Stevensville

Corn Pudding

6 eggs
2 (16-oz.) cans creamed corn
1 cup milk
1/2 cup flour
2 tbs. sugar
1/2 tsp. salt
1/2 cup butter
Paprika to taste

Beat eggs well. Add corn, milk, flour, sugar, and salt. Mix well. Melt butter in a 7 x 12-inch baking dish. Pour in corn mixture. Bake 50 minutes at 350 degrees, or until firm and brown on top. Sprinkle with paprika. Serves 10.

Lynn Pennebaker Strate
Missoula

216

Stuffed Eggplant

2 medium eggplants
2 cups dry bread crumbs
1/2 cup plus 2 tbs. butter, melted
1 tsp. oregano
1/4 tsp. thyme
1/8 tsp. nutmeg
2 tbs. finely diced onion
1 tbs. finely diced celery
1/3 cup finely diced fresh mushroom
1/2 tsp. salt (optional)
1/4 tsp. pepper
2 eggs, beaten
4 tbs. grated Parmesan cheese

Parboil unpeeled eggplants in 4-6 cups water for 15 minutes, or until tender but firm. This helps take away bitterness. Cut in half.

While eggplants are cooling, combine crumbs, 1/2 cup butter, oregano, thyme, nutmeg, salt and pepper, onion, celery, mushroom, and eggs. Scoop out eggplant pulp and add to crumb mixture. Place eggplant halves in shallow baking dish. Spoon filling into halves, and sprinkle with Parmesan cheese. Drizzle with 2 tbs. melted butter. Cover with foil and bake for 20 minutes at 375 degrees. Remove foil and bake another 10 minutes, until stuffing is lightly browned. Serves 8.

Elaine Kyriss
Billings

Onion Lovers' Delight

6 cups sliced sweet onion
3/4 cup Italian dressing
1/4 tsp. crushed oregano leaves
1 green pepper, sliced
1/2 cup grated Parmesan cheese

Separate onions into rings. Heat 1/2 cup dressing in large skillet. Add onion and oregano. Saute over low heat until onions are transparent, stirring often. Add remaining dressing and green pepper. Sprinkle cheese over onions. Cover skillet and let stand for 1 minute with heat turned off. Serves 8-10.

Laura Hicks
Troy

217

Scalloped Onions and Celery

12 small white onions
2 tbs. butter
1/8 tsp. pepper
2 tbs. flour
1 large stalk celery
1 1/2 cups milk
1/2 cup coarse cracker
  crumbs

Peel onions and cut celery into 1/2-inch lengths. Parboil each in separate pans about 20 minutes. Drain. Arrange onions and celery in baking dish.

In saucepan, melt butter and stir in flour and pepper to make smooth paste. Gradually add milk, and cook until thickened. Season. Pour sauce over vegetables, cover with crumbs, and dot with small pieces of butter. Bake 20 minutes at 325 degrees, or until crumbs are brown. Serves 6.

Dorothy Stack
Missoula

Campfire Lemon-Onion Delight

1 large onion
1 lemon
1 tbs. butter

Chop onion into 6 pieces. Chop lemon into 8 pieces. Combine both, dot with butter, and wrap in double-strength foil. Cook in hot campfire coals (not directly in fire) for 30 minutes. Eat right out of foil.

Fred King
Helena

Cheesy Spinach Bake

1 (15-oz.) can spinach, drained OR 2 (10-oz.) packages frozen spinach, thawed and drained
4 eggs, beaten
1 cup milk
1 cup shredded Swiss cheese
1 cup firm, white bread cubes
1/2 cup sliced onion
1/4 cup grated Parmesan cheese

Combine all ingredients and pour into 1-quart baking dish. Cover and bake 25-30 minutes at 375 degrees. Serves 6.

Gladys Hrasky
Billings

Spinach Artichoke Casserole

2 (8 1/2-oz) cans artichoke hearts, packed in water
1/2 cup butter
8 oz. cream cheese
2 (10-oz.) packages frozen spinach, cooked and drained OR 1 bunch fresh spinach, chopped
1/2 tsp. salt
Dash of pepper
1 tbs. lemon juice

Cut artichoke hearts into quarters and spread in bottom of greased 9 x 13-inch baking dish. In a saucepan, melt butter and cream cheese together over low heat. Add spinach, salt, pepper, and lemon juice. Spread spinach mixture over artichoke hearts. Bake 15 minutes at 350 degrees. Serves 12-15.

Mary Schneider
West Glacier

219

Country Scalloped Tomatoes

1/4 cup chopped onion
1/4 cup chopped green
  pepper
1/4 cup butter
6 medium tomatoes, peeled
  and sliced
1/2 tsp. salt
1/4 tsp. pepper
1 tbs. sugar
1/8 tsp. basil leaves
1 1/2 cups toasted bread
  cubes

Cook onion and green pepper in butter until soft. Arrange half of tomato slices in a 2-quart casserole. Top with half of seasonings and bread cubes and all of the green pepper mixture. Top with remaining tomato slices, seasonings, and bread cubes. Bake 30 minutes at 350 degrees. Serves 6.

Patty Howse
Great Falls

Baked Tomatoes

2 lbs. tomatoes
6 slices bacon
1 clove garlic, chopped
1 onion, chopped fine
1/2 lb. fresh mushrooms,
  sliced
1 tsp. seasoned salt
1/2 tsp. oregano
2 tbs. flour
6 tbs. grated Parmesan
  cheese
Butter
Seasoned salt to taste

Fry bacon and add garlic, onion, mushrooms, and seasonings. Thicken mixture with flour. Cut tomatoes 1/2-inch thick and arrange half the slices in a casserole dish. Sprinkle with seasoned salt. Add half of bacon mixture and sprinkle with half of Parmesan cheese. Repeat each layer. Dot with butter and bake 40 minutes at 350 degrees.

(Variation: Eggplant may be substituted for tomatoes.)

Dorothy Boulton
Bozeman

220

Marinated Sliced Tomatoes

4 large tomatoes, sliced
1/4 cup salad oil
1 tbs. lemon juice
1/2 tsp. crushed garlic
1/2 tsp. salt
1 1/2 tsp. dried basil
Chopped parsley as desired
Dash of pepper

Mix all ingredients except tomatoes together and pour over sliced tomatoes. Chill before serving. Serves 4-6.

Gladine Nehus
Great Falls

Turnips au Gratin

1 lb. medium turnips, cut into
   1/4-inch slices
2 medium onions, cut into
   1/4-inch slices
1/4 tsp. sugar
2 tbs. butter, melted
1 tbs. flour
1 cup milk
1/8 tsp. cayenne pepper
1/8 tsp. white pepper
1/4 tsp. salt
1/2 cup shredded American
   cheese
1/4 tsp. paprika
2/3 cup soft bread crumbs

Combine turnips, onion, and sugar in Dutch oven. Cover with water and bring to a boil. Reduce heat and simmer 8 minutes, or until vegetables are just tender. Drain and set aside.

Melt 1 tbs. butter in a heavy saucepan over low heat. Add flour, stirring constantly. Gradually add milk; cook over medium heat, stirring constantly, until thickened and bubbly. Add seasoning and cheese; stir until cheese melts. Remove from heat.

Put half the onion-turnip mixture in bottom of a greased 1-quart casserole dish. Top with half the cheese sauce. Repeat layers. Combine 1 tbs. melted butter, paprika, and bread crumbs and sprinkle over casserole. Bake 25 minutes at 350 degrees, or until hot and bubbly. Serves 6-8.

Pam Johnson
Billings

221

Zucchini Linquist

1 small zucchini
1 medium onion
3 medium carrots
2 tbs. butter
2 tbs. lemon juice

Slice zucchini 1/4-inch thick. Cut onion into large chunks, separating layers. Cut carrots into 1/4-inch strips about 3-4 inches long.

Melt butter in large skillet, add vegetables, and saute until carrot is tender. Do not overcook. Add lemon juice and stir before serving. Serves 4-5.

Dawn Linquist
Columbia Falls

Mexican Ratatouille

1 large green pepper
1 large onion
1 large tomato
1 (4-oz.) can diced green
  chilies
1/2 cup shredded cheddar
  cheese
1/2 cup bread crumbs
Salt to taste

Slice all vegetables thin. Layer half in a 5 x 7-inch casserole dish and sprinkle with chili peppers and salt. Add another layer of vegetables and top with cheese and bread crumbs. Bake 20-30 minutes at 350 degrees, or until all vegetables are tender and top is browned. Serves 2-4.

Jackie Kieser
Kila

222

Breads

Quick White Bread

1 cup milk
2 tbs. shortening
1 1/2 tsp. sugar
1 1/2 tsp. salt
1 package dry yeast
1/2 cup lukewarm water
2-3 cups flour

Heat milk; add shortening, sugar, and salt. Dissolve yeast in warm water and add to milk mixture. Add 1 cup flour and beat thoroughly. Cover and set in warm place to rise until light, about 1 hour. Add enough flour to make a firm dough. Keep dough somewhat sticky. Knead on a slightly floured board until smooth and elastic to touch. Cover and set in warm place until dough triples in volume. Knead again. Shape into a loaf and put into a greased pan. Set in warm place and allow dough to double in volume. Bake 50-60 minutes at 350 degrees. Makes 1 loaf.

Dawn Zimmerman
Kalispell

French Bread

1 package dry yeast
2 cups warm water
1 tbs. sugar
2 tsp. salt
5 3/4 cups flour

Combine first 4 ingredients in a large bowl. Mix in flour gradually. Place dough in lightly oiled bowl and cover with damp cloth. Let rise until doubled in volume. Punch down and shape into 2 long rolls. Place loaves on oiled cookie sheet or in French bread pans and let rise until dough doubles in volume. Bake about 20 minutes at 425 degrees. Makes 2 loaves.

Mary Ellen Olmstead
Cut Bank

224

Lauri's Farmer Bread

2 packages dry yeast
3/4 cup warm water
3 1/4 cups boiling water
1/2 cup brown sugar, packed
2 tbs. salt
1/2 cup butter
1 large can evaporated milk
2 cups Zoom or Roman Meal cereal, uncooked
About 10 cups white flour
2 cups whole wheat flour

Stir yeast into warm water until dissolved. In a very large bowl, combine the boiling water, sugar, butter, and salt. Stir until butter is melted. Add milk and cereal, whole wheat flour, and 2 cups white flour. When cooled to warm, stir in yeast and add white flour to make moderately stiff dough. Turn out onto floured surface and knead until smooth and elastic, about 5-7 minutes.

Return dough to large greased bowl. Cover and let rise until dough doubles in volume, about 1 1/2 hours. Punch dough down. Divide into 6 equal portions, and let dough rest while you grease 6 round cake or pie pans. Knead dough into round flat shapes and fit into pans. Poke dough with fork at 1-inch intervals across entire loaf to prevent air pockets from forming. Let dough double in volume, about 1 hour. Bake 30 minutes at 375 degrees. To make tops soft and shiny, baste with butter while still warm. Makes 6 loaves.

Pat Lauri
Elliston

225

Special Whole Wheat Bread

**4 - 4 1/2 cups
  unbleached flour
2 cups whole wheat flour
2 packages dry yeast
1 tbs. salt
1 1/2 cups milk
1/2 cup water
1/2 cup small-curd cottage
  cheese
1/4 cup honey
1/4 cup butter**

Combine whole wheat flour, 1 cup unbleached flour, yeast, and salt in a large bowl. Mix well. In a saucepan, heat milk, water, cottage cheese, honey, and butter until warm (120-130 degrees). Butter need not melt. Add to flour mixture. Blend with electric mixer at low speed until moistened. Beat 3 more minutes at medium speed. By hand, gradually stir in remaining flour to make a firm dough.

Knead dough on a floured board until elastic. Place in a greased bowl, turn greased side up, cover, and let rise until doubled in volume, about 1 hour. Punch down and divide into 2 parts. Shape into loaves. Place in greased 9 x 5-inch loaf pans, cover, and let rise until doubled in volume again, about 1 hour. Bake 35-40 minutes at 375 degrees, or until loaves are golden brown and sound hollow when tapped. Remove from pans and cool on rack. Makes 2 loaves.

**Mary Schneider
West Glacier**

Swedish Rye Bread

2 packages dry yeast
1 1/2 cups warm water (105-115 degrees)
1/3 cup brown sugar
1/3 cup molasses
1 tbs. salt
1 tsp. anise or fennel seed, crushed
1 tbs. finely shredded orange peel
2 tbs. vegetable oil
2 1/2 cups medium rye flour
2 1/4 cups white flour

Dissolve yeast in warm water; stir in brown sugar, molasses, salt, anise seed, orange peel, oil, and rye flour. Beat until smooth. Stir in white flour gradually to make a soft dough.

Turn dough onto lightly floured surface. Cover and let rise 15 minutes. Knead until smooth and elastic, about 5 minutes. Place in greased bowl, cover, and let rise 1 hour. Punch down and divide into 2 parts. Shape each part into a round, slightly flattened, loaf. Place on greased cookie sheet. Let rise 1 hour. Bake 30-40 minutes at 350 degrees. Remove to wire rack to cool. Brush tops with butter. Makes 2 loaves.

LaVonne Brown
Cut Bank

Montana Sourdough Starter

2 cups flour
2 cups water
2 yeast cakes

Mix together in a small crock and let stand overnight before using. The starter can be stored in the refrigerator for a long time; it should be stirred now and then. Always leave at least 1 cup in crock, and never put leftover batter back into the crock. The starter can be replenished when low by adding 1 cup flour and 1 cup water.

Sunny Peters
Diamond N Ranch, Lame Deer

227

Sheepherder's Sourdough

1 cake compressed yeast OR
   1 package dry yeast
1/4 cup warm water
3 cups sourdough starter
2 tsp. salt
2 tbs. cooking oil
Several cups unbleached
   white flour

Dissolve yeast in warm water. Add sourdough starter, salt, and oil. Blend in 2 cups flour. Continue to add flour until soft dough forms. Knead for 15 minutes. Let rise in an oiled bowl covered by a damp cloth until doubled in volume. Punch down. Form into 2 loaves and place into oiled loaf pans. Let rise until double. Brush with egg if desired, and bake 25-35 minutes at 375 degrees.

Chef's note: "This recipe is for Helena, and we're at 4,000 feet elevation. Increase yeast for lower elevations, decrease for higher. Sourdough is unpredictable and is influenced by the phases of the moon, weather systems in the area, and any number of favorite mysteries. If you need sourdough starter, come to the Sweetgrass Bakery, and we'll get you started. Ours is over 100 years old now."

Sweetgrass Bakery
Helena

228

Sourdough-Like Beer Bread

5 - 5 1/2 cups flour
2 packages dry yeast
1/4 cup sugar
1 1/2 tsp. salt
1/2 cup water
1 1/2 cups dark beer
3 tbs. cooking oil
Cornmeal

In a large bowl, combine 2 cups of flour, yeast, sugar, and salt. Mix well. In a saucepan, heat water, beer, and oil until quite warm (120-130 degrees). Add to flour mixture. Blend at low speed with electric mixer until moistened; beat 3 minutes at medium speed.

By hand, gradually stir in remaining flour to make a soft dough. Knead on floured surface until smooth and elastic, about 5 minutes. Place in a greased bowl, turning to grease top. Cover and let rise in a warm place until doubled in volume, about 1 hour. Punch down and divide into 2 parts.

On lightly floured surface, roll or pat dough into a 7 x 11-inch rectangle. Starting at long side, roll up tightly. Pinch ends to seal. Place on a greased cookie sheet and sprinkle with cornmeal. Make 3-4 diagonal slashes across the top. Cover and let rise 30 minutes. Bake 30-35 minutes at 375 degrees. Makes 2 loaves.

Janel McCall
Helena

229

Mama's Golden Loaves

1/2 cup warm water
  (105-115 degrees)
Pinch of ground ginger
1/4 cup canola oil
2/3 cup honey
2 cups warm buttermilk
1 tsp. salt
2 packages dry yeast
1 cup bran cereal
1 1/2 cups quick-cooking
  rolled oats
2 eggs
3 cups whole wheat
  pastry flour
3 cups unbleached flour
1 tbs. poppy seeds
1 tbs. caraway seeds

In a large mixing bowl, dissolve the yeast in 1/2 cup warm water; add pinch of ginger to make the yeast work more quickly. Stir in oil, honey, warm buttermilk, and eggs. Then add oats, bran cereal, salt, and seeds; mix well. Add all the whole wheat flour and unbleached flour. Add small amount of white flour if necessary to make the dough moist but not sticky.

Turn dough onto floured surface and knead for 7-10 minutes. Place dough in a large greased dish. Turn dough to grease top. Cover with damp towel and let rise in a warm, draft-free area until doubled in volume, about 1 1/2 hours. Punch down dough and divide into 3 equal parts for loaves or into 24 rolls. Place into lightly greased pans and let rise until doubled in volume, about 1 1/2 hours. Heat oven to 350 degrees. Place loaves in oven and turn heat down to 325 degrees. Bake loaves about 30-40 minutes, rolls about 15-20 minutes. Cool loaves on wire racks. Cool rolls in pans. Makes 3 loaves or 24 rolls.

Mary-Anne Sward
Kalispell

Grandma's Oatmeal Bread

2 packages dry yeast OR 2
  cakes compressed yeast
1/2 cup lukewarm water
1 1/2 cups boiling water
1 cup quick-cooking
  rolled oats
1/2 cup molasses
1/3 cup shortening
1 tbs. salt
5 1/2 - 6 cups sifted flour
2 eggs, beaten

Moisten yeast with lukewarm water. In large bowl, combine boiling water, rolled oats, molasses, shortening, and salt. Cool to lukewarm. Add yeast mixture. Stir in about 2 cups of flour. Add eggs and beat well. Add remaining flour to make soft, slightly sticky dough. Grease top lightly. Cover tightly and place in refrigerator at least 2 hours.

Turn dough out onto well-floured surface and shape into 2 loaves. Place in greased 9 x 5 x 3-inch loaf pans. Cover and let rise in a warm place until doubled in volume, about 2 hours. Bake 40-50 minutes at 375 degrees. Makes 2 loaves.

Bob Lehman
Kalispell

The way to health and vitality

The desire for buoyant carriage, vibrant good health and sustained vitality is natural to every woman. To achieve this you must be properly nourished. The eating of MORE bread at meals—and between meals is the result of modern woman's new attitude toward diet. She eats bread with everything... it is the GOOD companion of other foods....

1936 advertisement for Purity Bread Co., Billings

231

Dilly Casserole Bread

1 package dry yeast
1/4 cup warm water
1 cup cottage cheese,
  heated to lukewarm
2 tbs. sugar
1 egg
1 tbs. minced onion
1 tbs. butter
2 tsp. dill seed
1 tsp. salt
1/4 tsp. baking soda
2 1/4 - 2 1/2 cups sifted flour

Soften yeast in warm water. In a large bowl, combine cottage cheese, sugar, onion, butter, dill seed, salt, soda, egg, and yeast mixture. Add flour to form a stiff batter, beating well after each addition. Cover and let rise in a warm place until light and doubled in volume, about 1 hour.

Stir down batter. Turn into well-greased 8-inch round casserole dish. Let rise in warm place until light, 30-40 minutes. Bake 40-50 minutes at 350 degrees until golden brown. Brush with butter and sprinkle with salt if desired. Makes 1 loaf.

Susie Miller
Bozeman

I've been baking on the railroad

(Cooks for the railroad gangs had ovens that were) almost square holes, really wider than high dug back in the banks along the railroad tracks, with rock in the bottom to hold the heat.... (The cooks) built extra hot fires a few hours before the baking, then cleaned the fire out at baking time. Most had a heavy piece of metal for a door and closed the door tight all around to hold the heat. Besides the breads, baked beans, roasts, and other baked dishes (were) cooked in this manner.... Many old timers remember seeing these ovens all along the tracks....

Grandma's Favorite Recipes
compiled by Range Riders Reps, Miles City

232

Orasnica (Croatian Nut Bread)

1 package dry yeast
1/4 cup warm water
1/4 cup plus 1 tsp. sugar
3/4 cup milk, scalded
1 tsp. salt
1/4 cup butter
2 eggs
4-5 cups flour

Filling:
1/2 cup butter
1/2 cup sugar
1/2 cup brown sugar
2 eggs
1 tsp. vanilla
1 tsp. lemon extract
1/4 cup warm milk
4 cups chopped nuts

To make dough: Dissolve yeast and 1 tsp. sugar in warm water. In a large bowl, mix together 1/4 cup sugar, salt, butter, and scalded milk. When cool, add eggs, yeast mixture, and 4 cups flour. Continue adding flour until soft dough is formed. Knead until soft and place in warm bowl. Cover with damp, warm towel and let rise in a warm place until doubled in volume. Turn dough onto pastry cloth and divide in half. Let rest 10 minutes.

To make filling: Cream all filling ingredients except nuts together. Add nuts and mix well. Roll out each piece of dough until 1/8-inch thick. Spread filling over dough. Roll up and twist into an S shape. Put into 2 pans, 8 x 8 or 9 x 9. Let rise 50 minutes. Bake 1 hour at 325 degrees. Cover with foil if browning too much. Makes 2 loaves.

Sue Heffron
Helena

233

Sweet Egg Twist

2 packages dry yeast
1/2 cup warm water
  (110-115 degrees)
1/2 cup butter, melted
1 1/2 cups milk, heated to
  lukewarm
1 cup sugar
6-8 cups flour
1 tsp. salt
1 tsp. ground cardamom
4 eggs, beaten lightly
1/2 cup golden raisins

Glaze:
1 egg yolk
1 tbs. milk

Dissolve yeast in warm water and let rest. Combine butter, milk, sugar, salt, cardamom, eggs, raisins, and 2 cups flour; stir into yeast mixture. Blend in additional flour—up to 6 cups—until dough can be handled easily. Let rest for 15 minutes.

Knead dough until smooth. Place in an oiled bowl and let rise until doubled in volume, about 1 hour. Punch down and allow to rise again for 30 minutes. Divide dough in half. Divide each half into 3 sections. Roll each section into a long roll and braid 3 sections together. Place the 2 large braided loaves onto oiled cookie sheets. Allow to rise about 20 minutes.

Before baking, brush tops of loaves with glaze made by combining egg yolk and milk. Bake 30-35 minutes at 350 degrees, or until loaves are golden brown. This recipe can be halved if desired, or 3 medium loaves can be made rather than 2 large loaves.

Mary Ann Bigelow
Missoula

Refrigerator Rolls

2 packages dry yeast
2 1/2 cups warm water
3/4 cup sugar
4 eggs
2/3 cup cooking oil
1 1/2 tsp. salt
8-10 cups flour

Soften yeast in 1/2 cup water. Mix in remaining ingredients except flour and blend well. Add 8-10 cups of flour gradually, until dough is firm but sticky. Place in a large bowl and let sit overnight in the refrigerator. Drop dough onto a floured board. Roll out, cut into pie-shaped wedges, and roll up like crescent rolls. Let rise 1 hour. Bake 15-20 minutes at 350 degrees. Makes 24-30 rolls.

Barbara Vander Pas
Florence

Fancy Butter Rolls

4 1/2 - 5 cups flour
1 cup butter
1/2 cup plus 1 tsp. sugar
1/2 tsp. salt
2 eggs, beaten
1 cup milk
1 package dry yeast
1/4 cup warm water

Dissolve yeast in warm water to which 1 tsp. sugar has been added. Let sit 10 minutes. In large bowl, mix 3 cups flour and 1/2 cup sugar together. Cut in butter. Add eggs, milk, yeast, salt, and about 2 more cups flour to make a soft, sticky dough. Knead with a spoon until smooth. Cover and place in a cool place overnight.

Divide dough into 6 parts. Roll out each part, spread with melted butter if desired, and cut into 8 pie-shaped wedges. Roll each wedge to form a crescent. Let rise until doubled in volume. Bake 15-20 minutes at 350 degrees. Makes 48 rolls.

Hilde Basile
Bozeman

235

Butter Fleck Rolls

2 packages dry yeast
1/3 cup warm water
1/4 cup sugar
1/4 cup butter
2 tsp. salt
1 cup milk, scalded
2 eggs
5 - 5 1/2 cups sifted flour

Soften the yeast in warm water. In a large bowl, combine sugar, butter, salt, eggs, yeast, and milk (cooled to warm). Add flour gradually, beating well after each addition. Cover and let rise in a warm place until doubled in volume.

Turn dough onto floured board. Roll out thin and spread with softened butter. Cut into 1 x 2-inch lengths. Stack 5 pieces high and put on end in a greased muffin pan. Let rise 35-40 minutes. Bake 12-15 minutes at 400 degrees. Makes 9-12 rolls.

Doris Roberts
Columbia Falls

Potato Rolls

1 package dry yeast
1/4 cup warm water
1/2 cup hot mashed potato
1/4 cup butter
1/4 cup sugar
1 1/2 tsp. salt
1 cup warm milk
1 egg, beaten
4 - 4 1/2 cups flour

Dissolve yeast in warm water. Mix together egg, potato, butter, sugar, salt, and milk. Add yeast. Mix in enough flour to make a soft dough. Knead 2-3 minutes. Let rise for 1 hour, or until doubled in volume. Shape into rolls and let rise 30 minutes. Bake 10-15 minutes at 400 degrees, or until nicely browned. Makes 24 rolls.

Kathleen Papich
Anaconda

236

Cracked-Wheat Crescents

1 package dry yeast
1/2 cup warm water
   (105-115 degrees)
2 tsp. plus 2 1/2 tbs. honey
3/4 cup milk
2 tbs. butter
1 tsp. salt
1 large egg, lightly beaten
1/4 cup bulgur wheat
   (optional)
2 cups whole wheat flour
2 cups or more white flour
1/4 cup melted butter
1/4 cup grated Parmesan
   cheese
1/4 tsp. garlic salt

Dissolve yeast in warm water in large mixing bowl. Stir in 2 tsp. honey. Let stand 10 minutes. In a small saucepan, combine milk, 2 tbs. butter, 2 1/2 tbs. honey, and salt. Heat until butter melts and mixture is lukewarm. Pour milk mixture into yeast mixture. Mix in egg.

Beat in bulgur wheat, if desired, and then add whole wheat flour, 1 cup at a time. Beat well after each addition. Add enough white flour to make a soft, manageable dough. Knead dough on lightly floured board 8-10 minutes, until dough is smooth and elastic. Place in large greased bowl. Cover and let rise in warm place until doubled in volume, about 1 hour. Punch dough down. Knead on floured board about 30 seconds. Shape dough into a ball.

With a rolling pin, roll the ball into a 12-inch circle about 1/4-inch thick. Brush on melted butter. Combine Parmesan cheese and garlic salt and sprinkle evenly over butter. Cut dough into 16 pie-shaped wedges. Roll each wedge beginning with rounded side. Place rolls, with points underneath, on large greased baking sheets. Curve ends to form crescent shapes. Let rise in a warm place 20 minutes. Bake 15-20 minutes at 400 degrees, or until rolls are golden brown. Makes 16.

Martha A. Larson
Great Falls

237

Mom's Biscuits

5 cups flour
1 tsp. salt
1 tsp. baking soda
3 tsp. baking powder
3 tbs. sugar
1 package dry yeast
1/2 cup warm water
3/4 cup shortening
2 cups buttermilk

Dissolve yeast in warm water. In a large bowl, mix the dry ingredients. Blend in shortening, and then add buttermilk and yeast mixture. Mix well with a wooden spoon or hands. Drop pieces of dough onto baking sheets and bake 15-20 minutes at 400 degrees. Makes about 24.

Toni Lewis
Plains

Bread Sticks

1 1/2 cups hot water
1 1/2 cups cooking oil
12 oz. beer
2 packages dry yeast
2 tsp. salt
About 9 cups flour

Mix in order given. Let rise once until doubled in volume. Punch down dough and roll out to make sticks. Lay on greased baking sheets. Wet hands with water and moisten sticks. Shake on salt, dill weed, anise, celery seed, garlic salt, onion salt, or poppy seed as desired. Bake 35 minutes at 350 degrees. Makes 48 sticks.

Zelda Fink
Fairfield

English Muffins

1 cup milk
2 tbs. sugar
1 tsp. salt
1/4 cup butter
1 cup warm water
1 package dry yeast
About 5 1/2 cups unsifted
  flour
Cornmeal

Scald milk; stir in sugar, salt, and butter and cool to lukewarm. Dissolve yeast in warm water in a large warm bowl. Stir in milk mixture. Add 3 cups flour and beat until smooth. Add enough additional flour to make a soft dough. Turn out onto a lightly floured board and knead until smooth and elastic, about 8-10 minutes.

Place dough in a greased bowl, turning to grease top. Cover and let rise in a warm place, free from draft, until doubled in volume, about 1 hour. Punch down and divide in half. On a board heavily sprinkled with cornmeal, roll each piece to a thickness of 1/2 inch. Cut into 3-inch circles with cookie cutter. Cover and let rest on board for 30 minutes.

Carefully place rounds of dough on lightly greased medium-hot griddle, cornmeal side down. Bake until bottom is well-browned, about 15 minutes. Turn and bake about 15 minutes longer. Makes 12-18 muffins.

Shirley A. Goldsmith
Great Falls

239

Orange-Topped Crescent Rolls

1 package dry yeast
1/4 cup warm water
1 cup sugar
1 tsp. salt
2 eggs, beaten
1/2 cup sour cream
1/4 cup plus 2 tbs. melted butter
3-5 cups flour
3/4 cup coconut
2 tbs. grated orange peel
2 tsp. cinnamon

Topping:
3/4 cup sugar
1/2 cup half and half
2 tbs. orange juice
1/4 cup butter

Soften yeast in warm water in large bowl. Beat in 1/4 cup sugar, salt, eggs, sour cream, and 1/4 cup butter. With an electric mixer, beat in 2 cups flour. Add remaining flour gradually until batter becomes quite stiff. Knead with wooden spoon until smooth and elastic. Cover and let rise 2 hours in lightly greased bowl. Knead dough 15 times. Divide in half and roll into 2 (12-inch) circles. Spread with remaining butter.

To make filling: Combine 3/4 cup sugar, cinnamon, coconut, and orange peel. Sprinkle over dough circles. Cut each circle into 12 wedges and roll up, beginning at wide edge. Place in buttered 9 x 13-inch pan, curving ends slightly to form crescent shapes. Let rise 1 hour. Bake 30 minutes at 350 degrees.

Meanwhile, combine topping ingredients in saucepan. Boil 3 minutes, stirring often. Pour over hot crescent rolls. Sprinkle tops of rolls with coconut and broil until coconut is toasted. Makes 24 rolls.

Donna McColloch
Colstrip

Pumpkin Cinnamon Rolls

2 packages dry yeast
1/2 cup warm water
1 tsp. sugar
3/4 cup milk
2 tbs. butter
1 cup brown sugar
1/2 tsp. ground ginger
1/4 tsp. ground cloves
1 egg, beaten
3/4 cup pureed pumpkin
4-5 cups flour
1/4 cup melted butter
3/4 cup raisins
2 tsp. cinnamon

Soften yeast with 1 tsp. sugar in warm water. In a saucepan, mix together milk, 2 tbs. butter, 1/4 cup brown sugar, and spices; scald. Slowly add beaten egg and pumpkin to milk mixture. Blend in softened yeast. Mix 2 cups flour into liquid and blend well. Add enough of the remaining flour to make a moderately stiff dough.

Turn dough out onto lightly floured surface; knead until smooth and elastic, 5-8 minutes. Shape into a ball and place in a lightly greased bowl, turning once to grease top. Cover and let rise in a warm place until doubled in volume, about 1 hour. Roll dough into a rectangle 1/4-inch thick. Brush with melted butter. Sprinkle with 3/4 cup brown sugar, raisins, and cinnamon.

Roll up, starting with long side; seal seam by pinching together. Slice into 1-inch rolls and place cut-side-down in a greased pan. Cover and let rise until doubled in volume, about 45 minutes. Bake 18-20 minutes at 375 degrees. Makes about 12.

Deborah L. Cox
Billings

241

Old-Fashioned Brown Bread

2 cups buttermilk
1/2 cup dark molasses
1 cup raisins
1 cup whole wheat flour
1 cup rye flour
1 cup yellow cornmeal
1 tsp. baking soda
1/2 tsp. salt (optional)
Boiling water

Blend together buttermilk and molasses. Stir in raisins. Thoroughly combine flours, cornmeal, baking soda, and salt. Stir into buttermilk mixture and blend well. Grease 3 (20-oz.) or 4 (16-oz.) empty, clean food cans. Divide dough among cans.

Cover cans tightly with foil and place on rack set in large Dutch oven. Pour boiling water into Dutch oven to a depth of 1 inch. Cover and simmer, steaming bread for 2 1/2 - 3 hours. Add boiling water as needed. Remove bread from cans and cool on rack. Makes 3-4 loaves.

Elaine Kyriss
Billings

Chili Corn Bread

1 cup butter
1 cup sugar
4 eggs
4 oz. diced green chillies
1 (16-oz.) can creamed corn
1/2 cup shredded Monterey Jack cheese
1/2 cup shredded cheddar cheese
1 cup flour
1 cup yellow cornmeal
4 tsp. baking powder

In a mixing bowl, cream butter and sugar. Add eggs one at a time, and mix well after each one. Add chilies, corn, and cheese, and blend well. Blend in dry ingredients. Pour batter into greased and floured 9 x 13-inch pan. Place in 350-degree oven. Immediately reduce heat to 300 degrees and bake 1 hour. Serves 12.

Linda Kauffman
Stevensville

Indian Puris (Fried Bread Puffs)

2 cups sifted flour
1/4 cup butter, melted
1 tsp. salt
About 6 tbs. water
Cooking oil

Sift flour and salt into a large bowl. Add butter, mixing well with a fork. Stir in water gradually, mixing to make a soft, pliable dough. Knead dough 5-9 minutes on a lightly floured surface, until it is shiny and satiny. Roll out dough 1/8-inch thick. Cut into 3-inch rounds. In a skillet, heat at least 2 inches of oil to 360 degrees. Drop in rounds, frying 30 seconds on each side. Makes about 24.

Vickie Menard
Helena

Cloud Nine Baking Powder Biscuits

2 cups sifted all-purpose flour
1 tbs. sugar
1/2 tsp. salt
1 egg, beaten
4 tsp. baking powder
1/2 cup shortening
2/3 cup milk

Sift together dry ingredients. Cut in shortening until mixture resembles coarse crumbs. Combine egg and milk, and add to flour mixture all at once. Stir until dough follows the fork around the bowl. Roll out dough on a floured surface to 1/2-inch thick. Cut with 2-inch round biscuit cutter. Bake 8-10 minutes at 400 degrees. For drop biscuits, increase milk to 3/4 cup. Makes 1 dozen.

Johanna Pearson
Great Falls

Whole Wheat Biscuits

4 cups whole wheat flour
2 tbs. sugar
1 1/2 tsp. salt
1/2 tsp. cream of tartar
2 tsp. baking powder
1 1/2 tsp. baking soda
1 cup shortening
1 1/2 cups milk

Mix all dry ingredients together. Place shortening in the middle of the dry ingredients and pour milk over it. With hands, squeeze and mix the shortening and milk, working in the dry ingredients until a ball of dough forms. Roll dough out about 3/4-inch thick on a floured board and cut into rounds. Bake on an ungreased cookie sheet at 400 degrees until brown. Makes 20.

Chef's note: "This makes a heavy biscuit. It is best served for breakfast or with homemade soups."

Pam Johnson
Billings

Trail Biscuit Mix

5 lbs. flour
2 1/2 cups powdered milk
3/4 cup baking powder
3 tbs. salt
2 tbs. cream of tartar
1/2 cup sugar
2 lbs. shortening

Stir all dry ingredients together in a large pan. Cut in shortening to form coarse crumbs. Store at room temperature in a covered container. To use, add milk or water to bring to desired consistency for biscuits, pancakes, or waffles. Makes about 28 cups.

Gloria Guessen
Missoula

Dumplings

3/4 cup sifted flour
2 1/2 tsp. baking powder
1/2 tsp. salt
1 egg
1/3 cup milk

Sift flour, baking powder, and salt together. Beat the egg, add the milk, and mix with the dry ingredients. Drop by small spoonfuls into chicken gravy, broth, or soup, cover tightly, and cook 15 minutes. Do not remove cover while dumplings are cooking, because if steam escapes they will not be light. Makes 8.

Hazel Bethel
Baker

Corinne's Banana Bread

1/3 cup shortening
1 cup sugar
1 egg, well-beaten
2 cups bran flakes
1 1/2 cups flour
2 tsp. baking powder
1/2 tsp. salt
1/2 cup chopped walnuts
1 1/2 cups mashed banana
2 tbs. water
1 tsp. vanilla

Cream sugar and shortening well. Add egg and bran flakes. In a separate bowl, sift together flour, baking powder, and salt. Add nuts. Combine bananas and water, and add to creamed mixture alternately with dry ingredients. Stir in vanilla. Pour batter into 5 x 9-inch greased and floured pan. Bake about 1 hour and 10 minutes at 350 degrees. Makes 1 (1-lb.) loaf.

Diane Browder
Great Falls

245

Applesauce Nut Bread

1 cup sugar
1 cup applesauce
1/3 cup cooking oil
2 eggs
3 tbs. milk
2 cups flour
1 tsp. soda
1/2 tsp. baking powder
1 tsp. cinnamon
1/2 tsp. salt
1/2 tsp. nutmeg
3/4 cup chopped walnuts

Topping:
1/4 cup brown sugar
1/2 tsp. cinnamon
1/4 cup chopped walnuts

Mix sugar, applesauce, oil, eggs, and milk. In a separate bowl, combine dry ingredients. Add applesauce mixture and nuts and stir just enough to mix well. Pour into 9 x 5 x 3 -inch pan. Combine topping ingredients and sprinkle over batter. Bake 1 hour at 350 degrees. Cover loosely with foil after the first 30 minutes to keep bread from getting too brown. Remove from pan and cool on rack. Makes 1 (1-lb.) loaf.

Martha Broderson
Cascade

Buckboard butter

Nearly every family of homesteaders had a milk cow. A very handy animal to bring west, as she gave them milk, cream, and butter. The making of butter was easy and every home had its dasher type churn to make cream into butter. It wasn't unusual to find a homesteader driving his wagon someplace with a churn full of cream in his wagon. The bouncing and jarring of the wagon churned his butter as he went on his business.

Tag Rittel
Recipes and Remedies of the Pioneers

246

Apple Bread

1/2 cup shortening
1/2 cup sugar
1/4 cup brown sugar
2 eggs
1 cup diced apple
1 tsp. vanilla
1 cup chopped nuts
2 cups flour
1 tsp. baking powder
1/2 tsp. salt
1 tsp. baking soda
2 tbs. warm water

Dissolve baking soda in warm water. Combine all ingredients and pour into three 5 3/4 x 3 1/4-inch pans. Bake 1 hour at 350 degrees. Makes 3 loaves.

June Halgren
Great Falls

Apple Fritters

1 cup flour
1 tsp. baking powder
1 tbs. sugar
1/4 tsp. salt
1/4 cup milk
1 egg, beaten
2 cups peeled, chopped apple

Sift together dry ingredients. Mix together egg and milk and add to dry ingredients. Stir in apple. Drop by heaping tablespoons into hot oil. Fry on both sides until golden. Sprinkle with powdered sugar.

Pat Heintzman
Great Falls

247

Fresh Strawberry Bread

1/2 cup butter
1 cup sugar
1/2 tsp. almond extract
2 eggs, separated
2 cups flour
1 tsp. baking powder
1 tsp. baking soda
1 cup crushed strawberries

Cream butter, sugar, and extract. Beat in egg yolks. In a separate bowl, sift dry ingredients. Add flour mixture to creamed mixture alternately with strawberries. Beat egg whites until stiff. Fold into batter. Line a 9 x 5-inch pan with greased waxed paper. Pour in batter and bake 50-60 minutes at 350 degrees. Cool 15 minutes before removing from pan. Makes 1 loaf.

**Sue Kaul
Belgrade**

Peach Bread

1 1/4 cups pureed peaches
1/3 cup milk
1 egg
3 tbs. cooking oil
2 1/2 cups flour
3/4 cup sugar
3 1/2 tsp. baking powder
1/2 tsp. allspice
1/2 tsp. cinnamon
1/2 tsp. salt
1/3 cup chopped walnuts
1/4 cup brown sugar

Mix first 10 ingredients together in a large bowl. Beat for 30 seconds, or just until all ingredients are moistened. Pour batter into lightly greased 9 x 5 x 3-inch loaf pan. Mix walnuts and brown sugar together and sprinkle over top of batter. Bake 60-70 minutes at 350 degrees, or until toothpick inserted in center comes out clean. Cool 10 minutes before removing from pan. Makes 1 loaf.

**Judy Reed
Missoula**

248

Huckleberry Nut Bread

2 eggs
1 cup sugar
3 tbs. melted shortening
1 cup milk
3 cups flour
1 tsp. salt
4 tsp. baking powder
1 cup fresh huckleberries
1/2 cup chopped walnuts

Beat eggs and add sugar gradually. Mix thoroughly. Add melted shortening and milk. Sift flour with salt and baking powder. Add to huckleberries and nuts. Combine huckleberry-flour mixture with egg-milk mixture, mixing only until dry ingredients are moistened. Pour batter into greased and floured 9 x 5-inch loaf pan and bake 50-60 minutes at 350 degrees. Makes 1 loaf.

Judy Reed
Missoula

Cranberry Bread

3 large oranges
4 cups flour
1 3/4 cups sugar
1 tbs. baking powder
1 1/2 tsp. salt
1 tsp. baking soda
1/2 cup butter
2 eggs
2 cups fresh cranberries,
   coarsely chopped
1 cup seedless raisins

From oranges, grate 1 tbs. peel and squeeze 1 1/2 cups juice. Set aside. In a large bowl, mix flour, sugar, baking powder, salt, and baking soda. Cut in butter until mixture resembles coarse crumbs. Set aside.

In a medium bowl with a fork, beat eggs, orange juice, and peel until blended. Stir into flour mixture just until flour is moistened. Gently fold in cranberries and raisins. Spoon batter into 2 greased and floured 9 x 5 x 3-inch loaf pans. Bake 1 hour and 10 minutes at 350 degrees. Cool bread 10 minutes in pan before removing. Makes 2 loaves.

Patti Billet
Missoula

249

Rhubarb Bread

1 1/2 cups brown sugar
2/3 cup cooking oil
1 egg, beaten
1 tsp. vanilla
1 cup buttermilk
1 tsp. grated orange peel
2 1/2 cups flour
1 tsp. baking soda
1/2 tsp. salt
1 1/2 cups rhubarb, finely
  diced
1 cup chopped walnuts
Juice of 1 orange
1/2 cup sugar

Mix together first 9 ingredients. Stir in rhubarb and nuts. Pour batter into 2 loaf pans and bake 50 minutes at 350 degrees. Remove bread from oven and make syrup by blending orange juice and sugar. Poke holes into tops of loaves with a fork and pour syrup over. Makes 2 loaves.

June Halgren
Great Falls

Fig Rum Loaf

1 1/2 cups dried figs, cut into
  small pieces
1 cup sugar
3 tbs. butter
1/2 tsp. salt
1 1/3 cups boiling water
1 1/2 cups flour
1 1/2 tsp. baking soda
1 tsp. baking powder
1 egg
3 tbs. dark Jamaican rum
1 tbs. grated orange peel
3/4 cup chopped walnuts

Combine figs, sugar, butter, and salt in large mixing bowl. Add boiling water. Let cool to room temperature (butter does not have to melt). In separate bowl, sift together flour, baking soda, and baking powder. Add to fig mixture along with egg, rum, and orange peel. Beat with an electric mixer at medium speed until well-blended. Stir in nuts. Pour batter into greased 9 x 5-inch loaf pan. Bake 65-75 minutes at 350 degrees. Cool on rack 10 minutes. Remove from pan and finish cooling. Wrap and let sit 24 hours before serving. Makes 1 loaf.

Birdie Joers
Augusta

250

Prune Walnut Bread

1 1/2 cups chopped prunes
1 cup boiling water
1/3 cup honey
1 egg, beaten
1 tsp. vanilla
2 1/4 cups flour
2/3 cup sugar
2 tbs. melted butter
1 tsp. baking soda
1 tsp. salt
1 cup chopped walnuts

Combine prunes and boiling water. Cover and set aside for 20 minutes. Then add honey, egg, and vanilla. Sift together dry ingredients and add to prune mixture. Add melted butter and nuts. Pour into greased loaf pan and bake 1 hour at 325 degrees. Makes 1 loaf.

Eve McCauley
Helena

Zucchini Nut Bread

3 eggs
1 cup cooking oil
2 1/2 cups grated zucchini
1 1/2 cups sugar
3 tsp. vanilla
1 1/2 shot glasses rum or
    brandy
3 cups flour
1 1/2 tsp. baking soda
3 tsp. cinnamon
1/4 tsp. baking powder
1 cup crushed walnuts

Blend together first 6 ingredients. Add dry ingredients and mix well. Stir in nuts. Spoon batter into 2 greased and floured loaf pans. Bake 1 hour at 350 degrees. Makes 2 (1-lb.) loaves.

Shirley Smith
Butte

251

Chocolate Almond Zucchini Bread

3 cups sifted flour
2 cups sugar
1 1/4 tsp. baking powder
1 tsp. baking soda
1 tsp. cinnamon
1 cup toasted sliced almonds
1 cup cooking oil
1 tsp. vanilla
3 eggs
2 squares unsweetened
    chocolate, melted
2 cups shredded zucchini

Sift together first 5 ingredients. Mix oil, vanilla, and eggs until well-blended. Stir in chocolate, zucchini, and almonds. Mix in dry ingredients until just blended. Pour into 2 greased loaf pans. Bake 1 hour at 350 degrees. Cool in pans 10 minutes. Makes 2 (1-lb.) loaves.

Sue Kaul
Belgrade

Pumpkin Bread

6 eggs
2 cups canola oil
1 cup sugar
3/4 cup brown sugar
1 tbs. vanilla
5-6 cups grated raw pumpkin
7 cups flour
2 tsp. baking soda
2 tsp. baking powder
1 tbs. cinnamon
1 1/2 tsp. ground cloves
1 1/2 tsp. ground nutmeg
1 cup raisins, diced apple, or
    cranberries cut in half
1/2 - 1 cup chopped nuts

In a large mixing bowl, mix together eggs, oil, sugars, vanilla, and pumpkin. In a separate bowl, mix together dry ingredients. Combine pumpkin and flour mixtures. Add fruit and nuts. If using raisins, soak them first in warm water until plump and then drain. Pour batter into 4 greased loaf pans. Bake 50-60 minutes at 350 degrees. Loaves are done when a toothpick inserted in center comes out clean. Makes 4 (1-lb.) loaves.

John H. McEwen
Helena

252

Desserts

Chocolate Pound Cake

1 (4-oz.) package German sweet chocolate
2 cups sugar
1 cup butter
4 eggs
2 tsp. vanilla
1 cup buttermilk
3 cups sifted flour
1/4 tsp. baking soda
1/2 tsp. salt

Glaze:
1 (4-oz.) package German sweet chocolate
1 tbs. shortening
1/4 cup water
1 cup powdered sugar
Dash of salt
1/2 tsp. vanilla

To make cake: Melt chocolate in top of a double boiler. Cool and set aside. In a large bowl, cream together sugar and butter. Add eggs and vanilla. In a separate bowl, sift together flour, baking soda, and salt. Add buttermilk and flour mixture to creamed mixture. Mix well. Stir in chocolate until well-blended. Pour batter into a well-greased and floured 9-inch tube pan or bundt pan. Bake 1 1/2 hours at 300 degrees. Remove from pan immediately, and wrap in foil until cool.

To make glaze: Melt chocolate and shortening over low heat. Combine sugar and salt in a medium bowl. Gradually stir in melted chocolate. Add vanilla and blend well. For a thinner glaze, add a small amount of water. Drizzle over cake. Serves 12-16.

Sharon Gliko
Great Falls

254

Sauerkraut Chocolate Cake

2/3 cup butter
1 1/2 cups sugar
3 eggs
1 tsp. vanilla
2 1/4 cups flour
1/2 cup unsweetened baking
   cocoa
1 tsp. baking powder
1 tsp. baking soda
1/2 tsp. salt
1 cup water
2/3 cup sauerkraut, rinsed,
drained, and chopped
1/2 cup chopped nuts

Cream together butter and sugar. Beat in eggs and vanilla. Sift together dry ingredients. Add 1/3 at a time, alternating with water, to creamed mixture. Stir in sauerkraut and nuts. Line the bottom of a 7 x 10-inch baking pan with greased wax paper. Pour batter into pan. Bake about 35 minutes at 350 degrees, or until center springs back when lightly pressed with fingertip. Serves 12.

F.A. Wamack
Lewistown

Sour-Cream Chocolate Chip Cake

6 tbs. butter
1 cup plus 1 tbs. sugar
2 eggs
1 1/3 cups flour
1 tsp. baking soda
1 1/2 tsp. baking powder
1 tsp. cinnamon
1 cup sour cream
6 oz. chocolate chips

Cream together butter and 1 cup sugar. Beat in eggs one at a time. Blend in sifted dry ingredients. Add sour cream and mix well. Pour batter into greased and floured 9 x 13-inch baking pan. Scatter chocolate chips over batter, and sprinkle with 1 tbs. sugar. Bake 35 minutes at 350 degrees. Serves 12.

Sue Kaul
Belgrade

255

White Chocolate Cake

1/4 lb. white chocolate
1 cup butter
2 cups sugar
4 eggs, beaten
1 cup buttermilk
1 cup chopped pecans
1 cup flaked coconut
2 1/2 cups sifted flour
1 tsp. baking powder
1/4 tsp. salt
1 tsp. vanilla

Icing:
2 cups sugar
1 cup butter
1/4 lb. white chocolate,
   grated
1 (5 3/4-oz.) can evaporated
   milk
1 tsp. vanilla

Melt chocolate over hot water in double boiler. Cream together butter and sugar, and add eggs and melted chocolate. Sift dry ingredients. Add them, alternating with buttermilk, to creamed mixture. Stir in vanilla, coconut, and lightly floured nuts. Pour batter into greased 9 x 13-inch baking pan or 2 (9-inch) round pans. Bake 20-30 minutes at 350 degrees. Serves 12.

To make icing: Cook icing ingredients in saucepan until mixture reaches soft-ball stage. Beat until thick. Allow to cool before icing cake.

Ida Seidler Bishop
Great Falls

Mocha Oatmeal Cake

2 tbs. instant coffee granules
1 1/3 cups boiling water
1 cup quick-cooking
   rolled oats
1/2 cup butter, softened
1 cup sugar
1 cup brown sugar
1 1/2 cups flour
1 tsp. vanilla
2 eggs
1 tsp. baking soda
1/2 tsp. salt
2 tbs. unsweetened baking
   cocoa

Frosting:
3 tbs. butter, softened
2 cups sifted powdered sugar
1 tsp. vanilla

Combine coffee granules and boiling water. Set aside 2 tbs. coffee for use in frosting. Pour remaining coffee over oats in a medium bowl. Stir to combine. Cover and let stand 20 minutes. In a separate bowl, cream butter. Gradually add sugars, beating until fluffy. Blend in vanilla and eggs. Add oat mixture and blend well. In another bowl, sift together flour, soda, salt, and cocoa. Add to creamed mixture, blending well. Pour batter into greased and floured 9 x 9-inch pan. Bake 50-55 minutes at 350 degrees.

To make frosting: Cream frosting ingredients together, adding 2 tbs. reserved instant coffee. Frost cooled cake; decorate with chocolate curls if desired. Serves 9.

Jeanene Jukkala
Missoula

Mocha Roll

6 eggs, separated
1 cup sugar
1 tsp. vanilla
1/2 cup sifted flour

Filling:
1 cup whipping cream
2 tbs. sugar
1 tbs. unsweetened baking
  cocoa
1 tsp. instant coffee granules

Beat egg whites until foamy. Add sugar and beat until thick and glossy, about 7-8 minutes. Set aside. Add vanilla to egg yolks, and beat until thick and lemony in color. Fold yolks into whites, and then fold in sifted flour. Pour batter into an 11 x 16-inch cookie sheet lined with greased aluminum foil. Bake 15 minutes at 350 degrees. Turn cake out onto a towel sprinkled with powdered sugar. Roll up cake in towel, starting with long edge, and let it cool.

In a chilled mixing bowl, combine filling ingredients and beat until stiff. Unroll the cake, spread it with filling, and roll it back up without the towel, like a jelly roll. Serves 8.

Theresa Maleski
Helena

Indian Bitterroot Pudding

Use about 1/2 cup of roots per serving. Par-boil the roots for a few minutes. Drain and add fresh water. Cook until tender. Sweeten with wild honey to suit taste. Add 1 teaspoon bone marrow per serving. Thicken with the scrapings from the inner side of a fresh skin.

Julie Rock-Above
First Ladies' Cook Book

Coffee Regal Cake

1 1/2 cups sugar
1/2 cup butter
1 tbs. shortening
4 eggs, separated
1 cup cold strong coffee
1 tbs. brandy or vanilla
1/2 tsp. ground cloves
1/2 tsp. nutmeg
1 tbs. cinnamon
2 tsp. baking powder
1/2 lb. raisins or currants,
    dredged in flour
1/2 cup chopped nuts
2 1/2 cups flour

Frosting:
1/4 cup shortening
1 lb. powdered sugar
1 tsp. vanilla
Strong coffee as needed

Cream butter, shortening, and sugar. Add egg yolks and beat well. Add coffee, flour, baking powder, and spices. Fold in beaten egg whites. Add raisins, nuts, and vanilla or brandy. Pour batter into 2 greased and floured 8-inch layer pans. Bake 30-45 minutes at 350 degrees, until a toothpick inserted in the center comes out clean.

To make frosting: Beat together shortening, vanilla, and sugar. Add coffee a little at a time to reach spreading consistency. Frost cooled cake. Serves 8.

Nancy Matthews McCaffree
Forsyth

259

Hungarian Cream Cake

2 cups sifted cake flour
2 tsp. baking powder
1 1/4 cups whipping cream
2 eggs, beaten well
1 tsp. vanilla
1/2 tsp. salt
1 cup sugar

Sift flour, baking powder, and salt together 3 times. Add sugar to eggs and beat well. To egg mixture, alternately add flour and cream. Beat well after each addition until smooth. Add vanilla. Pour into greased 5 x 9-inch loaf pan, and bake 1 hour at 350 degrees. Serves 6.

Annabelle Anderson
Bozeman

Empress Sponge Cake

1 cup sifted cake flour
1 1/4 cup sugar
1 1/2 tsp. grated lemon peel
2 tbs. cold water
7 eggs, separated
1 1/2 tbs. lemon juice
1/4 tsp. salt
1/2 tsp. cream of tartar
1/2 tsp. vanilla

Sift flour once, measure into a bowl, and sift 4 more times. In a separate bowl, combine 1/2 cup sugar, lemon peel, water, and egg yolks, and beat until very thick. Add lemon juice gradually, beating constantly. Stir in flour until just blended.

In another bowl, beat egg whites and salt until mixture forms moist peaks. Add cream of tartar and beat until stiff enough to stand in soft peaks. Add remaining sugar gradually, beating well. Add vanilla. Fold in egg yolk mixture and turn into an ungreased 10-inch tube pan. Bake 45-50 minutes at 350 degrees. Invert pan and cool 1 hour. Serves 12-24.

Lucille Hudson
Polson

Carrot Cake

Cake:
1 1/4 cups corn oil
2 cups sugar
2 cups flour
2 tsp. cinnamon
2 tsp. baking powder
1 tsp. baking soda
1 tsp. salt
4 eggs
4 cups grated carrot
1 cup chopped pecans
1 cup raisins

Filling:
1 1/2 cups sugar
1/4 cup flour
3/4 tsp. salt
1 1/2 cups whipping cream
3/4 cup unsalted butter
1 1/4 cups chopped pecans
2 tsp. vanilla

Frosting:
8 oz. unsalted butter,
  softened
8 oz. cream cheese
1 lb. powdered sugar
1 tsp. vanilla
1 1/2 cups shredded coconut

To make cake: In a large bowl, whisk together corn oil and sugar. Add eggs. Stir in all dry ingredients. Stir in carrot, raisins, and pecans. Pour batter into greased and floured 10-inch tube pan. Bake 70 minutes at 350 degrees. Cool completely.

To make filling: In a heavy saucepan, blend sugar, flour, and salt. Stir in cream. Add butter and cook over low heat until melted. Simmer 20-30 minutes until golden brown. Cool to lukewarm, add nuts and vanilla, and cool completely. Refrigerate until thick.

To make frosting: Cream butter and cream cheese together. Beat in sugar and vanilla. If too soft to spread, chill.

To assemble: With a serrated knife, split cake into 3 layers. Spread filling between layers; spread frosting over top and sides of cake. Pat coconut onto sides of cake. Cake is best when served chilled. Serves 12-16.

Kelly Estes
Elk Canyon Ranch
White Sulphur Springs

261

German Rhubarb Cake

4 cups diced rhubarb
3/4 plus 2/3 cup sugar
1 cup plus 2 tbs. flour
1/2 tsp. baking powder
1/2 cup butter
3 eggs

Beat together butter, 3/4 cup sugar, 1 whole egg, and 2 egg yolks until creamy. Add flour and baking powder. Pour batter into greased spring-form pan. Top with diced rhubarb. Bake 50 minutes at 375 degrees. Beat together remaining 2 egg whites and 2/3 cup sugar. Spread over hot cake. Bake 10 minutes more at 400 degrees. Serves 8.

Renate Lehmann
Helena

Granny's Green Apple Cake

5 large Granny Smith apples
2 eggs
3/4 cup cooking oil
2 cups sugar
2 tsp. vanilla
2 cups flour
2 tsp. cinnamon
1 tsp. baking soda
1/4 tsp. salt
1 cup chopped nuts

Icing:
8 oz. cream cheese
3 tbs. butter
2 tsp. vanilla
2 cups powdered sugar

Beat together eggs and oil until foamy. Add sugar and vanilla and mix well. Blend in flour, cinnamon, baking soda, and salt. Peel apples, slice, and add to batter along with nuts. Mix well. Pour batter into lightly greased 9 x 13-inch baking pan. Bake 45-60 minutes at 350 degrees, or until cake is golden brown. Cool completely.

To make icing: Combine icing ingredients and beat to blend well. Frost cooled cake. Serves 12-16.

Holly Cook
Ulm

262

Apple Cake with Caramel Sauce

1 cup sugar
1 egg
1/4 cup butter
1 cup flour
1 tsp. baking soda
1/2 tsp. salt
1/2 tsp. nutmeg
1/2 tsp. cinnamon
2 cups peeled apple slices

Sauce:
1/2 cup sugar
1/2 cup brown sugar
1 tsp. vanilla
1 tbs. butter
1/2 cup half and half

Combine cake ingredients and mix well. Pour into greased 9 x 9-inch baking pan, and bake about 40 minutes at 350 degrees.

Bring sauce ingredients to a boil. Serve hot over slices of cake. Serves 9.

Karen Sauer
Billings

Snow cream

We only had snow cream in the coldest of weather, when the mercury dipped far below zero. The snow would fall in feathery softness and accumulate in great piles of pure white, dry snow—no dust, no soot, no pollution. Mamma whipped up a big bowl of cream until it stood in peaks and added sugar and extract. She folded the feathery snow into the whipped cream until the cream could absorb no more. That was snow cream! A fluffy white mound of creamy, frosty goodness!

Louise K. Nickey
Cookery of the Prairie Homesteader

263

Dutch Applesauce Cake

2 cups sifted flour
1 tsp. baking soda
1 tsp. cinnamon
1/2 tsp. ground cloves
1/2 tsp. nutmeg
1/4 tsp. salt
1/2 cup butter
1 cup brown sugar
1 cup unsweetened
  applesauce
1 cup raisins
Chopped nuts (optional)

Sift together first 6 ingredients. In a separate bowl, cream butter and add sugar gradually. Continue creaming until fluffy. Alternately add dry ingredients and applesauce to creamed mixture. Blend well. Stir in raisins and nuts, if desired. Pour batter into greased 5 x 9-inch loaf pan, and bake 35 minutes at 350 degrees. Cake is done when toothpick inserted in center comes out clean. Serves 6-8.

Chef's note: "My mother brought her sister's Pennsylvania Dutch cookbook with her to north-central Montana years ago. Many people enjoyed her delicious cooking."

Merrie Johnson
Corvallis

Yum-Yum Cake

 15 oz. seeded muscat raisins
2 1/2 cups cold water
2 tbs. cooking oil
1 1/2 cups sugar
Pinch of salt
4 cups flour
1 tsp. baking soda
2 tbs. cinnamon
1 tsp. ground cloves
1 tsp. nutmeg
1 cup chopped walnuts

Combine first 5 ingredients in a saucepan and bring to a boil. Simmer 10-20 minutes; cool completely. Add sifted dry ingredients and mix thoroughly. Add nuts and mix again. Pour batter into 2 greased 5 x 9-inch loaf pans. Bake 1 hour 15 minutes at 325 degrees. Serves 12-16.

Bernadine Lohman
Butte

Pecan Loaf Cake

1 lb. butter
2 1/4 cups sugar
6 eggs, separated
4 cups broken pecans
1 lb. cut candied cherries
1 lb. cut candied pineapple
2 oz. lemon extract
4 1/2 cups flour
1 tsp. baking powder

Cream together butter and sugar. Add well-beaten egg yolks. Dredge pecans, cherries, and pineapple in flour and add to creamed mixture. Stir in lemon extract. Sift flour together with baking powder. Add to creamed mixture. Beat egg whites until stiff and fold into batter. Mix thoroughly. Pour batter into large greased and floured angel-food cake pan. Pack batter firmly. Bake 5 hours at 250 degrees, with a pan of hot water on racks above and below cake. Serves 16-20.

Dorothy Boulton
Bozeman

Observations on pastry

An adept in pastry never leaves any part of it adhering to the board or dish used in making. The best thing to make it upon is a slab of marble or slate; which substance causes less waste, being cold and smooth. The coolest part of the house and day should be chosen for the process; the hands should be previously washed in very hot water; and the less they touch the paste the better and lighter it will prove; nor should it be rolled much. In whatever way paste is made, wetting it much will render it tough. Salt butter of the best quality makes a fine crust; for sweet things, wash it.

Housekeepers Almanac
1866

265

Fruit Cake

4 cups very warm water
2 packages dry yeast
2 tbs. sugar
Flour as needed
3 cups brown sugar
2 cups butter, softened
6 eggs
1/2 cup molasses
1 1/2 cups powdered milk
1 or more containers candied
   fruit mix
3 handfuls dark raisins
3 handfuls light raisins
3 handfuls chopped nuts
1 tbs. cinnamon
1/2 tsp. ground cloves
1/2 tsp. nutmeg
1/2 tsp. allspice
1 tsp. baking soda
1 cup wine or brandy

In a large bowl, stir yeast and 2 tbs. sugar into warm water. Add enough flour to make a dough that will just drop off spoon. Cover and let rise for 2 hours. Add next 5 ingredients in order given. Beat well and add fruits and nuts. Stir in spices and wine or brandy.

Mix in enough flour to make a dough that will cling to the mixing spoon. Pour batter into 2 lightly greased 5 x 9-inch loaf pans. Bake 2 hours at 350 degrees. Cake will be moister if cooked in a covered casserole dish; remove lid during last 20 minutes of baking. Serves 12-16.

Donna McCulloch
Colstrip

266

Raspberry Walnut Torte

1 (10-oz.) package frozen raspberries, thawed
1/2 cup butter, softened
1/3 cup powdered sugar
1 1/4 cups flour
3/4 cup finely chopped walnuts
2 large eggs
1 cup sugar
1/2 tsp. baking powder
1/2 tsp. salt
1 tsp. vanilla
Vanilla ice cream

Sauce:
2 tbs. cornstarch
1/4 cup sugar
1/2 cup water
1/2 cup raspberry syrup
1 tbs. lemon juice

Drain raspberries, reserving 1/2 cup syrup for sauce. Cream together butter and powdered sugar. Gradually beat in 1 cup flour until blended. Press mixture over bottom of 9-inch spring-form pan. Bake 15 minutes at 350 degrees. Cool completely.

Spoon raspberries over crust and sprinkle with walnuts. Beat together eggs and sugar. Add remaining 1/4 cup flour, baking powder, salt, and vanilla; beat until well-blended. Pour over nuts, spreading as necessary. Bake 30-35 minutes at 350 degrees, or until golden. Remove from spring form and cool on wire rack; cut into squares. Serve at room temperature with ice cream and sauce.

To make sauce: In a 1-quart saucepan, stir together cornstarch and 1/2 cup sugar. Gradually stir in water and raspberry syrup. Simmer over moderate heat, stirring constantly, until thickened and clear. Remove from heat and stir in lemon juice. Serve hot over torte. Serves 9.

Mary A. Johnson
Great Falls

Cinnamon Torte

1 1/2 cups butter
2 eggs
1 1/2 cups sugar
2 3/4 cups flour
Pinch of baking soda
2 tbs. cinnamon
3 pints whipping cream
4 tbs. powdered sugar
1/2 tsp. vanilla
2 tbs. unsweetened baking
  cocoa
1/2 tsp. instant coffee
  granules
1/2 square grated semi-
  sweet chocolate

Beat together butter, eggs, and sugar at low speed until fluffy. Add flour, soda, and cinnamon, and mix well. Form into 10-12 balls. Press balls into bottoms of 2 (8-inch) round cake pans, and bake 8-12 minutes at 350 degrees. Refrigerate until cool.

Whip cream and add powdered sugar and vanilla. Reserve 3/4 cup for icing; into it mix the cocoa, coffee granules, and chocolate.

To assemble: Put plain whipped cream between the crust layers, and ice the top layer. Do not cover sides. Refrigerate overnight before serving. Serves 12-16.

Tamara Kittelson-Aldred
Missoula

Cheesecake

2 cups cottage cheese
1/4 cup melted butter
4 eggs
1 1/2 cups sugar
16 oz. cream cheese
1/4 cup lemon juice
2 tsp. vanilla
1/4 tsp. salt
2 cups sour cream
1/4 cup flour

Crust:
2 cups graham cracker
   crumbs
1/2 cup sugar
6 tbs. melted butter
1/8 tsp. allspice
1/16 tsp. nutmeg

Combine crust ingredients and press onto bottom and sides of 9-inch spring-form pan. Combine cake ingredients in blender. Mix until smooth. Pour into crust and bake 1 1/2 hours at 300 degrees. Turn off oven and let cake sit inside until completely cooled. Serves 12.

Patti Sharpe
Great Falls

269

Amaretto Cheesecake

Crust:
2 cups crushed bran flakes
3 tbs. butter, melted
2 tbs. water
2 tsp. brown sugar
1/2 tsp. cinnamon

Filling:
2 eggs, separated
1/2 cup honey
1 3/4 cups cream cheese, softened
2 1/2 tsp. amaretto or almond flavoring
1 1/2 cups sour cream or yogurt
1/2 cup slivered almonds

Mix crust ingredients together and press into 9-inch spring-form pan or pie plate. Beat egg whites until stiff but not dry. Set aside. In a large bowl, beat egg yolks and cream cheese until smooth. Add honey and amaretto, mix well, and fold in egg whites. Pour into pan. Bake 40-45 minutes at 325 degrees, or until light brown. Remove from oven and cool. Top with sour cream and almonds. Remove from pan. Serves 8.

(Variation: For chocolate amaretto cheesecake, melt 1 oz. unsweetened baking chocolate over low heat. Cool. Add to cheesecake ingredients before baking. Increase honey to 3/4 cup.)

Deb Strohmyer
Libby

Pumpkin Cheesecake

1/3 cup butter
1/3 cup sugar
1 egg
1 1/4 cups flour
16 oz. cream cheese
3/4 cup sugar
16 oz. pureed pumpkin
1 tsp. cinnamon
1/4 tsp. nutmeg
1/4 tsp. ginger
1/4 tsp. ground cloves
Dash of salt
2 eggs

Cream butter and sugar; blend in egg and flour. Press into bottom and 2 inches up into the sides of a 9-inch spring-form pan. Bake 5 minutes at 400 degrees.

Combine cream cheese and sugar. Blend in remaining ingredients and mix well. Pour into spring-form pan and bake 50 minutes at 350 degrees. Loosen cake from rim of pan. Chill thoroughly. Serves 8-10.

Gayle Carpenter
Helena

A good time was had by all

The first dance in the history of Big Elk Creek, a small town to the north of our (Sweet Grass) county, was given at the home of one of our prominent stockgrowers a few nights ago, which proved to be a grand and most enjoyable affair indeed....

The dance lasted until four in the morning. Everybody went home voting it was the dance of the season. The menu: Linn Haven oysters, Haute Sauce, Bisque of lobster, Amontillado Sherry, Diamond back Terrapin, Celery, Pommery Sec, Jersey Capons in Mushroom Sauce, Petis pois, Veuve Clicquot, Red head ducks, Lettuce salad, Chambertin, Plom biere, Assorted cakes, Orange Water Ice, Roman Punch, Strontia water, Fruits, Cafe Noir.

Clipping from The Big Elk Budget, 1885

Limey Cheesecake

1 1/4 cups chocolate wafer crumbs
1/4 cup melted butter
1 envelope unflavored gelatin
1/4 cup cold water
2 egg yolks
3/4 cup lime juice
1/3 cup honey
1 (14-oz.) can sweetened condensed milk
16 oz. cream cheese
2 cups whipped cream
2 drops green food coloring

Combine crumbs and butter and press into bottom of a 9-inch spring-form pan. Bake 10 minutes at 325 degrees. Cool.

Soften gelatin in water. Stir over low heat until dissolved. Beat egg yolks. Add lime juice and honey and blend in gelatin. Cook, stirring constantly, over medium heat for 5 minutes. Cool.

Cream together condensed milk and cream cheese until smooth. Slowly add gelatin mixture; blend thoroughly. Mix in food coloring. Fold in whipped cream and pour over crust. Chill until firm. Serves 8-10.

Deborah L. Cox
Billings

Crunchy Peanut-Butter Cookies

3/4 cup butter
1 1/4 cup crunchy peanut butter
3/4 cup sugar
3/4 cup brown sugar
1 tsp. vanilla
1 egg
1 1/4 cups unbleached flour
1 tsp. baking soda
1 tsp. salt

Cream together butter, peanut butter, and sugars. Add vanilla and egg and mix well. Sift together the flour, baking soda, and salt and gradually add to the creamed mixture, mixing well. Drop by heaping teaspoonfuls onto ungreased cookie sheets. Dip a fork in sugar or flour and press down on each ball of dough twice to create a checkerboard pattern. Bake 8-12 minutes at 350 degrees. Makes about 3 dozen.

Dawn M. Sturman
Bozeman

Monster Cookies

1 lb. butter
4 cups sugar
4 cups brown sugar
12 eggs
3 lbs. crunchy peanut butter
4 tsp. vanilla
1 tbs. light corn syrup
8 tsp. baking soda
18 cups quick-cooking rolled oats
1-2 lbs. M & M candies
4 cups chocolate chips

In very large bowl, cream together butter, sugars, syrup, peanut butter, and vanilla. Beat in eggs. Stir in soda, oats, M & Ms, and chocolate chips. Scoop dough with an ice-cream scoop onto cookie sheets, arranging balls 2-3 inches apart. Bake at 300 degrees until browned. Makes about 3 dozen.

Chef's note: "This recipe won a blue ribbon at the Montana State Fair."

Aimee Hachigian
Ulm

Gobs

1/2 cup shortening
2 cups sugar
2 eggs
1 tsp. vanilla
3/4 cup milk
1/4 cup vinegar
1/2 cup boiling water
4 cups flour
2 tsp. baking soda
1 tsp. baking powder
1/2 tsp. salt
1/2 cup unsweetened baking
  cocoa

Filling:
1 lb. powdered sugar
1/2 lb. butter
1 tsp. vanilla
4-6 tbs. milk

Mix milk and vinegar together and let stand 5 minutes. Mix together dry ingredients except sugar and set aside. Cream sugar and shortening. Add eggs and vanilla and beat well. Carefully add boiling water to creamed mixture, and then alternately add sour milk and dry ingredients. Batter will be thick.

Drop by tablespoonfuls onto greased baking sheets and bake 10-15 minutes at 350 degrees. Cool cookies completely.

To make filling: Soften butter and beat in vanilla. Alternately add powdered sugar and milk until creamy. Fit 2 cookies together with filling spread between. Makes about 4 dozen.

Karen Dodson
Butte

274

Chocolate Haystacks

3 cups sugar
3/4 cup milk
5 tbs. unsweetened baking
    cocoa
3/4 cup butter
1/3 cup light corn syrup
1/2 tsp. salt
2 tsp. vanilla
1 cup flaked coconut
1 1/2 cups chow mein
    noodles
3 cups quick-cooking
    rolled oats

Combine sugar, cocoa, butter, and corn syrup in a large saucepan. Bring to a boil and continue to cook to 200 degrees. Remove from heat and stir in salt and vanilla. Add remaining ingredients. Drop by tablespoonfuls onto waxed paper. Allow to cool and harden. Makes about 50.

Mary-Anne Sward
Kalispell

Chocolate Pecan Drop Cookies

1/2 cup butter
1 cup brown sugar
1 egg, beaten
1 tsp. vanilla
2 oz. unsweetened baking
    chocolate, melted
1 2/3 cups cake flour
1/2 tsp. salt
1/2 tsp. baking soda
1/2 cup milk
1/2 cup chopped pecans
Chocolate frosting
1/4 cup pecan halves

Cream together butter and sugar. Add egg, vanilla, and melted chocolate. Blend well. Sift dry ingredients together. Add alternately with milk to creamed mixture. Add chopped nuts. Drop by teaspoonfuls, 2 inches apart, onto greased cookie sheets. Bake 10-12 minutes at 350 degrees. Frost while warm with chocolate frosting and decorate with pecan halves. Makes 3 dozen.

Agnes Van Oosten
Livingston

275

Rocky Chocolate Chip Cookies

5 cups whole wheat flour
5 cups white flour
2 cups brown sugar
2 cups sugar
1 cup oat bran
1 tbs. baking powder
1 tbs. baking soda
2 tsp. salt
8 egg whites
2 cups skim milk
1 cup cooking oil
1 tbs. vanilla
8 cups quick-cooking rolled
   oats
8 oz. semi-sweet chocolate
   chips

In a large bowl, mix first 8 ingredients together. In a separate bowl, combine next 4 ingredients. Add wet ingredients to dry ingredients and mix thoroughly. Mix in oats and chips with your hands. Mold into balls. Add water if ingredients will not hold together. Place balls on ungreased cookie sheets and bake 20 minutes at 350 degrees, or until lightly browned. Makes 100 cookies.

Mary Musil
Helena

Incredible Banana Cookies

2 1/2 cups flour
1/2 tsp. salt
2 tsp. baking powder
1/4 tsp. baking soda
2/3 cup shortening
1 cup sugar
2 eggs
1/2 tsp. vanilla
1 cup chocolate chips
1 cup mashed banana

Mix first 4 ingredients together. In a separate bowl, cream shortening and sugar; add eggs, vanilla, banana, and chocolate chips. Blend well and add to dry ingredients. Drop by teaspoonfuls onto greased cookie sheets. Bake 8-12 minutes at 375 degrees. Makes about 4 dozen.

Rita Hartman
Billings

276

Oatmeal Plus Cookies

1 cup butter
1 cup vegetable shortening
3 tbs. cooking oil
2 cups brown sugar
3/4 cup sugar
2 large eggs
1/4 cup water
1 tsp. vanilla
2 cups flour
1 tsp. salt
1 tsp. baking soda
1 1/2 tsp. ground cloves
1 cup chopped nuts
5 cups quick-cooking
  rolled oats
1 cup cornflakes
1 cup chopped raisins

Beat butter, shortening, oil and sugars together. Add eggs, water, and vanilla, and cream together. In a separate bowl, mix flour, salt, cloves, and baking soda. Add to creamed mixture. Stir in oats, nuts, and raisins. Fold in cornflakes and drop by teaspoonfuls onto greased cookie sheets. Bake 12 minutes at 350 degrees. Makes about 5 dozen.

Phyllis Skelton Marshik
Helena

Licorice Snaps

2 1/2 cups flour
1 cup sugar
1 cup brown sugar
1 tsp. baking soda
1/2 tsp. salt
1/2 tsp. ground cloves
1/2 tsp. cinnamon
1 cup butter, softened
1 egg
1 tbs. anise flavoring
1/2 cup chopped pecans

Combine all ingredients together in a large bowl. Blend well. Divide dough in half and shape into 2 (10-inch) rolls. Wrap in waxed paper and chill 4 hours. Cut into 1/4-inch slices. Arrange on ungreased cookie sheets. Bake 10-12 minutes at 375 degrees. Makes about 6 dozen.

Mrs. John M. Kralich
Big Sandy

Legendary Lodge Pumpkin Cookies

1 cup cooking oil
1 cup sugar
1 cup canned pumpkin
1 egg
2 cups flour
1 tsp. baking soda
1 tsp. cinnamon
1/4 tsp. allspice
1/4 tsp. nutmeg
1/2 tsp. salt
1 cup raisins
1/2 cup chopped walnuts
  (optional)

Frosting:
3 tbs. butter
4 tsp. milk
1/2 cup brown sugar
1 cup powdered sugar
3/4 tsp. vanilla

Cream oil, sugar, pumpkin, and egg together. Add dry ingredients and mix well. Stir in raisins and nuts. Drop onto greased cookie sheet, and bake 10-12 minutes at 350 degrees.

To make frosting: Heat butter, milk, and brown sugar until sugar has dissolved. Cool. Add powdered sugar and vanilla. Frost cookies when cool. Makes about 4 dozen.

Margaret Brown
Helena

Lemonade Cookies

1 cup butter
1 cup sugar
2 eggs
3 cups sifted flour
1 tsp. baking soda
1 (6-oz.) can frozen
  lemonade concentrate,
  thawed

Cream butter and sugar together. Add eggs and beat until light and fluffy. Add flour and soda to creamed mixture alternately with 1/2 cup lemonade concentrate. Mix well. Drop by teaspoonfuls onto greased cookie sheets. Bake 8-10 minutes at 400 degrees. Do not overbake. Brush hot cookies lightly with remaining lemonade concentrate, and sprinkle with sugar. Makes about 5 dozen.

Connie Blasdel
Kalispell

Fork Cookies

1/2 cup shortening
1/2 cup butter
1 1/2 cups sugar
1 tsp. vanilla
2 eggs
1 cup ground raisins
4 cups flour
1 tsp. baking powder
2 tbs. orange juice
1/2 cup chopped nuts
Grated peel of 1 orange

Mix all ingredients together in large bowl. Drop by teaspoonfuls onto a greased cookie sheet; then press with a fork. Bake 10-12 minutes at 325 degrees. Makes about 6 dozen.

Gladine Nehus
Great Falls

Bohemian Yeast Cookies

1 package dry yeast
1/4 cup warm water
3 cups sifted flour
3/4 tsp. salt
1 cup butter
2 egg yolks
2/3 cup sour cream
1 tsp. vanilla
Powdered sugar

Filling:
2 cups seedless raisins or
   dates
1/2 cup water
1/4 cup sugar
2 tbs. lemon juice
1/2 cup chopped walnuts

Sprinkle yeast over warm water. Sift flour and salt together; cut in butter until mixture resembles meal. Combine egg yolks, cream, and vanilla. Add yeast. Add to the flour mixture and blend until all flour is moistened. Shape dough into a ball, wrap in plastic wrap or waxed paper, and refrigerate several hours or overnight.

To make filling: Cook all filling ingredients except nuts together in saucepan until thick. Remove from heat and add nuts.

Sprinkle surface of dough with powdered sugar. Divide into 4 portions. Roll out each portion into a rectangle about 1/4-inch thick. Cut into 2 x 4-inch strips. Spread filling in thin layer on each strip. Roll each like a jelly roll. Arrange on greased cookie sheets and bake 10 minutes at 350 degrees.

Bonita M. Anderson
Sidney

Austrian Nut Butter Cookies

1 cup sifted flour
1/2 cup sugar
2/3 cup ground hazelnuts,
  walnuts, or pecans
1/2 cup butter, softened

Filling:
2 tbs. butter
1/3 cup sifted powdered
  sugar
1 square unsweetened
  baking chocolate, melted

Frosting:
1 tbs. butter
1/8 cup sifted powdered
  sugar
1 egg yolk
1 square unsweetened
  baking chocolate, melted

Sift flour and sugar together into a large bowl. Add nuts. Blend in butter to form dough. Chill 1-2 hours. Roll out on floured pastry cloth or board to 1/8-inch thickness. Cut into rounds with 2-inch cookie cutter. Place on ungreased cookie sheets. Bake 7-10 minutes at 375 degrees, until light golden brown.

To make filling: Cream butter and powdered sugar together. Blend in melted chocolate. Sandwich 2 cookies together with filling spread between.

To make frosting: Cream butter and powdered sugar together. Add melted chocolate and egg yolk; blend well. To serve cookies in Austrian manner, spread top of each "sandwich" thinly with jam and then with frosting. Sprinkle with slivered almonds before frosting sets. Makes 12-18.

Ida Seidler Bishop
Great Falls

281

Austrian "Peaches"

3/4 cup butter, softened
1/2 cup milk
1 cup sugar
2 eggs
1 tsp. baking powder
1 tsp. vanilla
3 3/4 cups unsifted flour
2/3 cup apricot jam
1/4 cup chocolate chips,
   melted and cooled
1/3 cup finely chopped
   filberts, walnuts, or pecans
2 tsp. rum or sherry
1/3 cup orange sugar
   (see instructions)
2/3 cup yellow-gold sugar
   (see instructions)
Slices of green gumdrops
Pieces of cinnamon sticks

Mix together butter, milk, sugar, eggs, baking powder, vanilla, and 2 cups flour. Beat well. Stir in remaining flour. Roll into 3/4-inch balls. Place 1 inch apart on ungreased baking sheet. Bake 15-20 minutes at 325 degrees, until bottoms are browned. Cool on wire racks.

Place tip of a small knife in center of flat side of cookie. Carefully turn knife and rotate cookie to hollow out. Reserve crumbs. Mix 1 1/2 cups crumbs, jam, chocolate, nuts, and rum. Fill hollowed cookies with this mixture. Place 2 cookies, flat sides together. Press one end more closed than other so that "pit" shows. Brush each "peach" lightly with water. Dip part of one side of cookie in orange sugar for blush. Roll entire cookie in yellow-gold sugar. Set aside to dry, first inserting a piece of cinnamon stick for a "stem." Slices of green gumdrops may be used for "leaves." Makes about 3 dozen.

Orange sugar: Measure 1/3 cup sugar into shallow ovenproof dish. Add a few drops of yellow food coloring and 1 drop red food coloring. Rub color evenly into sugar with back of spoon. Heat in oven at 400 degrees, stirring occasionally, until dry.

Yellow-gold sugar: Make as for orange sugar, using 2/3 cup sugar and yellow food coloring. When dry, stir in a tiny amount of orange sugar.

Katherine Jean Neimi
Great Falls

Pecan Tassies

6 oz. cream cheese, softened
1 cup butter, softened
2 cups flour
About 24 maraschino
   cherries (optional)

Filling:
2 eggs, slightly beaten
1 1/2 cups brown sugar
1 1/2 cups chopped pecans
2 tbs. melted butter
1 tsp. vanilla
1/2 cup raisins (optional)

In large bowl, cream the cheese, butter, and flour. Wrap dough and refrigerate for 30 minutes. Pinch off small pieces of dough, roll into balls, and press into small (1 3/4-inch) tart pans.

In medium bowl, combine filling ingredients. Add raisins if desired. Spoon 1 1/4 tsp. filling into each pan. Top with cherry if desired. Bake 25 minutes at 350 degrees. Makes about 2 dozen.

Renny Torgerson
Dagmar

Polish Chrusciki (Elephant Ears)

1 cup whipping cream
6 egg yolks, beaten well
4 cups flour
1/2 tsp. salt
3 tbs. sugar
2 tbs. rum

Mix all ingredients and knead on floured board until smooth. Roll out paper-thin. With a pastry wheel, cut strips 3/4 inch wide and 3 inches long. Cut gash in center and twist ends through. Fry in 375-degree oil until light brown. Drain on absorbent paper and sprinkle with powdered sugar when cool.

Virginia Lesniak
Billings

283

Montana Backpacker Bars

1 cup butter
1 1/2 cups brown sugar
1 cup quick-cooking oats
1 cup whole wheat flour
1 cup white flour
1/2 cup wheat germ
4 tsp. grated orange peel
4 eggs, lightly beaten
2 cups whole almonds
1 cup chocolate chips
1/2 cup chopped dates
   or figs
1/2 cup chopped dried
   apricots
1/2 cup shredded coconut

Cream butter with 1 cup brown sugar. Stir in oats, flours, wheat germ, and orange peel. Press mixture into bottom of an ungreased 9 x 13-inch baking pan. Combine eggs, almonds, chocolate chips, dates, apricots, coconut, and remaining 1/2 cup brown sugar in another large bowl, and mix gently but thoroughly. Pour over butter mixture, spreading evenly. Bake 30-35 minutes at 350 degrees. Cool before cutting into bars. Makes about 2 dozen bars.

Rosie Endean
Bozeman

Rocky Road Brownies

12 oz. chocolate chips
1 cup butter
3 cups flour
2 cups sugar
1 tsp. baking powder
1 tsp. vanilla
1/2 tsp. salt
4 eggs
4 cups miniature
   marshmallows
2 cups chopped nuts

Melt butter and 1 cup chocolate chips together over low heat. Cool. Mix flour, sugar, baking powder, vanilla, salt, eggs, and chocolate mixture. Spread in an ungreased jelly-roll pan. Bake 15 minutes at 375 degrees. Sprinkle remaining chips and nuts over top of brownies. Top with marshmallows. Bake another 15-20 minutes. Cut when cooled. Makes 3-4 dozen.

Vicki Uehling
Big Timber

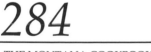

284

Chip 'n Coffee Bars

2 eggs
2 cups brown sugar
1 cup cooking oil
2 tsp. vanilla
1 1/2 tsp. instant coffee
  granules
1 cup hot water
2 cups unsifted flour
1 cup whole wheat flour
1 tsp. salt
1 tsp. baking soda
12 oz. chocolate chips
1 cup chopped nuts

Glaze:
1 cup powdered sugar
1 tbs. butter
1/2 tsp. instant coffee
  granules
1 1/2 tbs. hot water

Beat eggs until light and fluffy. Add brown sugar, oil, vanilla, and coffee granules dissolved in hot water. Blend well. In a separate bowl, combine flours, salt, and soda, and beat into egg mixture. Spread batter into a greased 10 x 15-inch rimmed cookie sheet. Sprinkle chocolate chips and nuts over top. Bake 30 minutes at 350 degrees.

To make glaze: Dissolve coffee granules in hot water. Blend in remaining ingredients and drizzle over bars. Makes 4 dozen.

Carol Ann Johnson
Missoula

Thick 'n Chewy Chocolate Bars

1 cup butter
1/2 cup brown sugar
1/2 cup sugar
2 eggs
1 tsp. vanilla
1 1/4 cups flour
1 tsp. baking soda
1 1/2 cups quick-cooking
  rolled oats
12 oz. chocolate chips
1 cup chopped nuts

Cream together butter and sugars. Blend in eggs and vanilla. Mix together flour and baking soda, and add to creamed mixture. Stir in oats, chocolate chips, and nuts. Spread in well-greased 9 x 13-inch baking pan. Bake 25-30 minutes at 375 degrees. Cool before cutting into bars. Makes 2 dozen.

Sue Kaul
Belgrade

Orange Slice Bars

1 cup orange-slice candy,
  cut fine
1/2 cup finely chopped
  walnuts
2 cups flour
1 tsp. baking powder
Pinch of salt
4 eggs, beaten
2 cups brown sugar
1 tsp. vanilla

Icing:
1 1/2 cups powdered sugar
2 tbs. orange juice
2 tbs. melted butter

Mix together orange slices, walnuts, flour, baking powder, and salt. In a separate bowl, mix together beaten eggs, brown sugar, and vanilla. Add to candy-nut mixture. When blended well, spread into a large baking sheet and bake 15-20 minutes at 350 degrees. Cool.

Mix icing ingredients together and spread on cooled bars. Makes 2-3 dozen.

Jeanie Greenfield
Helena

286

Lemon Squares

1 cup butter
1/2 cup plus 2 cups sugar
2 cups plus 4 tbs. flour
4 eggs, beaten
4 tbs. fresh lemon juice
Grated peel of 2 lemons
Powdered sugar

Blend butter, 1/2 cup sugar, and 2 cups flour together. Press into bottom of a 9 x 13-inch pan. Bake 20 minutes at 350 degrees.

Combine eggs, lemon juice, lemon peel, 2 cups sugar, and 4 tbs. flour. Pour over hot crust. Return to oven and bake 25 minutes at 350 degrees. Remove, cool slightly, and loosen edges from pan. Sift powdered sugar over bars. Makes about 2 dozen.

Judy Cummings
Highwood

Paul's Pumpkin Bars

4 eggs
1 2/3 cups sugar
1 cup cooking oil
1 (16-oz.) can pumpkin
2 cups flour
2 tsp. baking powder
2 tsp. cinnamon
1 tsp. salt
1 tsp. baking soda

Icing:
3 oz. cream cheese, softened
1/2 cup butter, softened
1 tsp. vanilla
2 cups sifted powdered sugar

Beat together eggs, sugar, oil, and pumpkin until light and fluffy. Stir together flour, baking powder, cinnamon, salt, and baking soda. Add to pumpkin mixture and mix thoroughly. Spread batter in ungreased 10 x 15-inch baking pan. Bake 30 minutes at 350 degrees. Cool.

To make icing: Cream together cream cheese, butter, and vanilla. Add powdered sugar gradually, beating until smooth. Frost cooled bars and cut. Makes 3 dozen.

Mrs. Lloyd Paynter
Butte

Farmer's Market Zucchini Bars

1 cup cooking oil
2 cups sugar
2 cups grated, unpeeled
    zucchini
4 eggs
2 cups flour
2 tsp. baking powder
1 tsp. baking soda
1/4 tsp. salt
2 tsp. cinnamon
1 tsp. pumpkin pie spice

Frosting:
3 oz. cream cheese
1 tsp. vanilla
1/2 cup butter
1 tsp. milk
1 3/4 cups powdered sugar

Sift together flour, baking powder, baking soda, salt, and spices. Add other ingredients in order given. Blend well. Pour batter into a 10 x 15-inch pan, and bake 30 minutes at 350 degrees.

Beat all frosting ingredients together and frost cooled bars. Makes 2-3 dozen.

June Halgren
Great Falls

Paper-Bag Apple Pie

1 unbaked 9-inch pie shell
3-4 large baking apples
1/2 cup sugar
2 tbs. flour
1/2 tsp. cinnamon or nutmeg
2 tbs. lemon juice

Topping:
1/2 cup sugar
1/2 cup flour
1/2 cup butter

Peel, core, and cut up apples. In a large bowl, combine sugar, flour, and spices. Add apple and toss to coat well. Spoon into unbaked pie shell and drizzle with lemon juice.

To make topping: Combine sugar and flour in small bowl. Cut in butter. Sprinkle over top of apples. Slide pie into a large brown paper bag. Fold open end over twice. Bake 1 hour at 425 degrees. Split bag open to cool. Serves 6-8.

Selma C. Conner
Harlem

Sugarless Apple Pie

6 red or Granny Smith apples
1 (6-oz.) can frozen apple
   juice concentrate, thawed
1 1/2 - 2 tsp. cornstarch
1 tsp. cinnamon or nutmeg
Pastry for 9-inch,
   double-crust pie

Peel and slice apples. Simmer 5 minutes in apple juice concentrate. Add cinnamon and cornstarch that has been mixed with a little water. Cook until thick. If apples are very juicy, you may need to add a little more cornstarch mixed with water. Pour apples into pie shell. Put on top crust. Bake about 20 minutes at 450 degrees, reduce heat to 350 degrees, and bake another 20-30 minutes, until pie is brown and crust is done. Serves 6-8.

Joy Fulton
Great Falls

289

Fresh Peach Pie

1 unbaked pie shell
5-6 peaches, peeled and
　halved
2 eggs, separated
1 tbs. flour
1 cup sugar
4 tbs. butter, softened

Place peach halves cut-side-up in pie shell. Mix together egg yolks, flour, sugar, and butter. Beat egg whites until stiff, and fold into yolk mixture. Pour over peaches. Bake 15 minutes at 450 degrees, reduce heat to 325 degrees, and bake another 45 minutes. Serve topped with whipped cream. Serves 6-8.

Bonnie Fastje
Wilsall

Huckleberry Pie

4 cups huckleberries
1 1/4 - 1 1/2 cups sugar
　(to taste)
1/3 cup flour
Dash of salt
1 tbs. lemon juice (optional)
1 tbs. butter
Pastry for 9-inch double-crust
　pie

Mix together sugar, flour, and salt. Toss huckleberries in flour mixture. Add lemon juice if desired. Set aside while preparing pastry. Spoon huckleberries into pie crust, dot with butter, sprinkle with lemon juice if desired, and cover with top crust. Slit top to let steam escape. Bake 40-50 minutes at 425 degrees. Serves 6-8.

Dolores Williams
Ulm

290

Huckleberry Cream Pie

1 (9-inch) graham-cracker
crust OR 1 baked 9-inch
pie shell
8 oz. whipping cream,
whipped
1 (14-oz.) can sweetened
condensed milk, chilled
Juice of 1 lemon
1 cup huckleberries
(with juice)

Mix together condensed milk and lemon juice.
Chill until slightly thick. Fold in whipped
cream and mix well. Add berries with juice.
Pour into pie crust. Chill 4 hours. Serves 6-8.

Roni Frank
Trout Creek

Grandma Moses' Strawberry Pie

4 cups strawberries,
stems removed
3/4 cup water
1 cup sugar
3 tbs. cornstarch
1 tsp. lemon juice
1 tbs. butter
Prepared pie crust

Put all but 1 cup strawberries into prepared pie
crust. In a saucepan, combine the 1 cup berries
and water and boil 3-4 minutes. Mix the sugar
and cornstarch together and add to the berry
syrup. Cook slowly, until thick and clear. Add
lemon juice and butter to syrup, cool, and pour
over berries. Served with whipped cream.
Serves 8.

Betty Stav
Deer Lodge

Orange Pie

1 cup orange juice
2 tbs. melted butter
3 eggs, separated
1/2 tsp. lemon flavoring
3/4 cup sugar
3 tbs. flour
1/2 tsp. vanilla
1 (9-inch) graham-cracker
  pie crust
Graham cracker crumbs

Mix juice, butter, sugar, flour, and egg yolks together, and cook until thick. Beat egg whites until stiff. Add flavorings to butter-yolk mixture; then fold in egg whites. Pour into crust and sprinkle with graham cracker crumbs. Store in refrigerator. Serves 6-8.

Ruby Bruce
Parker

Fresh Raspberry Rhubarb Pie

Pastry for 9-inch, double-
  crust pie
1 2/3 cups sugar
1/3 cup tapioca
2 cups chopped rhubarb
2 cups raspberries
2 tbs. butter

Mix sugar and tapioca. Mix together raspberries and rhubarb, and turn half of fruit into pastry-lined pie plate. Sprinkle with half the sugar mixture. Repeat with remaining fruit and sugar mixture; dot with butter. Cover with top crust, cut slits to allow steam to escape, seal, and flute edge. Sprinkle with sugar if desired.

Cover edge of crust with 2- to 3-inch strip of aluminum foil to prevent excessive browning. Remove foil during last 15 minutes of baking. Bake 40-50 minutes at 425 degrees, until crust is brown and juice begins to bubble through slits in crust. Serves 6-8.

Pamela K. Rausch
Missoula

Sour Cream Rhubarb Pie

1 cup sour cream
2 tbs. flour
1 tsp. vanilla
3/4 cup sugar
1/4 tsp. salt
1 egg
2 cups diced rhubarb
1/2 tsp. cinnamon
Pastry for 9-inch,
   single-crust pie

Topping:
1/4 cup butter
1/3 cup flour
1/2 cup brown sugar

Mix pie ingredients together and bake in an unbaked pie shell for 25 minutes at 400 degrees. Mix topping ingredients together and pour over pie. Bake another 20 minutes at 400 degrees. Serves 6-8.

Maryleen Sanford
Reedpoint

Sour Cream Lemon Pie

1 cup sugar
3 1/2 tbs. cornstarch
1 tbs. grated lemon peel
3 egg yolks, slightly beaten
1/4 cup lemon juice
1 cup milk
1/4 cup butter
1 cup sour cream
1 baked 9-inch pie shell
1 cup whipping cream,
   whipped

Combine sugar, cornstarch, lemon peel, juice, egg yolks, and milk in heavy saucepan. Cook over medium heat until thick. Stir in butter and cool mixture to room temperature. Stir in sour cream. Pour filling into pie shell. Cover with whipped cream and garnish with lemon slices. Store in refrigerator. Serves 6-8.

Pat Burlison
Red Lodge

Famous Cajun Pie

2 eggs
1/2 cup flour
1/2 cup sugar
1/2 cup brown sugar
1/2 cup butter, melted and
  cooled
6 oz. semi-sweet chocolate
  chips
1 cup chopped walnuts
1 unbaked 9-inch pie shell
Whipped cream or ice cream

In a large bowl, beat eggs until foamy. Add flour and sugars and beat until well-blended. Blend in melted butter. Stir in chocolate chips and nuts. Pour into pie shell. Bake 1 hour at 325 degrees. Serve warm topped with whipped cream or ice cream. Serves 8.

Debra Cruce
Missoula

Pineapple Chiffon Pie

1 1/2 tbs. unflavored gelatin
1/2 cup cold water
1 cup crushed pineapple
  (with juice)
3/4 cup sugar
1 tbs. lemon juice
1/2 tsp. salt
3 eggs, separated
1/2 cup whipping cream
Whipped cream (optional)
Maraschino cherries
  (optional)
1 (9-inch) baked pie shell

Soak gelatin in cold water. Heat pineapple and juice. Add sugar, lemon juice, and salt; then add gelatin. Beat egg yolks slightly, and pour in pineapple mixture. Let cool until syrupy.

In a separate bowl, beat egg whites until stiff; then beat in whipping cream. Fold a little at a time into syrupy mixture. Pour into pie shell. Allow to set. May be topped with whipped cream and garnished with maraschino cherries. Serves 6-8.

Gloria Broksle
Twin Bridges

Margarita Mud Pie

1 3/4 cups crushed
    chocolate wafers
1/2 cup unsalted butter,
    softened
1/4 cup thawed frozen
    lemonade concentrate
3 tbs. tequila
4 tsp. fresh lime juice
1 tbs. triple sec
2 tsp. grated lime peel
3 drops green food coloring
    (optional)
5 cups vanilla ice cream,
    softened
Sweetened whipped cream
1 lime, sliced thin

Blend cookie crumbs and butter in small bowl. Press into bottom and up sides of a 9-inch pie plate. Bake 12 minutes at 350 degrees. Cool completely.

In a large bowl, mix together lemonade, tequila, lime juice, triple sec, lime peel, and food coloring. Add ice cream and mix well. Do not let ice cream melt. Spoon mixture into prepared crust. Cover with plastic and freeze overnight. Garnish with whipped cream and lime slices. Serves 6-8.

Patti Billet
Missoula

A Mexican cure for headache

Proper diet and exercise, cheerfulness of mind, and agreeable social intercourse will do more towards regulating the stomach and bowels in those predisposed to this dreadful pain than any plan of medical treatment which can be suggested. However, vinegar bandages, applied to the temples and forehead, give great relief.

Fisher's Improved House-Keeper's Almanac
1860

White Russian Pie

1 envelope unflavored
    gelatin
3 large eggs, separated
1/4 cup kahlua
1/2 cup whipping cream,
    whipped
1/4 cup cold water
7 tbs. sugar
3 tbs. vodka
1 graham cracker crust

Topping:
3 tbs. kahlua
1 cup whipping cream,
    whipped

Sprinkle gelatin over cold water and allow to stand for 5 minutes. Then dissolve gelatin by heating in top of double boiler. Beat egg yolks with 4 tbs. sugar at high speed until thick. Beat dissolved gelatin slowly into yolk mixture. Stir in kahlua and vodka. Cook, stirring occasionally, until mixture begins to thicken slightly.

In another bowl, beat egg whites to form soft peaks. Add 3 tbs. sugar, one at a time, to make meringue. Fold into gelatin mixture. Add whipped cream. Chill mixture a few minutes, until it mounds easily on spoon. Turn into prepared crust and chill. Make topping by mixing kahlua into whipped cream. Spread over pie before serving. Store in refrigerator. Serves 6-8.

Gayle Raunig-Corrigeux
Great Falls

Sky-High Coconut Cream Pie

Filling:
4 egg yolks
2 cups milk
1/4 cup grated coconut
1 tbs. butter
1/2 cup sugar
2 heaping tsp. cornstarch
Pinch of salt
1 tsp. vanilla
   (or more to taste)

Crust:
1 cup shortening
1/4 tsp. salt
5 tbs. water
3 cups flour
1 tbs. vinegar
1 egg

Meringue:
4-6 egg whites
1 tbs. sugar per egg white
Grated coconut

To make filling: Combine milk, sugar, salt, and coconut in saucepan. Bring almost to a boil. Mix cornstarch and egg yolks together with a little water and add to milk mixture. Cook over low heat, stirring constantly, until thick. Add butter and vanilla. Cool.

To make crust: Blend flour, shortening, and salt. Beat egg and add water and vinegar. Add liquid mixture to dry ingredients. Mix well by hand. Roll out and shape into a pie plate. Bake 12 minutes at 425 degrees.

To make meringue: Beat egg whites until stiff. Gradually add 1 tbs. sugar for each egg white used. Beat well. Pour cooled filling into baked pie shell. Spread top with meringue, making sure to spread to edges of pastry. Sprinkle with coconut. Bake briefly at 400 degrees, until meringue has browned. Serves 6-8.

Robin Arbuckle Jones
Great Falls

297

Paradise Pumpkin Pie

8 oz. cream cheese
1/4 cup plus 1/2 cup sugar
1/2 tsp. vanilla
4 eggs, beaten
1 1/4 cups pureed pumpkin
1 tsp. cinnamon
1 1/2 cups evaporated milk
1/4 tsp. ginger
1/4 tsp. nutmeg
Dash of salt
1 unbaked pie shell

Cream together cream cheese, 1/4 cup sugar, and vanilla. Add 2 eggs, mix well, and set aside. Combine pumpkin, 1/2 cup sugar, milk, spices, and 2 eggs, and blend well. Spoon cream cheese mixture into unbaked pie shell. Carefully ladle pumpkin mixture over cheese. Bake 65-70 minutes at 350 degrees. Pumpkin mixture will sink to bottom, and cream cheese will rise to top. Serves 6-8.

Rosie Endean
Bozeman

Green Tomato Pie

3 cups sliced green tomato
1 1/3 cup sugar
3 tbs. flour
1/4 tsp. salt
4 tsp. grated lemon peel
6 tbs. lemon juice
3 tbs. butter
3/4 tsp. cinnamon
Pastry for 9-inch double-crust
  pie

Combine first 8 ingredients in a bowl and pour into a pastry-lined pie plate. Cover with top crust. Pierce crust with fork to allow steam to escape. Bake 10 minutes at 450 degrees, reduce heat to 350 degrees, and bake another 30 minutes. Serves 6-8.

Gloria Guessen
Missoula

298

Washington Nut Pie

3 eggs, beaten
3 tbs. butter, melted
1 cup light corn syrup
1/2 cup sugar
Vanilla to taste
Pinch of salt
1/2 - 1 cup chopped walnuts
Pastry for 9-inch,
　　single-crust pie

Combine all ingredients and pour into a pastry-lined pie plate. Bake 40-50 minutes at 375 degrees, or until a knife inserted in the center comes out clean.

Chef's note: "This pie is not quite as sweet as pecan pie and is more economical to make."

Emily Peck
Billings

Macadamia-Nut Cream Pie

1/2 cup sugar
1/4 cup cornstarch
Pinch of salt
3 egg yolks
2 cups milk
1 tbs. butter
1 1/2 cups whipping cream
2 tbs. kahlua
1/2 cup chopped
　　macadamia nuts
1 baked 9-inch pie shell

Combine sugar, cornstarch, salt, and egg yolks in a small bowl and beat well. Heat milk until not quite boiling and stir in sugar mixture. Cook, stirring, until thickened, about 3 minutes. Remove from heat and stir in butter. Cover surface with waxed paper and refrigerate until completely chilled.

Beat whipping cream and fold 1/2 cup into the chilled mixture along with kahlua and nuts. Pour into pie shell. To serve, top with remaining whipped cream and garnish with macadamia nuts. Serves 8-10.

Rebecca Smith
Missoula

Almond Fruit Tart

Shell:
1/2 cup butter, softened
1/2 cup sugar
1 egg yolk
1 tsp. vanilla
1/2 tsp. almond extract
1 1/2 cups flour
1/2 cup slivered almonds,
  toasted

Filling:
8 oz. cream cheese, softened
2 tbs. sugar
2 tbs. amaretto liqueur
1 tsp. vanilla

Topping:
Sliced fruit
1/4 cup apricot jam
1 tbs. water
Slivered almonds

To make shell: Cream together butter and sugar. Beat in egg yolk, vanilla, and extract. Mix in flour and almonds and gather dough into a ball. Press dough into an 11-inch tart pan, bringing dough evenly up sides of the pan. Prick shell with fork and bake about 10 minutes at 375 degrees, or until golden brown. Cool and set aside.

To make filling: Beat cream cheese and sugar together until creamy. Add liqueur and vanilla and beat well. Spread into cooled tart shell and chill until firm.

To top: Whisk jam and water together over medium heat until jam has melted; boil 30 seconds. Arrange sliced fruit over filling (use kiwis, strawberries, blueberries, peaches, or whatever is on hand). Drizzle with glaze and garnish with slivered almonds. Serves 8-12.

Rebecca Smith
Missoula

Frozen Banana-Split Dessert

2 cups graham cracker
  crumbs
1/4 cup butter, melted
3 bananas, sliced
1/2 gallon vanilla ice cream
6 oz. chocolate chips
1/2 cup butter
1 cup evaporated milk
2 cups powdered sugar
1 cup whipping cream,
  whipped
1/2 cup chopped nuts

Blend together graham cracker crumbs and melted butter. Press into a 9 x 13-inch pan. Cover with banana slices and then ice cream. Freeze. In a saucepan, mix together chocolate chips, 1/2 cup butter, milk, and powdered sugar. Heat until chips and butter have melted and then cook 15 minutes. Cool, pour over ice cream, and freeze. Spread dessert with whipped cream and sprinkle with nuts. Freeze. Serves 9-12.

Susan Jenson
Sidney

Overnight Cherry Dessert

1/2 lb. vanilla wafer crumbs
1/2 cup butter
1 cup powdered sugar
2 eggs, separated
1 cup whipping cream,
  whipped
1/2 cup chopped walnuts
1 (6-oz.) jar maraschino
  cherries, cut fine (with
  juice)

Butter an 8 x 8-inch pan and spread with 1/3 vanilla wafer crumbs. Cream together butter and powdered sugar. Add egg yolks. Beat egg whites until fluffy and add to creamed mixture. Spread over crumbs. Top with another 1/3 crumbs. Combine whipped cream, nuts, and cherries, and spread over second layer of crumbs. Top with remaining crumbs and refrigerate overnight. Serves 9.

Inez O. Kienitz
Plentywood

301

Raspberry Dessert

2 (10-oz.) packages frozen
  raspberries (with syrup)
1 cup water
1/2 cup sugar
2 tsp. lemon juice
4 tbs. cornstarch
1/4 cup cold water
50 large marshmallows
1 cup milk
2 cups whipping cream,
  whipped
1 1/4 cups graham cracker
  crumbs
1/4 cup chopped nuts
1/4 cup butter, melted

Heat raspberries with 1 cup water, sugar, and lemon juice. Dissolve cornstarch into 1/4 cup cold water and stir into raspberries. Cook until thickened and clear. Cool.

Melt marshmallows in milk in top of double boiler; cool thoroughly. Fold in whipped cream. Mix graham cracker crumbs, nuts, and butter. Press into bottom of a 9 x 13-inch pan. Spread crust with marshmallow-cream mixture. Top with raspberry mixture. Refrigerate until firm. Serves 15-18.

Gloria Broksle
Twin Bridges

An old Indian recipe

If hair begins to thin, kill a groundhog in the month of August, take the fat from the entrails and render out. Massage this into the scalp morning and night.

Elsie J. Cummings and Wavie J. Charlton
Survival: Pioneer, Indian, and Wilderness Lore

Frosty Fudge Mousse

Crust:
1 cup vanilla wafer crumbs
3 tbs. butter, melted
1/2 cup chopped almonds or
   walnuts

Filling:
1 cup chocolate milk
1/2 cup semi-sweet
   chocolate chips
1/8 tsp. salt
5 cups miniature
   marshmallows
1 tsp. vanilla
1 cup whipping cream,
   whipped

To make crust: Mix together crumbs and butter. Press into bottom of a 9 x 9-inch baking pan. Sprinkle with nuts. Bake 10 minutes at 300 degrees. Cool.

To make filling: Heat chocolate milk, chips, and salt over low heat, stirring constantly until chips melt. Add marshmallows and continue heating until melted. Stir often. Remove from heat and add vanilla. Fold in whipped cream. Pour filling over crust. Freeze until firm. Remove from freezer 10 minutes before cutting. Serves 9.

LaVonne Brown
Cut Bank

Hasty Pudding

2 cups brown sugar
4 cups water
4 tbs. butter
1 cup raisins
1 cup sugar
2 cups flour
4 tsp. baking powder
1/2 tsp. salt
1 cup milk

Combine brown sugar, water, 2 tbs. butter, and raisins in a 9 x 13-inch baking pan. Bring mixture to a boil and cook 10 minutes. Cream sugar and remaining 2 tbs. butter. Mix together sugar, flour, baking powder, and salt. Add dry ingredients to creamed mixture alternately with milk. Drop batter by spoonfuls into the boiling raisin mixture and bake 20 minutes at 375 degrees. Serves 12.

Doris S. Peterson
Helena

303

Old-Fashioned Bread Pudding

4 cups cubed stale bread
4 eggs
3 cups milk
3/4 cup sugar
Pinch of salt
1/4 tsp. cinnamon
1/8 tsp. nutmeg
1 tsp. vanilla

Butter a 2-quart casserole and put bread cubes into it. Blend remaining ingredients together, and pour over bread, pressing down any cubes that float. Cover and bake about 1 hour at 350 degrees, or until knife inserted in center comes out clean. Serves 8.

(Variations: Add 1/2 cup raisins, 1 cup chopped apple, and/or 1/4 cup chopped nuts.)

Doris Ekstrom
Ekstrom Stage Station
Rock Creek

Huckleberry Crunch

3/4 cup sugar
1 cup water
2 tbs. cornstarch
4 cups huckleberries
1 tsp. vanilla
1 cup flour
1/2 cup brown sugar
3/4 cup quick-cooking rolled oats
1 tsp. cinnamon
1/2 cup butter

In a saucepan, mix together sugar, water, and cornstarch. Bring to a boil. Remove from heat and add huckleberries and vanilla. Set aside.

Mix together flour, brown sugar, oats, and cinnamon. Cut in butter until crumbly. Spread half the flour mixture in the bottom of a 9 x 13-inch baking pan. Top with huckleberry mixture. Sprinkle with remaining flour mixture. Bake 45 minutes at 375 degrees for metal pan, or at 350 degrees for glass pan. Serve warm or cooled. Garnish with whipped cream if desired. Serves 12-15.

Jean Waldherr
Kalispell

Palacinkes (Croation Crepes)

Crepes:
1 cup flour
2 tbs. sugar
Pinch of salt
3 eggs
1 cup milk
2 tbs. cooking oil

Filling:
16 oz. small-curd cottage
   cheese, drained
16 oz. ricotta cheese
2-3 egg yolks
1 tsp. lemon juice
1/3 cup sugar

Whole milk or half and half

To make crepes: Mix all crepe ingredients together and pour a small amount at a time into a small, hot, oiled skillet. Tilt pan so that batter covers bottom in a thin layer. Let cook briefly until browned; then turn like a pancake to brown other side. Remove from pan. Continue until all batter is cooked.

Mix filling ingredients together and spoon some into middle of each crepe. Roll up crepes and arrange in baking dish. Pour milk or half and half over crepes just so that it covers bottom of pan. Bake 20-25 minutes at 350 degrees. Cover with a fruit glaze and whipped cream, if desired. Makes about 10 crepes.

Sue Heffron
Helena

305

Baklava

1 lb. phyllo dough
1 lb. walnuts, ground
1 lb. clarified butter

Syrup:
1 cup water
2 cups honey
1 cup sugar
1/4 cup lemon juice
   (or to taste)

Boil syrup ingredients together and cool. Brush butter on bottom of 9 x 13-inch baking pan. Cover bottom with 1 sheet of phyllo dough. Brush with butter and add another phyllo sheet. Continue in this way until half the phyllo dough is stacked. Arrange ground walnuts over last sheet. Resume stacking sheets, buttering after each, until all phyllo dough is used. Cut through all layers to make diamond shapes, and bake at 350 degrees until lightly browned. Cool thoroughly.

Pour cold syrup over cold baklava in pan at least 1 hour before serving. Some syrup may be left over. Serves 12-16.

Chef's note: "This won a blue ribbon at the Montana State Fair."

Aimee Hachigian
Ulm

Flower Pots

Per serving:
1/2 - 1 cup ice cream or
frozen yogurt
2-inch diameter flower pot
Plastic straw
2 crushed chocolate wafers
Fresh flower
"Gummy worm" candy
(optional)

Thoroughly wash and dry as many flower pots as you need. Stand a straw in the center of each pot and fill around it with ice cream or frozen yogurt. Sprinkle top with crushed wafers to resemble dirt. Clip the straws down to "dirt" level. Freeze overnight.

Just before serving, put a fresh flower into each straw. Arrange a "gummy worm" on the top of each pot for an added effect.

Robin Arbuckle Jones
Great Falls

Almond Roca

1 cup sliced almonds
1 cup butter
1 cup sugar
1 tbs. corn syrup
3 tbs. water
3 oz. semi-sweet chocolate
  chips

Mix all ingredients except almonds and chips. Cook over medium heat until mixture reaches a temperature of 300 degrees on a candy thermometer—hard-crack stage. Remove from heat. Mix in almonds, saving a few for garnish. Spread onto a cookie sheet. Sprinkle with chocolate chips, and spread when chips have softened. Crush reserved almonds and sprinkle over top. Let cool completely. Break into pieces.

Kathy Eskestrand
Havre

Peanut Brittle

1 tbs. butter
1 tsp. vanilla
1/2 tsp. salt
2 tsp. fresh baking soda
1 (16-oz.) bag raw peanuts
2 cups sugar
1 cup light corn syrup

Premeasure salt, soda, vanilla, and butter. In heavy saucepan over medium heat, stir sugar and corn syrup until mixture comes to a heavy boil. Add raw peanuts and continue cooking until peanuts turn a light golden brown. Remove from heat and quickly add premeasured ingredients. Stir until blended and pour onto cookie sheet that has been buttered and then lightly sprinkled with sugar. When the bottom of the cookie sheet is cool to the touch, use the end of a table knife to break peanut brittle.

Chef's note: "If you use Spanish peanuts, remove most of the skins so that you can see when the peanuts are light brown. Cashews work well also."

Ruth Kohlenberger
Deer Lodge

Salted Nut Roll

16 oz. salted peanuts
3 tbs. butter
1 (12-oz.) package peanut
  butter chips
1 (10-oz.) package miniature
  marshmallows
1 (14-oz.) can sweetened
  condensed milk

Grease a 9 x 13-inch baking pan. Sprinkle half the peanuts in the pan. Melt remaining ingredients in a saucepan until smooth. Pour over peanuts. Press remaining peanuts into top. Allow to cool completely, and then cut into pieces. Store in refrigerator. Makes 24 pieces.

Judy Kuhl
Helena

308

Brunch

Venison Quiche

1 (9-inch) unbaked pie shell
1/2 lb. ground venison or
   venison sausage
1/2 cup sliced onions
1 (4-oz.) can chopped
   green chilies
1 cup shredded mozzarella
   cheese
1 cup shredded Swiss cheese
2 tbs. flour
1 cup milk
1/2 tsp. hot sauce
4 eggs, beaten

Line pie shell with aluminum foil. Bake 5 minutes at 450 degrees. Remove foil and bake 5 more minutes. In a skillet, brown meat and onion; drain well. Stir in chilies and set aside.

In a saucepan, combine cheese and flour and add milk. Cook and stir over medium heat until cheese is melted. Add hot sauce. Gradually blend milk mixture into beaten eggs; then add meat mixture. Pour into pie shell. Bake 20-25 minutes at 325 degrees. Let stand 10 minutes before serving. Serves 6-8.

Cindy Miller
Missoula

Sunday Morning Spectacular

4 slices bacon
1/2 lb. dried beef
2 (4-oz.) cans button
   mushrooms, drained
1/2 cup butter
1/2 cup flour
4 cups milk
Pepper to taste
16 eggs
1/4 tsp. salt
1 cup evaporated milk

Saute bacon and drain off excess fat. Add beef, mushrooms, 1/4 cup butter, flour, milk, and pepper. Stir until thick and smooth. Beat eggs, salt, and evaporated milk together. Scramble eggs in 1/4 cup butter. Layer sauce and eggs in casserole dish, beginning and ending with sauce. Bake covered for 1 hour at 300 degrees. Serves 12.

Mike Grove
White Sulphur Springs

Chicken Zucchini Crescent Pie

4 cups sliced zucchini
1/2 onion, chopped
2 cups cooked
   chicken chunks
1/2 cup butter
2 tbs. parsley flakes
1/2 tsp. salt
1/2 tsp. pepper
1/4 tsp. garlic powder
1/4 tsp. oregano
1/2 tsp. basil
2 eggs, beaten well
8 oz. mozzarella cheese,
   shredded
1 (8-oz.) package refrigerator
   crescent dinner rolls

Cook zucchini and onion in butter about 10 minutes. Stir in parsley and seasonings. In a large bowl, blend eggs and cheese. Stir in vegetable mixture and chicken. Separate dinner rolls and place in 8 x 12-inch baking dish or 10-inch pie plate. Press together to form crust. Pour in chicken-vegetable mixture. Bake 30 minutes at 375 degrees, or until knife inserted into center comes out clean. Let stand 10 minutes before serving. Serves 6-8.

Renny Torgerson
Dagmar

Scrambled Avocado Eggs

3 eggs, beaten
Light cream
Salt and pepper to taste
1/2 avocado, diced
1 tbs. butter

Beat eggs slightly in small bowl. Pour in enough light cream to cover eggs, add salt and pepper to taste, and beat well. Stir avocado into eggs. Melt butter in skillet until browned. Pour in egg-avocado mixture and cook as for scrambled eggs. Serves 2.

Mrs. J.W. Penkake
Lewistown

311

Chili Relleno Casserole

2 (4-oz.) cans whole
   green chilies
1 (12-oz.) can
   evaporated milk
4 eggs
1/4 cup flour
10 oz. grated cheddar
   cheese
10 oz. grated Monterey
   Jack cheese

Beat together milk, eggs, and flour. Set aside. Cut open chilies and remove seeds. In an 8 x 12-inch baking dish, arrange 1 can of chilies. Sprinkle with half the 2 cheeses. Top with another layer of chilies and another of cheese. Pour milk mixture over all. Sprinkle with salt. Bake 1 hour at 350 degrees. Let sit for 5 minutes before cutting. Serves 6.

Sherry Joyce
Kalispell

Egg and Sausage Casserole

10-12 eggs, beaten
3 cups milk
4 slices bread, cubed
1 tsp. salt
1 1/2 tsp. dry mustard
2 lbs. pork sausage
1 1/2 cups shredded
   American cheese
1 onion, chopped

Brown sausage and drain. Place cubed bread in bottom of a greased, deep 9 x 13-inch baking dish. Layer sausage over bread and then cheese over sausage. Beat together milk, eggs, salt, mustard, and onion. Pour over sausage and cheese. Refrigerate overnight. Bake 1 - 1 1/2 hours at 350 degrees, or until set. Serves 12.

Ina Gackle
Plentywood

Mexican Cornbread Squares

1 (10-oz.) package
cornbread mix
1 (9-oz.) can creamed corn
2 eggs
2 tbs. milk
3/4 cup shredded cheddar
cheese
2 cups cooked, diced
roast beef
1/4 cup salsa
1 (4 1/2-oz.) can diced
green chilies
1/2 cup shredded Monterey
Jack cheese

Sauce:
1 (16-oz.) can Mexican-style
stewed tomatoes
1 cup salsa
1 tsp. hot sauce
1/2 tsp. Worcestershire sauce
1/2 tsp. ground cumin

In a bowl, combine cornbread mix, corn, eggs, milk, and cheddar cheese. Stir to blend. Spread half of batter in a greased 8 x 8-inch baking dish. Combine beef, salsa, and green chilies. Spread over batter. Sprinkle with Monterey Jack cheese. Top with remaining batter. Bake 35 minutes at 350 degrees. Let stand 5 minutes before serving.

Meanwhile, combine sauce ingredients in saucepan and cook over medium heat until hot. Pour over cornbread squares. Serves 6.

Penny Rubner
Great Falls

313

Sausage Cornbread

1 cup sifted flour
1/4 cup sugar
4 tbs. baking powder
3/4 tsp. salt
1 cup yellow cornmeal
1 lb. bulk sausage
2 eggs
1 cup milk
1/2 cup shortening

Brown sausage and drain, reserving 3 tbs. pan drippings. Put sausage and drippings in a baking pan. Stir dry ingredients together. Add slightly beaten eggs, milk, and shortening. Beat just until moistened. Pour over sausage and bake 20-25 minutes at 425 degrees. Serves 6-8.

Lillian A. Dove
Missoula

Double-Bran Muffins

2 cups oat bran
2 cups bran flakes
2 1/2 cups skim milk
1/2 cup cooking oil
3 egg whites
1 cup flour
1/3 cup brown sugar
2 tbs. baking powder
1/2 tsp. salt

In a bowl, combine cereal and milk; let stand 5 minutes. Combine flour, brown sugar, baking powder, and salt; set aside. Mix oil and egg whites into cereal mixture. Stir in flour mixture until just blended. Spoon batter into muffin tin sprayed with non-stick spray. Bake 18-20 minutes at 400 degrees. Makes about 24 muffins.

(Variations: Add 1 cup chopped walnuts, 2 mashed bananas, and/or 1 tsp. grated orange peel.)

Joan A. Christianson
Libby

One-Month Muffins

2 cups bran cereal
1 cup boiling water
1 1/4 cups sugar
1/2 cup shortening
2 eggs
2 cups buttermilk
2 3/4 cups flour
1/2 tsp. salt
2 1/2 tsp. baking soda
1 tsp. baking powder
1 cup raisins
1/2 cup chopped dates

Pour water over cereal. Cream together sugar, shortening, and eggs. Add to cereal. Stir in buttermilk and mix well. Blend in remaining ingredients and mix well. Place in a tightly covered bowl and keep refrigerated. Will keep for 1 month.

To use, scoop into muffin tin lined with papers, and bake 15-20 minutes at 375 degrees. Makes 24-30 muffins.

Laura Hicks
Troy

Oatmeal Muffins

1 cup quick-cooking
  rolled oats
1 cup buttermilk
1/3 cup butter, softened
1 cup brown sugar
1 egg
1 cup flour
1 tsp. baking powder
1 tsp. baking soda
1/2 tsp. salt
1/4 cup raisins, chopped
  dates, or walnuts (optional)

Stir together oats and buttermilk and set aside. Cream together butter and brown sugar. Add egg and mix well. Sift dry ingredients together. Add creamed mixture to oats and mix well. Add flour mixture and mix well again. Add raisins, dates, or nuts as desired. Fill muffin cups 2/3 full and bake 20 minutes at 400 degrees. Makes 12-15 muffins.

Juliette W. Hoffmann
Bozeman

315

Lemon Poppy- Seed Muffins

3/4 cup butter, softened
1 cup sugar
2 eggs
2/3 cup milk
1/3 cup lemon juice
3 cups flour
4 tsp. baking powder
1/2 tsp. salt
1/4 cup poppy seeds
4 tsp. grated lemon peel

Glaze:
2 cups powdered sugar
1/4 cup lemon juice
1 tsp. vanilla

Cream butter and sugar together. Beat eggs, milk, and lemon juice in a separate bowl. In yet another bowl, mix flour, baking powder, and salt. Alternately add dry and wet ingredients to butter-sugar mixture. Stir in poppy seeds and lemon peel. Divide batter among muffin cups, and bake 25 minutes at 350 degrees.

Meanwhile, combine glaze ingredients. Allow muffins to cool 10 minutes and then dip tops, one by one, into the glaze. Let dry. Makes 12 muffins.

Kelly Estes
White Sulphur Springs

Gingerbread Muffins

2 1/2 cups flour
1 cup light molasses
1 cup buttermilk
1 cup chopped pecans
1/4 cup sugar
1/2 cup shortening
1 1/2 tsp. baking soda
1 tsp. cinnamon
1 tsp. ginger
1/4 tsp. nutmeg
1 egg

Mix all ingredients together and blend until just moistened. Beat 2 minutes. Fill muffin cups half full and bake 20-25 minutes at 375 degrees. Makes 24 muffins.

Sue Kaul
Belgrade

316

Whole Wheat Surprise Muffins

1 1/2 cups whole wheat
   pastry flour
1 cup unbleached flour
2 tsp. baking powder
1 tsp. baking soda
1 egg
3 tbs. canola oil
1 cup buttermilk
1/2 cup honey
1 tsp. poppy seeds
3/4 cup grated carrot
1/2 cup cream cheese
1/2 cup orange marmalade

In a medium bowl, stir together dry ingredients. Blend in honey, egg, oil, and buttermilk until smooth. Fold in grated carrot and poppy seeds. Fill greased muffin cups 1/2 full of batter. Drop about 1 tsp. cream cheese and 1 tsp. orange marmalade into center of each muffin. Cover cream cheese and marmalade with remaining batter. Bake 15-20 minutes at 400 degrees. Makes 12 muffins.

Mary-Anne Sward
Kalispell

Surprise Muffins

3/4 cup chopped pecans
   (optional)
1 cup milk
1 egg, beaten
1/4 cup cooking oil
1 1/4 cups flour
3/4 cup cornmeal
1/4 cup sugar
4 tsp. baking powder
1/2 tsp. salt
1/2 cup fruit preserves

Grease a 12-muffin tin. Use 1/2 cup chopped nuts to coat sides and bottoms of individual cups (optional). In a medium bowl, combine milk, oil, and egg. Stir in dry ingredients, mixing well. Fill cups 1/3 full. Spoon a teaspoonful of preserves into the center of each muffin cup. Cover with remaining batter. Sprinkle tops of muffins with remaining nuts. Bake 15-17 minutes at 425 degrees. Makes 12 muffins.

Pat Heintzman
Great Falls

317

Banana Date Nut Muffins

1 1/2 cups unsifted flour
1 cup wheat germ
1/3 cup sugar
3 tsp. baking powder
1/2 tsp. salt
1 cup mashed banana
1 cup chopped dates
1/2 cup chopped walnuts
   or pecans
1/2 cup milk
1/4 cup cooking oil
2 eggs

Measure dry ingredients into a bowl. Stir well to blend. Stir in dates and nuts. In a separate bowl, combine milk, oil, mashed banana, and eggs. Beat slightly. Add liquid ingredients to dry ingredients all at once. Stir just until all ingredients are moistened. Fill well-greased muffin cups 2/3 full. Bake 20-25 minutes at 400 degrees. Makes about 18 muffins.

Edna H. Shaffer
Deer Lodge

Wild-Rice Blueberry Muffins

3 tbs. butter
1/2 cup sugar
1/2 cup water
1 egg
1/2 cup sweetened
   condensed milk
2 cups flour, sifted
2 tsp. baking powder
1 1/2 cups blueberries
1 cup cooked wild rice

Blend softened butter with sugar. Add water, egg, milk, flour, and baking powder. Stir just until smooth. Fold in blueberries and wild rice. Spoon into well-oiled muffin cups. Bake 20-25 minutes at 375 degrees. Makes about 12 muffins.

M. Kjellgren
Great Falls

318

Rhubarb Muffins

1 1/2 cups brown sugar
1/2 cup cooking oil
1 egg
2 tsp. vanilla
1 cup buttermilk
2 cups diced rhubarb
1/2 cup chopped nuts
2 1/2 cups flour
1 tsp. baking soda
1 tsp. baking powder
1/2 tsp. salt

Topping:
1 tsp. melted butter
1/2 cup sugar
1 tsp. cinnamon

Combine sugar, oil, egg, vanilla, and buttermilk. Stir in rhubarb. Sift dry ingredients together and add to batter. Fill muffin cups about 2/3 full of batter. Mix topping ingredients together and sprinkle over tops of muffins. Bake 20-25 minutes at 375 degrees. Makes 24 muffins.

Helen Donaldson
Billings

319

Blueberry Orange Coffee Cake

2 cups flour, sifted
1/2 cup sugar
3 tsp. baking powder
1/2 tsp. salt
1 egg, slightly beaten
1/2 cup milk
1/2 cup cooking oil
1 cup blueberries
2 tsp. grated orange peel
1/2 cup orange juice
2 tbs. butter
1/2 cup brown sugar
1 tsp. cinnamon
1/2 cup chopped walnuts

In a large bowl, sift together flour, sugar, baking powder, and salt. Combine egg, milk, and oil. Add all at once to dry ingredients and mix. Combine blueberries, orange peel, and orange juice, and stir into batter just until blended. Spread batter evenly in greased 7 x 12-inch baking pan. Combine brown sugar, butter, cinnamon, and nuts and sprinkle over batter. Bake 25-30 minutes at 375 degrees. Serve warm. Serves 6-8.

Lillian McGinnis
Great Falls

Breakfast at high noon

Last Monday the Homer Club celebrated its eleventh anniversary at the charming home of Mrs. T.W. Buzzo by giving an elaborate breakfast at high noon.... For three hours the ladies discussed the elaborate menu, which consisted of:

First: Waldorf—mixed fruits served in orange cups;
Second: Snow fish with lobster sauce and cucumbers;
Third: Omelette al La Itallianne;
Fourth: Lamb de Maintennon, peas, potatoes, Lyonnaise;
Fifth: French waffles with Yankee Maple syrup, and German honey.

Butte newspaper clipping of May 20, 1902
reprinted in Butte's Heritage Cookbook

Mel's Cinnamon Rolls

2 cups milk
6 tbs. butter
3 tbs. dry yeast
1 cup warm water
2 tsp. salt
2 eggs
1/2 cup brown sugar
1/2 cup honey
5 cups whole wheat flour
5 cups white flour

Topping:
3/4 cup sugar
1/4 cup brown sugar
5 tsp. cinnamon
6 tbs. butter

Over medium heat, scald milk and add butter, stirring to melt. Add yeast to warm water and let sit for 1 minute. In a large bowl, mix salt, brown sugar, whole wheat flour, and 3 cups white flour. Blend in yeast mixture, scalded milk, eggs, and honey. Add remaining 2 cups of flour a little at a time, until dough is no longer sticky.

Knead dough 8-12 minutes, cover, and let rise in a greased bowl until doubled in volume. Roll dough out to form rectangle. Melt topping butter and spread over dough. Mix together sugars and cinnamon and sprinkle over butter. Starting with the long edge, roll dough. Seal edges. Cut thick slices and arrange on cookie sheet. Bake 10-12 minutes at 350 degrees. Makes 18 rolls.

Melanie Mumbower
Butte

Old-Fashioned Raisin Griddle Cookies

3 1/2 cups sifted flour
1 cup sugar
1 1/2 tsp. baking powder
1 tsp. salt
1/2 tsp. baking soda
1 tsp. nutmeg
1/4 cup shortening
1 egg, beaten
1/2 cup milk
1 cup raisins

Sift dry ingredients together. Cut in shortening. Combine egg and milk, blend, and add with raisins to dry mixture. Stir until mixture will hold together, adding a bit more milk if necessary. Roll or pat out dough 1/4" thick on floured board. Cut with a 2-inch round cookie cutter or shape by hand.

Heat griddle or skillet to 380 degrees. Oil lightly. Place cookies on griddle and turn when bottom is brown and top puffy. Brown other side. Serve hot off the griddle or cooled.

David Angove
Helena

Diamond N Sourdough Pancakes

1-2 cups sourdough starter
1 egg
1 cup flour
1 tbs. cooking oil
1/4 cup powdered milk
Pinch of salt
1 tsp. baking soda
2 tbs. sugar

Mix first 5 ingredients together and beat well. Add salt, soda, and sugar. Beat until smooth and let rest a few minutes. Bake on a very hot griddle until golden brown; flip and brown other side. Serves 6.

Sunny Peters
Diamond N Ranch
Lame Deer

Ginger Pancakes with Lemon Sauce

2 cups biscuit mix
1 egg
1 1/3 cups milk
1 1/2 tsp. ginger
1 tsp. cinnamon
1/2 tsp. ground cloves
8 oz. cream cheese, softened
Milk as needed

Lemon sauce:
1/4 cup butter
1 cup sugar
1/4 cup water
1 egg, beaten well
Grated peel of 1 lemon
3 tbs. lemon juice

Beat first 6 ingredients together until smooth. Cook pancakes on griddle or in skillet until browned on both sides. Place half of pancakes on serving plates. Top with creamed cheese that has been whipped with a little milk. Arrange remaining pancakes over cream cheese. Top with lemon sauce. Serves 8.

To make sauce: Heat all ingredients to boiling over medium heat, stirring constantly.

Mickey Senechal
Grass Range

Pumpkin Pancakes

1 cup buttermilk
1/4 cup sugar
2 tbs. shortening
1 tsp. baking powder
1/2 tsp. salt
1/2 tsp. baking soda
1 egg, slightly beaten
1 cup flour
3/4 tsp. pumpkin pie spice
1/2 cup canned pumpkin or
   squash

Combine all ingredients and beat until smooth. Cook on griddle or in skillet until browned on both sides, turning once. Serves 4.

Joyce Tranberg
Lakeside

Sour Cream Apple Pancakes

3/4 cup flour
1/4 cup sugar
1/2 tsp. baking soda
1/2 tsp. salt
1/4 tsp. cinnamon
1 1/2 cups grated apple
1 1/4 cups sour cream
1 egg, slightly beaten
1 tsp. vanilla

In a large bowl, combine all dry ingredients. In another large bowl, combine remaining ingredients and mix well. Add to dry ingredients and stir until just blended.

Pour 1/4 cup batter onto greased, preheated griddle and flatten slightly. Cook 3-5 minutes, flipping once. Serves 4.

Patti Billet
Missoula

Fresh Strawberry Puff Pancake

1/4 cup butter
3 eggs
1 1/2 cups milk
6 tbs. sugar
3/4 cup flour, unsifted
1/4 tsp. salt
About 3 cups strawberries,
    halved
Sour cream to taste
Brown sugar to taste

Place butter in a 9-inch spring-form pan. Place pan in 425-degree oven until butter melts and bubbles, about 2-5 minutes. Meanwhile, beat together eggs, milk, 4 tbs. sugar, flour, and salt until smooth. Pour batter all at once into hot butter. Return to oven and bake 30 minutes, or until edges are puffed and brown.

Sprinkle strawberries with remaining sugar and stir to coat evenly. When pancake is done, remove from oven and spoon strawberries into center. Cut into wedges and serve with sour cream and brown sugar. Serves 4.

Lillian McGinnis
Great Falls

Oatmeal Pancakes with Orange Sauce

2 cups milk
1 1/2 cup quick-cooking
   rolled oats
1 cup flour
2 1/2 tsp. baking powder
1/4 cup wheat germ
1 tsp. salt
2 tbs. sugar
2 eggs, beaten
1/3 cup cooking oil

Sauce:
1 cup sugar
2 tbs. lemon juice
2 cups orange juice
2 tbs. cornstarch
1/4 cup butter

To make sauce: Mix sugar and cornstarch together in saucepan over medium heat. Stir in juices. Cook, stirring constantly, until mixture is thick and clear. Remove from heat and blend in butter. Keep warm.

To make pancakes: Mix oats into milk and let stand a few minutes. Sift together dry ingredients. Stir eggs and oil into oat mixture. Add dry ingredients. Bake on moderately hot griddle, turning once. Serve with warm sauce. Serves 4.

Sharon M. Fox
Missoula

Corn Waffles

2 cups flour
2 tsp. baking powder
1 tsp. salt
2 cups canned corn
1 cup milk
4 tbs. sugar
2 eggs
4 tbs. butter, melted

Sift together dry ingredients. In a separate bowl, combine eggs, milk, and corn. Stir in dry ingredients. Add melted butter and bake on hot waffle iron until steam has stopped seeping from the iron, about 5-6 minutes. Waffles should be nicely browned. Makes 5-6 waffles.

Dorothy Stack
Missoula

Breakfast Take-Alongs

2/3 cup butter
2/3 cup sugar
1 egg
1 tsp. vanilla
3/4 cup flour
1/2 tsp. baking soda
6 slices bacon, fried and
   crumbled
1/2 tsp. salt
1 1/2 cups quick-cooking
   rolled oats
1 cup shredded cheddar
   cheese
1/2 cup wheat germ or finely
   chopped nuts

Beat together butter, sugar, egg, and vanilla. Combine flour, soda, and salt, and add to butter mixture. Mix well. Stir in oats, cheese, wheat germ (or nuts), and bacon. Drop by rounded tablespoonfuls onto greased cookie sheet. Bake 12-14 minutes at 350 degrees, or until edges are golden brown. Cool 1 minute and remove to wire rack to finish cooling. Makes about 3 dozen.

Carolyn Lehman
Kalispell

Stuffed French Toast

8 slices bread
16 oz. cream cheese, cubed
12 eggs
1/3 cup maple syrup
2 cups milk

Remove crusts from bread and cut into cubes. Arrange half the bread cubes in the bottom of a 9 x 13-inch baking dish. Add cubed cream cheese. Top with remaining bread cubes. Beat together eggs, syrup, and milk. Pour over bread and cheese. Cover and let sit overnight in the refrigerator. Bake 45 minutes at 375 degrees. Serves 9.

Carol Ann Johnson
Missoula

326

French Toast with Sauteed Fruit

Toast:
4 eggs
1 cup milk
2 tbs. sugar
Juice of one orange
Juice of 1/2 lime
1 1/2 tsp. vanilla
8 (1/2-inch-thick) slices
   French bread

Fruit:
1 cup sliced strawberries
1 cup sliced apple
1 cup sliced orange
1 cup raspberry jam
3 tbs. butter
1 tsp. nutmeg
4 tbs. triple sec

Stir together all French toast ingredients except the bread. Set mixture aside. Melt butter and saute fruit. Add raspberry jam, triple sec, and nutmeg to fruit. Reduce heat and gently and occasionally stir until fruit is hot.

Dip slices of bread in egg mixture, coating both sides thoroughly. Cook on griddle or in skillet over medium heat until both sides are brown, turning just once. Place French toast on serving plates and glaze with 1/2 - 3/4 cup sauteed fruit. Sprinkle with powdered sugar. Serves 8.

The Sanders' Bed & Breakfast
Helena

Relief for teething babies

Teething babies were given a piece of cooked fatty bacon rind to chew when teething. A cloth was dipped in sage tea with a little alum and honey in it, and the gums rubbed with the mother's cloth-covered forefinger to help relieve swollen gums of teething babies.

Elsie J. Cummings and Wavie J. Charlton
Survival: Pioneer, Indian, and Wilderness Lore

327

Toasted Homemade Cereal

4 cups rolled oats
2 cups raw wheat germ
1 cup hulled sunflower seeds
1/2 cup sesame seeds
1 cup chopped walnuts
1/2 cup flaked coconut
3/4 cup brown sugar
3/4 cup cooking oil
1/3 cup water
2 tbs. vanilla

Combine all ingredients and mix well. Spread in shallow pan. Bake 1 hour at 275 degrees, stirring every 15 minutes. Cool and store in a tight container. Makes 8-9 cups.

Dorothy Boulton
Bozeman

Joe McGregor's recipe for pancakes

The following will sufficiently satisfy or kill eight people. Break two barnyard pearls into a mixing bowl. Add two lunch fangs full of beet dust, two fingers and a thumb of ocean dust, one large or two small squirts of swine bosom oil. Work this concoction over briskly with a blunt stick or spoon. Add two mickeys of Midvale Creek. Add four man-sized handfuls of wheat dust, one thumb and a finger of Arm & Hammer silver polish, three thumbs and three fingers of Jack Screw powder. Whip the hell out of the above with blunt stick or basting spoon until smooth & gentle. Turn out on hot griddle, lightly oiled. When little bubbles show up, like warts on a toad's back, turn over. Leave on griddle until all possibility of a creamy center in circles of torture has passed. Serve on warm plate with fried swine bosom or little pigs in tights, plenty of home-made larrup and a dish of hard oil also.

from The Glacier Park Women's Club's Cook Book
1941

Miscellaneous

Spicy Sweet Spaghetti Sauce

1/4 cup olive oil
3 cloves garlic, sliced
1 (15-oz.) can tomato sauce
1 (6-oz.) can tomato paste
1 cup water
3 tbs. sugar
1 small stick cinnamon
1 lb. mild or hot Italian
  sausage, bulk
  or individual

If using individual sausage, cut sausage into serving-sized pieces; brown sausage and drain excess fat. Push meat to side of pan, add olive oil and garlic and cook until garlic is browned. Add remaining ingredients. Simmer, stirring often, for 1 hour. Remove cinnamon stick before serving. Makes about 3 cups.

Birdie Joers
Augusta

Eggplant Spaghetti Sauce

1/2 cup cooking oil
3 cups diced eggplant
1 medium onion, chopped
1 (8-oz.) can tomato sauce
1 (6-oz.) can tomato paste
3/4 cup water
1 tsp. sugar
1/2 tsp. salt
1/4 tsp. pepper
1/4 cup grated Parmesan
  cheese

Heat oil. Add eggplant and onion and cook until onion is browned on all sides. Add tomato sauce, tomato paste, water, sugar, salt, and pepper. Cover and cook over low heat for 20 minutes. Add cheese and cook 10 minutes, or until cheese melts. Makes about 4 cups.

Laura Hicks
Troy

330

Tomato Salsa

4 cups peeled and coarsely
   chopped tomato
2 cups chopped peppers
   (yellow banana peppers,
   green bell peppers, or
   both)
1 cup chopped jalapeno
   peppers
1 cup chopped onion
2 tsp. salt
2 tsp. cumin or coriander
2 tsp. celery seed
2 tsp. chili powder
5 large cloves garlic, minced
1/2 cup vinegar
1/2 cup sugar
1 (6-oz.) can tomato paste

Combine all ingredients in a large kettle and bring to a boil. Reduce heat and simmer for about 1 hour, stirring occasionally. Pour into sterile half-pint jars, leaving 1/2-inch head space. Put on lids and rings and process in a boiling water bath for 30 minutes. Makes about 10 half-pint jars.

Mary-Anne Sward
Kalispell

Peach Salsa

6 peaches
4 tomatoes
4 jalapeno peppers
4 tbs. lemon juice
1 cup red wine vinegar
1 cup sherry
4 tbs. honey
1 cup chopped green onion

Peel, pit, and chop peaches. Cut tomatoes into wedges and remove seeds. Remove membrane and seeds from jalapeno peppers and chop fine. Mix together all of the above. In a separate bowl, mix together lemon juice, sherry, vinegar, and honey, and add to peach mixture. Stir in green onions. Serves 15.

The Stovetop Restaurant and Deli
Helena

331

Barbecue Sauce

1 cup catsup
2/3 cup vinegar
1/3 cup Worcestershire sauce
2 tbs. lemon juice
1/2 tsp. liquid smoke
1/2 tsp. dry mustard
1/2 tsp. cayenne pepper
1 tsp. pepper
1/2 tsp. salt
1/2 tsp. sugar
1 tsp. barbecue spices
Minced garlic to taste
1 (12-oz.) can V-8 Juice

Combine all ingredients in a saucepan and bring to a boil. Simmer 30 minutes. Makes about 4 cups.

Harold A. Auer
Great Falls

Prime Rib Dressing

2 cups mayonnaise
1/2 tsp. onion salt
1/2 tsp. pepper
1 1/2 tbs. dry mustard
1/2 tsp. salt
1 1/2 tsp. red wine vinegar
1 1/2 tsp. malt vinegar
1/2 tsp. Worcestershire sauce
2 tbs. horseradish
1/4 cup sour cream
1 1/2 tbs. milk
1/4 cup crumbled Roquefort
   or blue cheese

Mix all ingredients together. Store in refrigerator. Makes 2 1/2 cups.

Rebecca Smith
Missoula

332

Ham Sauce

1 cup boiling water
1 beef bouillon cube
1/2 cup red wine vinegar
1 cup sugar
1 (9-oz.) jar prepared
   mustard
3 tbs. flour
3/4 cup cold water

Bring first 5 ingredients to a boil and thicken with flour mixed into cold water. Serve warm or cold with ham or roast beef. Sauce will keep well in the refrigerator. Makes about 2 1/2 cups.

Judie Murrill
Corvallis

Dijon-Style Mustard

2 large onions, sliced
2 garlic cloves, chopped
2 cups white or red wine
   vinegar
1/4 tsp. pepper or hot sauce
2 tsp. salt
1 cup dry mustard
1 tbs. cooking oil
2 tbs. honey

Place onion slices and chopped garlic in glass bowl. Add wine vinegar. Cover and let stand for 24 hours. Strain through a double layer of cheesecloth and set aside.

In a bowl, combine the pepper, salt, dry mustard, and 1/2 cup strained vinegar mixture. Bring remaining vinegar to a boil in a stainless steel pan. Gradually add the mustard mixture. Simmer 5 minutes. Cool with saucepan covered. Stir in oil and honey, and beat together with an electric mixer for 3 minutes. Store in refrigerator in sterilized jars. Makes 1 - 1 1/2 cups.

Mary M. Ross
Stevensville

333

Tenderizer Sauce or Marinade

1/3 cup fresh lemon juice
2 crushed garlic cloves
1 1/2 tsp. dried parsley flakes
1/2 cup wine vinegar
1 tbs. pepper
1 1/2 cups cooking oil
3/4 cup soy sauce
1/4 cup Worcestershire sauce
2 tbs. dry mustard
2 1/4 tsp. salt

Combine all ingredients and mix well. Marinate steak in this sauce overnight. Sauce may be stored in a tightly covered jar in the refrigerator. Makes 3 1/2 cups.

Ida Seidler Bishop
Great Falls

Thai Peanut Butter Sauce

1/2 cup crunchy peanut
  butter
1/2 cup soy sauce
1 tsp. hot sauce
1/4 cup honey
1/3 cup water
3 cloves garlic, minced
1/2 cup sesame oil

Blend in blender or food processor until thick, smooth paste is formed. Cover and refrigerate. Sauce is good over vegetables or pasta. Makes about 2 cups.

Laura Ryan Weatherly
Butte

Zucchini Relish

4 - 4 1/2 zucchinis, chopped
2 medium onions, chopped
1 red bell pepper, chopped
2 tbs. non-iodized salt
1 1/2 cups sugar
1 cup vinegar
1 cup water
2 tsp. celery seeds
1 tsp. turmeric
1 tsp. nutmeg
1/8 tsp. pepper

Coarsely grind zucchini, onion, and red pepper. Stir in salt. Cover and refrigerate overnight. Drain, rinse in cold water, and drain again.

In a large kettle, combine vegetables and remaining ingredients. Bring to a boil. Cover and simmer 10 minutes, stirring frequently. Ladle into sterilized pint jars, adjust lids, and process in a boiling water bath for 15 minutes. Makes 4 pints.

Ann Harding
Philipsburg

Corn Relish

4 cups corn
3 cups chopped tomato
1 1/2 cups chopped green
  pepper
3/4 cup chopped cucumber
1 cup chopped onion
1 cup sugar
2 cups vinegar
1 tbs. salt
1 tsp. celery seeds
1 tsp. mustard seeds

Combine first 5 ingredients in a large kettle and set aside. In a saucepan, mix remaining ingredients and heat to dissolve sugar. Pour over vegetables. Simmer 1 hour, stirring occasionally. Pour into sterilized pint jars, leaving 1/4-inch head room, and seal. Cook in a boiling water bath for 10 minutes to ensure sealing. Makes about 4 pints.

Marlyse Drogitis
Harrison

335

Jellied Moose Nose

1 upper jawbone of moose
1 onion
1 clove garlic
1 tbs. pickling spice
1 tsp. salt
1/2 tsp. pepper
1/4 cup vinegar

Cut the upper jawbone of the moose just below the eyes. Place in a large kettle of scalding water and boil for 45 minutes. Remove and chill in cold water. Pull out all hairs and wash thoroughly until no hairs remain.

Place the nose in a kettle and cover with fresh water. Add onion, garlic, spices, and vinegar. Bring to a boil, reduce the heat, and simmer until meat is tender. Refrigerate overnight in the liquid.

When cool, remove meat from broth and remove and discard bone and cartilege. Slice the meat thin and alternate layers of white and dark meat in a loaf pan. Pour broth over meat to cover. Let cool until jelly has set. Slice and serve cold.

Chef's note: "This makes for great dinner conversation, and believe it or not it ain't bad! Buffalo nose can be used in place of moose nose."

Ronald B. Tobias
Bozeman

336

Mincemeat

2 lbs. cooked beef, elk, or
   venison, coarsely ground
1 lb. suet
6 cups raisins
5 lbs. ground apples
2 lbs. currants
2 tsp. ground cloves
3 tsp. ground cinnamon
1 tsp. allspice
1 cup vinegar
4 cups grape or cranberry
   juice
6 3/4 cups sugar
1 lb. cranberries or pitted pie
   cherries
1 tbs. salt

Mix all ingredients together and cook until all are tender. Ladle into sterilized jars, adjust lids, and seal while mincemeat is hot in a boiling water bath for 10 minutes. Makes about 12 pints.

Zella Hunter
Townsend

A thank you to nature

Making jam and jelly is saying thank you to nature. You go out and walk in the hills and mountains, you bring home part of those hills and mountains, and then you put your bounty in glass jars. With love.

Kim Williams
Cookbook & Commentary

Spiced Peaches

2 1/2 lbs. fresh peaches
5 cups sugar
2 cups water
2 cups white vinegar
2 tsp. whole cloves
1 (12-inch) cinnamon stick

Break cinnamon stick into small pieces. Combine spices, sugar, water, and vinegar in a 6-quart kettle. Heat to boiling; reduce heat to keep hot but not boiling. Peel and pit peaches and cut into halves. Add peach halves to syrup and heat for 5 minutes. Pack fruit and syrup into hot, sterilized pint jars. Leave 1/2-inch head space. Adjust lids, and process in boiling water bath for 20 minutes. Makes 3 pints.

Elaine Kyriss
Billings

Huckleberry Jam

4 cups crushed huckleberries
1 package pectin
1 cup apple juice
6 cups sugar
1/4 cup lemon juice

Follow instructions in pectin package for cooking time, preparing jars, and sealing. Makes about 10 half-pint jars.

Patti Sharpe
Great Falls

338

Peach Holiday Jam

Juice of 1 lemon
1/2 lemon rind, grated
Juice of 1 orange
1 orange rind, grated
1/2 cup maraschino cherries, chopped
3 cups mashed peaches
1 cup whole green grapes
1 cup crushed pineapple (with liquid)
6 cups sugar
2 packages pectin

Follow instructions in pectin package for making jam. Makes 10-12 half-pint jars.

Caroline Emery
Philipsburg

Rosy Rhubarb Jam

5 cups rhubarb, cut into 1 1/2-inch pieces
1 cup crushed pineapple, drained
4 cups sugar
1 (3-oz.) package strawberry gelatin

Combine rhubarb, pineapple, and sugar in a saucepan. Place over low heat and stir gently until sugar is dissolved. Cook over medium heat until thick and clear, about 10-20 minutes. Remove from heat and stir in gelatin. Pour into sterilized jars, cover with paraffin, and seal. Makes about 4 cups.

Betty Stav
Deer Lodge

339

Chokecherry Syrup

1 gallon chokecherries
6 cups water
1 package pectin
3/4 cup fresh lemon juice
8 cups sugar

Wash cherries and put in a large kettle with 6 cups water. Bring to a boil and simmer 30 minutes. Let stand overnight. Process through a sieve and measure syrup; add water to make 8 cups. Add pectin and lemon juice to syrup. Bring to a boil and add sugar. Boil 4 minutes. Pour into sterilized jars and process in boiling water bath for 10 minutes. Makes about 8 cups.

Dorothy Boulton
Bozeman

The end of feasting

When we had an extra good dinner with many sweets and rich foods, Olive and I had to take a physic, whether we needed it or not. I remember castoria—it was effective and I rather liked the taste. It was the same with Syrup of Figs—that wasn't bad either. Then some neighbor gave Mamma a recipe for a homemade cathartic. The taste was terrible, I thought, but it certainly was most effective—and many a trip was made to the little house out back— even though the thermometer registered below zero.

Grind 1/2 pound seeded raisins, 1/2 pound figs, and 1 ounce senna leaves. Add 1 pound of brown sugar. Pour over this mixture 1/2 pint of boiling water. Stir thoroughly. One dose was one generous teaspoon of this concoction. As I have already remarked, it was effective.

Louise K. Nickey
Cookery of the Prairie Homesteader

Index

342

343

345

347

348

350

351

For more copies of
The Montana Cookbook

For additional copies of *The Montana Cookbook*, please see your local bookstore. You also may write to Falcon Press, P.O. Box 1718, Helena, MT 59624 or call toll-free 1-800-582-2665.

About Falcon Press

Falcon Press publishes a wide variety of quality books and calendars, including several titles on Montana. The *Montana Wildlife Viewing Guide* describes 113 easily accessible wildlife viewing areas and is part of a state-by-state series called Wildlife Viewing in America. *Montana on my Mind*, Montana's best-selling giftbook, was the first book in our America on my Mind series, which now includes large-format books on several states. *The Montana Calendar*, first published in 1974, features outstanding color photography by Michael S. Sample.

Other Montana books by Falcon Press include *Montana National Forests*, *The Hiker's Guide to Montana*, *The Hiker's Guide to Montana's Continental Divide Trail*, *The Floater's Guide to Montana*, *The Angler's Guide to Montana*, *The Hunter's Guide to Montana*, and *The Rockhound's Guide to Montana*.

Falcon Press also publishes recreational guidebooks, calendars, and full-color books on many other states and regions.

For more information on books and calendars by Falcon Press, please check wtih your local bookstore or call 1-800-582-2665 and ask for our free catalog. You also may write to Falcon Press Catalog, P.O. Box 1718, Helena, MT 59624.

352